UKRAINE'S
ECONOMIC REFORM

UKRAINE'S ECONOMIC REFORM

Obstacles, Errors, Lessons

RAPHAEL SHEN

Westport, Connecticut
London

Library of Congress Cataloging-in-Publication Data

Shen, Raphael.
 Ukraine's economic reform : obstacles, errors, lessons / Raphael
Shen.
   p.   cm.
 Includes bibliographical references and index.
 ISBN 0–275–95240–1 (alk. paper)
 1. Ukraine—Economic policy—1991–   2. Ukraine—Economic
conditions—1991–   I. Title.
HC340.19.S54   1996
338.947′71—dc20   95–50468

British Library Cataloguing in Publication Data is available.

Library of Congress Catalog Card Number: 95–50468
ISBN: 0–275–95240–1

First published in 1996

Praeger Publishers, 88 Post Road West, Westport, CT 06881
An imprint of Greenwood Publishing Group, Inc.

Printed in the United States of America

The paper used in this book complies with the
Permanent Paper Standard issued by the National
Information Standards Organization (Z39.48–1984).

10 9 8 7 6 5 4 3 2 1

Contents

Tables and Figures

TABLES

FIGURES

Acknowledgments

I wish to express my deep gratitude to Professor Ivan Lukinov (Vice Chairman, Ukrainian Academy of Sciences; Director, Institute of Economic Research, Ukrainian Academy of Sciences) for his generous and helpful assistance to me during my research visit to Ukraine in late 1994. With his introductions, I was granted invaluable interviews with leading academicians and prominent officials in Ukraine. With his guidance, I secured precious printed materials from government offices and academic institutions.

I am also deeply indebted to my students, Helene Dopierala (my graduate assistant), Angela Eaton, Eric Reynolds, Mary Beth Barnds, and Christopher Pellerito. Their assistance to me during various phases of this research project deserves more than a mere expression of sincere appreciation.

My gratitude is also due to Anne Dwyer who helped edit chapters of the manuscript as it progressed, and then the entire manuscript, once again, upon its completion. My gratitude goes also to Ann Reilly, who helped format, typeset, and finalize the camera-ready version of the manuscript. Ann, my sincerest of thanks.

I am also grateful for the contribution of Lydia Melnik who provided various materials which I needed to undertake this project.

Finally, I wish to acknowledge the kindness, hospitality, and warmth of my friends in Ukraine. May their dreams come true.

Introduction

Political and economic independence has been a novel experience for Ukraine. From the thirteenth century until 1991—excluding a brief two-year period of independence in 1917–1918—Ukraine's vast regions were occupied by neighboring powers. Its most recent overlord was the former Soviet Union (FSU). For nearly seven decades, Ukraine was an integral part of a rigidly structured and tightly controlled command system and was thoroughly integrated into the FSU politically, socially, and economically. Upon regaining independence in 1991, Ukraine inherited a state that is politically divided, ethnically mixed, and economically stagnant. Its economy was the most tightly controlled and closely supervised entity of all the FSU republics because its productive forces were of vital strategic importance to Moscow's long-term objectives. As a result, of all the FSU republics, Ukraine is most in need of reforming and restructuring its institutions and productive assets. Yet, it has had no experience in self-governance. Its decision makers have no precedents to fall back on for lessons in systemic transformation.

On the governmental level, since personal political life spans are shorter than national life spans, terms like "long-term" and "future" carry only abstract weight with Ukraine's decision makers. Irrespective of opportunity costs, which were institutionalized under the Soviet system, preserving the status quo has become an expedient option. Postponing difficult economic decisions has been a commonplace practice, and decision makers hasten to paint disjointed features of a market system over the facade of a structurally distorted and operationally dysfunctional economy, heedlessly overlooking crucial prerequisites to an orderly transition.

On the micro plane, the average management also lacks the fundamental attributes of adaptability, flexibility, and progressiveness essential for efficient decision-making processes. Risk taking and responsibility bearing were alien modi operandi during the Soviet era. Passivity, therefore, nearly fossilized from the practices of the past, lingers among Ukraine's management and workforce alike.

Aside from human and institutional deficiencies, Ukraine has also inherited from the FSU a highly specialized and integrated capital structure, a network of passive financial institutions, a bankrupt nonconvertible currency, a disrupted system of factor and product markets, and a mass of rapidly obsolescent capital assets having minimal salvage value. The newly independent Ukraine thus faces background forces more uniquely burdensome and distinctly complex for economic restructuring than other newly liberalized countires like Hungary, Poland, or the Czech Republic. It is incumbent on architects of reform and decision makers in Ukraine to implement a responsible and distinct approach to reform uniquely suited to Ukraine's current conditions.

The ideal and the real nevertheless do not habitually coincide. Even in advanced market economies with highly developed institutional and infrastructural support systems, enterprise restructuring or institutional reform always entails painfully delicate processes. In the United States, for instance, the United Auto Workers' rank and file, public school administrators, and medicare and welfare recipients are thus forever vigilant over the processes of recommended changes. Resistance or inertia toward changes involving future uncertainties is an instinctive reflex. This is particularly true in the newly independent Ukraine. Attempts at a systemic transformation in Ukraine are pervasively overshadowed by hidden obstacles from within and unanticipated disruptions from without. Attempts at economic restructuring and institutional reform thus pose formidable challenges to policy designers and decision makers alike.

In practice, effective macro policies require extensive and timely micro responsiveness. Reform designers and decision makers need to conscientiously examine an economy's relative strengths and weaknesses prior to responsibly effectuating deliberate and consistent macro policies. This has not been the case in Ukraine's reform experience.

This study examines the effects of Ukraine's integration with the FSU for seventy-three years, investigates Ukraine's inherited economic structure and functioning vis-à-vis reform obstacles, analyzes and evaluates its reform policies since regaining independence, presents an outline of practical lessons from its unique reform experiment, and concludes with recommendations for the government of Ukraine, as well as for the governments of other newly independent republics of the FSU.

UKRAINE'S ECONOMIC REFORM

Ukraine in Historical Perspective

Ukraine declared its independence from the former Soviet Union (FSU) on August 24, 1991. Excluding Russia, whose territories extend far into the Asian continent, Ukraine is the largest and the fourth most populous nation in Europe. Its 233,090 square miles of territory host a population of 52.2 million. At the beginning of 1993, 72.2 percent of Ukraine's inhabitants were natives, 22.1 percent were Russians, nearly 1 percent were Jews and 1 percent Belorussians, and the remainder included an array of other minorities from Moldova, Bulgaria, Poland, Hungary, and Romania. Ukraine's 4,039 miles of border front Belorussia to the north, Russia to the northeast and east, the Black Sea to the south, Moldova, Romania, and Hungary to the southwest, and Slovakia and Poland to the west.

Ukraine's current boundaries were delineated by the Soviet Union after World War II, when the regions inhabited by ethnic Ukrainians were designated the Ukrainian Soviet Socialist Republic. All members of the Commonwealth of Independent States (CIS) now recognize these boundaries of Ukraine as rightful and permanent.

Regions historically populated by ethnic Ukrainians were repeatedly invaded by the Mongols and the Tartars and, since the thirteenth century, were alternately occupied by, among others, Poland, Lithuania, Germany, Austria, Romania, and Russia. Though there had long been a Ukrainian people of common heritage, there was not a sovereign state of Ukraine until January 22, 1918, when a hastily formed Ukrainian Supreme Council proclaimed Ukraine an independent and sovereign state.

Ukraine's independence, however, lasted less than two years. Under political pressure and military threat from Moscow, Ukraine relinquished its status as a sovereign and independent state when it became a founding member of the Union of Soviet Socialist Republics (USSR). For nearly seven decades thereafter, Ukraine was known as the Ukrainian Soviet Socialist Republic. Ukraine reclaimed its sovereignty in 1991, but political sovereignty and economic independence have been a novel experience for Ukraine's decision makers. A brief overview of Ukraine's history and its people help highlight some background forces at work in this young nation's attempts at an independent existence.

GEOGRAPHICAL NOTES, HISTORICAL SKETCHES

In addition to Russia's famed Volga, Ural, and Don Rivers, Ukraine's own system of bountiful waterways was one of the earliest nurturing grounds for the emergence of a civilization in the vast steppe lands of eastern Europe. Its rich top soil, criss-crossed and enriched by more than 23,000 rivers and streams, enticed nomadic Slav tribes of the east to settle in the region in the fifth and sixth centuries. Traders from the south and the west, notably those from the Byzantine Empire and beyond, simultaneously began penetrating nascent commercial posts along the Dnieper and Don Rivers, establishing Kiev as the center for commercial and cultural exchanges in the region.

The Dnieper River, Ukraine's best known waterway and life stream of the city of Kiev, was the cradle of modern civilization for both Russia and the Ukraine. Orig-inating near Russia's Smolensk, the river runs southward toward Kiev, then mean-ders more than 650 miles, first southeast through the eastern portion of Ukraine, then southwest by Ukraine's port city of Knepropetrovsk, before finally emptying into the Black Sea.

The Viking leader Rulik and his seafaring warriors from across the Baltic Sea descended on the northern Russian city of Novgorod around the middle of the ninth century. Seizing trading posts along the Dnieper River as they traversed southeast and southward, Rulik's Vikings, also known as the Varangians or the Rus, established their center of command in the city of Kiev. They collected taxes, traded in slaves, controlled commercial flows along the river banks, and explored access routes to markets of the Byzantine Empire and beyond. A civilization blending the distinctive characteristics of the plain-dwelling Slavs and the venturesome Vikings began to emerge north of the Black Sea and the Sea of Azov during the ninth and the tenth centuries. It was called "Kievan-Rus," named after the city of Kiev and the Rus, or Vikings.

The early Kievan-Rus, known as the armed merchants of the region, kept the mounted Khazars of the east plains from expanding westward, consolidated their own levying authority, and extended their trading routes southward across the Black and Caspian Seas. The state of Kievan-Rus first evolved longitudinally along the region's north-south river system. Commercial links and taxation jurisdictions along river routes gave rise to quasi-formalized political and commercial unity among towns of Kievan-Rus territories. Toward the end of the first millennium, a Kievan state matured; its centers of power were based between the river city of Kiev to the south and the lake-based metropolis of Novgorod to the north.

Vladimir the Great (980–1015) envisioned the glories of the Byzantine Empire as a model for his own Kievan state. He accepted Byzantine Christianity, introduced it as a state religion, designated his sons and immediate family members as prince-administrators of commercial centers, and established the order of succession to his seat of power in Kiev.

Chaos, however, ensued upon Vladimir's death. Svyatopolk, Vladimir's second son, murdered three of his six brothers and established himself as the Great Prince Administrator of Kiev. It was not until 1019 that Yaroslav, Vladimir's fourth son and Svyatopolk's younger brother, descended upon Kiev with his mercenary Varangians from the northern city of Novogorod. Yaroslav, nicknamed the Wise, and his followers defeated Svyatopolk, consolidated the previously separate administrations of Novogorod in the north and Kiev in the south, and unified the rule of the Kievan state between 1019 and 1054. Under Yaroslav, Kiev enjoyed a period of political stability and military growth. Culture flourished, arts and letters thrived, religious faith took root, political alliances with powerful neighbors were formed, and commercial relationships expanded. Kiev became the political and cultural center of eastern Europe. These were the decades of crowning glory for the Kievan-Rus state.

Another power struggle followed Yaroslav's death in 1054. After more than two decades of armed conflict among princely families, Yaroslav's third son, Vsevolod, emerged in 1078 as the Great Prince of Kiev. He married a daughter of Byzantine Emperor Constantine Monomakh, increased Kievan-Rus's cultural and commercial contacts with Greco-Roman sovereignties, and strengthened political alliances with dominions of the Byzantine Empire. Vsevolod and his son Vladimir Monomakh continued Yaroslav's territorial consolidations of the Kievan-Rus state.

Again, territorial conflicts among the nobility erupted upon the death of Vladimir Monomakh. While southern princes vied for control of the great princely seat of Kiev, Yuri Dolgorouki, the eighth son of Vladimir Monomakh, marched north in 1147 and, with the cooperation of the Varangians, established a new seat of princely power, or principality, named Moscovia, southeast of Novgorod (Tremblay, 1979: 20).

Around this time, the ruling families of the northern principalities started to diversify their trade relationships, initiate new trade routes, and establish new settlements along the rivers of the northern and eastern territories of present-day Russia. The traders along the banks of the major southern rivers and the taxpaying settlers of fertile plains of the south meanwhile began migrating northward. These waves of northward migration began by the middle of the twelfth century and continued through the beginning of the thirteenth century. Many traders moved north in response to flourishing commercial prospects; farmers, on the other hand, fled the contentious south in favor of the emerging stablity of the north.

In time, commercial prosperity and political stability in the north—in contrast with frequent armed conflicts in the south—permitted the rise of Moscovia as the new political and cultural center. It displaced Kiev as the great seat of princely power and the paradigm of Russian cities. The Kievan-Rus state became disunited; the north burgeoned into what was to become the Tsardom of Muscovy, while territories of present-day Ukraine to the south gradually became the possessions of foreign powers.

Kiev was thoroughly pillaged first in 1169 by Andrew of Bogolyubovo, a northern prince. The Mongol Tartars began sweeping across the plains from the east during the first half of the thirteenth century, and Kiev was plundered in 1240 by Genghis Kahn's nephew Batu and his Golden Horde forces. So despoiled was Kiev that,

in the second half of the thirteenth century there were no princes in Kiev—even as nominees of the Horde. Some stray folk began to settle in the city, but the recurrent Tartar raids forced the Kievan Metropolitan Maxim—still "Metropolitan of all Russia"—to quit the south and establish himself with his retinue and belongings in the north at Vladimir on the Klyazma. According to the chronicler: "Then the whole of Kiev ran away." (Allen, 1963: 38)

While the southern part of modern-day Ukraine either came under the rule of the Golden Horde or was exposed to its repeated raids, the northern and western parts increasingly became a part of the Grand Duchy of Lithuania's domain during the early part of the fourteenth century. Gediminas, the Grand Duke of Lithuania (1316–1341), alluded to himself as the "King of Lithuania and Rus," for he was extending his reign eastward into present-day Ukraine and northward into the Russian territories. The traditionally important term "Kievan," a portion of the established expression for the state of Kievan-Rus, was expeditiously omitted from the Grand Duke's royal designation of his territorial domain (Chirovsky 1984: 3). Kiev henceforth became a symbol of past glories and a target of military conquests. Kievan-Rus as a unified political entity had by then ceased to exist. For nearly three centuries thereafter, much of present-day Ukraine came under the shared—and at times alternating—controls of its powerful neighbors.

The territorial expansion of Lithuania's domain eastward and southward promoted cultural, commercial, and population exchanges among the present states of Lithuania, Ukraine, and Belorussia. The three ethnically diverse peoples coexisted for centuries, mutually influencing and enriching each other's distinct histories. Although Ukrainian influence on Lithuania's arts, letters, social development, and cultural life was significantly more pronounced than the reverse, Ukraine's peasant-farmers remained subjects of the Grand Duchy of Lithuania, bound to the land, taxed, and conscripted for military service. Since the Grand Duchy's warriors, especially during the reign of the Grand Duke Algirdas (1341–1377), were the only military able to restrain the westward advances of the Golden Horde, Ukraine gained territorial security from its alliance with the Lithuanians. Life was also more bearable under Lithuanian rule because the ruling class did not interfere with the peasants' religious practices.

The fate of peasant-farmers changed drastically with the formation of the Polish-Lithuanian Commonwealth in 1569. As Poland's dominance over Lithuania grew, so did the Polish aristocracy's influence and claims in Ukrainian territories. By late sixteenth century, nearly all Ukrainian territories previously held by the Grand Duchy of Lithuania passed to Poland's control. The Polish nobles not only kept the peasants on their land as serfs, but also attempted to impose Roman Catholicism on a people who had for centuries practiced Byzantine Orthodoxy. The attempt was deliberate, purposeful, and methodical: those who relinquished the Orthodox faith in favor of Catholicism were granted recognition and privileges; those who resisted were overtly discriminated against and were relegated to the bottom of social, political, and economic stratum of the Commonwealth.

The Polish nobles who employed social and economic leverage to pressure the natives into leaving behind their Orthodox faith believed that the supplantating of a religion alien to the Polish tradition could assist political and military assimilation of a newly subjugated people. They were attempting to accomplish a political objective by dictating an overall religious conversion. Their efforts at proselytizing their Orthodox subjects intensified in the mid-1600s. It was under this oppressive milieu that a more clearly defined Ukrainian culture began to emerge. Resentment against Polish rule grew, feeding and nurturing an already existing sentiment of separatism and independence from Poland.

The emergence of a distinct political entity in the region later known as Ukraine was inspired by freedom-loving peasants who felt the burden of economic depriv-ation and social discrimination intolerable. Aversion to domination by external forces nurtured their longing for an autonomous and sovereign identity. They fled east and southward to the sparsely populated steppe lands situated in the central part of present-day Ukraine. These runaway peasants were the fore-runners of the Ukrainian people. They were varyingly alluded to as fugitives, warriors, frontiersmen, or wanderers, but they were collectively known as the *kozaks*, or the free, self-ruling Cossacks. The free Cossacks differed from another group of warriors known as the "registered" Cossacks, whom the Polish nobles and the Moscovy princes employed among their armed forces in defense against the Tartars from the plains.

The free Cossacks were armed, free-spirited former serfs who roved the plains between the Polish forces to the west, the Tartars to the south, and the steadily growing power of the Moscovy to the north and the east. To protect their inhabited territories, the free Cossacks fought off would-be intruders whenever and wherever necessary. In order to ensure their freedom, the Cossack warriors erected defensive structures called *siches* along the lower banks of the Dniper River. A *sich* was a structure surrounded by ditches and moats. An elected military ruler called an *ataman* directed the affairs of each of the *siches*, and the *atamans* gathered each year to select their commander in chief, who was called the *hetman*. The *hetman* had power over the affairs of all the *siches*. The assembly of *atamans* was called the *rada*. To this day, the Ukrainians refer to their parliament as the "Supreme Rada."

It was the *rada* that assigned diverse responsibilities to the *atamans* of various *siches*, including the defense of towns and villages within the Cossacks' domain. Aside from the earlier form of administrative rule during the days of Kievan-Rus, governance of people through a chain command of *rada, hetman*, and *atamans* was the earliest known form of self-government in Ukraine.

The free Cossacks' successes at remaining free from and independent of their powerful neighbors in time earned them recognition as gallant fighters. They sought to form themselves into an organized, independent political entity. This longing crystallized into a tangible reality with the appearance on the scene of a warrior named Bogdan Khmelnytsky. Khmelnytsky was a registered Cossack official who fled the Poles, joined the free Cossacks in the plains, and was ultimately elected *hetman* by his fellow free Cossack warriors. He led a series of successful campaigns against his former Polish overlords, and his military successes inspired the subjugated serfs in many parts of the former Kievan-Rus to rise in revolt against the landed gentry of the Polish aristocracy. As the free Cossacks advanced farther and farther west into the Polish-occupied Ukrainian territories, including the ancient city of L'Viv, a new political entity not only emerged but also caught the notice of its powerful neighbors. The Cossack-possessed self-governing territories between the Polish Empire to the west and the Grand Duchy of Moscovy to the east and north was referred to as *ukraina* or *okraina*, a Slavic term meaning borderland or frontier territory. The people inhabiting that poorly defined frontier region were called the Ukrainians. This was one of the two brief periods in history that Ukraine enjoyed a distinct and independent status as a self-governing state, the other being the two years following the Bolshevik revolution.

Despite Poland's steadily declining military strength during the second half of the seventeenth century, the Polish king and his noblemen remained intent on punishing the free Cossacks for the harm they had inflicted on Poland's vested interest in the region. Polish forces kept Ukraine's Cossacks vigilant and their sympathizers in the countryside anxious. Sustained armed conflicts between Khmelnytsky's Cossacks and the Polish king's forces steadily eroded both sides' stamina, providing Moscovy with a ready window for making inroads into both Ukrainian and Polish territories. By the time of Ivan the Terrible (1533–1584), the first tsar of the Russian Empire, Moscovy had already extended its domain far northward and eastward. Long before Khmelnytsky began his successful revolt against the Polish forces in Ukraine, Moscovy had long entertained ambitions to extend its domain southward and westward. When the exhausted Cossacks had finally to ally themselves with one of four powers for survival—the Poles to the west, the Crimean Tartars to the south, the sultan of Turkey, or the tsar of Moscovy—Khmelnytsky, with the approval of the *rada*, sent envoys to Tsar Alexey Mikhailovich. Khmelnytsky sought protection for the Cossacks' land and the people's religious freedom from their non-Orthodox neighbors. He placed Ukraine under the protection of Moscovy and pledged Ukraine's obeyance to the tsar. The people of Ukraine lost their first opportunity to establish for themselves a formalized independent and autonomous state.

The tsar took Ukraine under his protection in 1654, and Ukraine became a vassal of a growing Russian Empire. The Ukrainians were free to practice their Orthodox religion, which was identical with that of tsarist Russia's. However, the people found themselves under a new caste of masters from the north. Their fate remained unchanged: they remained serfs. As the Russian Empire kept up its all-directional expansion, a systematic integration and Russification program began in the southern regions of Ukraine. Moscow conscripted Cossack fighters for military expeditions, drafted Ukrainian laborers for building projects, banned the use of the Ukrainian language from schools, and exiled opponents to Siberia's vast wilderness.

Russia completely controlled Ukraine by the end of the eighteenth century. Following Catherine the Great's war against the Ottoman Empire, Russia appropriated the Tartar's stronghold of Crimea and appended it to its southern administrative command near Ukraine. Ukraine, together with the Crimean region, remained under tsarist rule until 1917, when the Bolshevik Revolution ended the rule of the Romanov dynasty.

Russia's provisional government under Lenin and Trotsky busied itself with eliminating anti-Bolshevik forces between 1917 and 1919. This helped to augment the voices of Ukrainians calling for independence. Ukrainian nationalism resurfaced. The congress of the people's representatives convened in Kiev in April 1917 and proclaimed Ukraine a sovereign and independent state. For the first time in Ukraine's history, a conventional government was formed. However, Ukraine's first experience with independence was short-lived. The government with Myhailo Hrushevsky as president and Volodymir Vinnichenko as prime minister, lasted for only two years. There was neither a peaceful environment nor sufficient time to crystallize the people's dream for an independent Ukraine, for the Bolsheviks were intent on sovietizing Ukraine. Moscow surreptitiously created a Ukrainian Soviet Socialist government in the city of Kharkov, directly challenging the authority of the Kiev government. As a further threat to Ukrainian sovereignty, German, Austrian, White Russian, and Polish forces alternately advanced into and retreated from different parts of Ukraine in 1918. Kiev's incipient government was forced to expend most of its inadequately synchronized energy fending off political assaults from within and military offensives from without. By December 1919, Russia's Bolshevik army had occupied all of Ukraine. Poland occupied the western portion of Ukraine between 1920 and 1939. Hungary and Romania each annexed a small portion of Ukraine's southwestern territories during the same period. All territories lost to these three countries in 1920 were reclaimed by the FSU toward the end of World War II. In addition, Ukraine was occupied by Germany during the period 1941–1944.

For a brief period, when German forces occupied Ukraine during World War II, Ukraine's hope of regaining independence from the Soviets resurfaced momentarily. The hope, however, quickly faded at the end of the war. Moscow not only reclaimed Ukraine as an integral part of the USSR, but also carved land masses from the eastern portions of Poland, Romania, and Czechoslovakia and incorporated them into the Ukrainian Soviet Socialist Republic. Ukraine was once again securely under Soviet dominion. Finally, in 1954, in commemoration of three centuries of union between Russia and Ukraine, Moscow transferred the idyllic vacation land of Crimea from Russia to Ukraine's jurisdiction. All in all, Ukraine's territory increased by 34.9 percent between 1939 and 1954.

The Ukrainian people were subject to nearly another half century of Soviet control. Finally, on August 24, 1991, the Supreme Rada declared Ukraine sovereign and independent for the second time in its history. Ukraine now ranks among the youngest of the independent states in the world.

THE PEOPLE

Nomadic Slavs had entered the steppe lands of present-day Ukraine by the eighth century A.D., settling along trade routes as dictated by waterways. Hunting and food gathering preceded settled cultivation of Ukraine's rich soil. By the middle of the ninth century, the Nordic explorers had descended southward from the Gulf of Finland, south to the coast of the Black Sea. During this time, Turkish warriors and Greek merchants ventured northward, while the Golden Horde continued its western movement. Most of the travelers came in search of gains or spoils; not infrequently, thousands of settlers were carted off as prizes. They were human cargo, uprooted from Ukrainian soil, transplanted into foreign lands, and used as slaves or traded as commodities.

Over the past millennium or more, the land of Ukraine has witnessed massive demographic movements. Some of the migration was voluntary, but other movements of people were the result of planning or coercion. Many settlers migrated northward in the twelfth century and thereafter, fleeing from endless armed conflicts among southern warring princes. For centuries, assorted waves of Lithuanians, Poles, Germans, Tartars, Greeks, Jews, Russians, and others were able to penetrate the ill-defined frontiers of Ukraine's domain.

The Ukrainians enjoyed relative peace and independence during the glorious decades of the free Cossacks. The Cossacks at that time were concerned with the defense of the *siches* and with planning and executing campaigns abroad, hunting, fishing, and simple farming. A primary objective of campaigns abroad was the freeing of Ukrainian captives held in foreign lands; the tragic fate of the people captured and sold by invaders was passionately branded into the soul of the free Cossacks. Freeing Ukrainians from foreign domination, religious persecution, and outside rule became a mission.

From the sixteenth century to World War II, Ukraine was the prey of foreign powers on a grand scale. The Ukrainians became pawns in a highly organized game of mass deportations and conscription. Tsarist administrations banished nationalist-minded intellectuals en masse and drafted hundreds of thousands of Ukrainians for construction projects in Russia. The Soviets exiled millions of Ukrainian dissidents, including peasants objecting to farm collectivization. They also injected millions of non-natives into Ukraine in order to implement the USSR's sovietization policy.

During World War II, Germany consigned masses of Ukrainians into its own workforce and absorbed large numbers of Ukrainian youth into its armed forces.

Ukraine was thus historically a point of contention for various foreign rivals: the Mongols and the Tartars, the Finns and the Jews, the Turks and the Greeks, the Serbs and the Germans, and the Poles and the Russians. Unless and until assimilated into Ukraine's cultural and social settings, the Poles remained Poles and the Tartars remained Tartars. Many of the city dwellers, in particular the non-natives from neighboring states, were storekeepers, merchants, traders, or administrators. The Ukrainian natives, on the other hand, were mostly farmers and Cossacks. It was in the countryside, in the people of simple living, that the soul and the spirit of Ukraine was most securely embodied.

LANGUAGE, NATIONAL IDENTITY

Russia, Ukraine, and Belorussia shared a common language based on the Cyrillic alphabet. Foreign incursions and shifting populations over the centuries interjected novel words and fresh expressions into daily usage in different parts of that vast region. These foreign influences, combined with differences in local usage, led to the creation of three distinct languages by the thirteenth century. These three different languages—Russian, Ukrainian, and Belorussian—continued to diverge as they evolved.

The development of the Ukrainian language expedited the process of shaping and crystallizing a uniquely Ukrainian identity; the language became a vehicle for uniting a people suffering from a shared tragic past. The language recorded the long history of aliens who repeatedly invaded, plundered, and left with innumerable human spoils, leaving behind accounts of tragedies that continuously enriched and embellished the already abundant sources of legends, lores, ballads, songs, and folk dances. For instance, in portraying the fate of Ukraine's people, a typical folk song laments: "Our hamlet has been burned and our goods plundered. The old mother has been killed and the wife carried off captive. The tambourines are heard from the valley. People are led to slaughter there, with nooses round their necks and chains that clatter on their feet" (quoted in Allen, 1963: 126).

Taras Shevchenko (1814–1861), Ukraine's most prominent and respected poet and artist, condensed and committed into Ukrainian the most painful pages of the nation's history. His ache for an independent homeland led him to lament over *hetman* Khmelnytsky's decision to grant suzerainty over Ukraine to the tsar of Russia, even though the legendary Cossack and his 1654 *rada* had no viable alternative. Shevchenko encapsulated the history of the Ukrainian people more as a serialized account of lament and pain than a song of freedom and joy. In depicting the collective fate of the Ukrainian people, he lamented:

In slavery I grew 'mid strangers,
Unwept by any kin of mine;
In slavery I now will lie,
And vanish without any sign.
I shall not leave the slightest trace
Upon our glorious Ukraine,
Upon our land, but not ours.   (Quoted in Chamberlin, 1944: 30–31)

Shevchenko and his colleagues circulated poetry, lamentations, and the accumu-lated wealth of folklore, legends, tales, and songs of past repressions. Countless narratives of national tragedies came alive through ballads, verse, lyrics, and other written expressions. The Ukrainian language became an all-purpose instrument for reviving, nurturing, and sustaining the nation's collective consciousness. It helped reawaken the people's longing for an independent homeland.

The people's aspiration for freedom from serfdom was not lost on their masters. The Russian Empire needed a pliable Ukraine whose people had no language of their own, who had no memory of their past, who had no master other than the tsar of Russia, and whose labor force could be drafted at will without organized resistance. The tsarist government exiled Shevchenko and his collaborators to remote regions of the empire, prohibited the publication of writings in Ukrainian, and directed the Ukrainians to embrace the Russian language as their own.

The Ukrainian language survived nonetheless; although messages from Ukraine's tragic past were prohibited from circulation in the people's own language, they were engraved in the soul of Ukrainian society. Melancholic lyrics and poignant narratives helped weave the fabric of Ukrainian culture, mold its temperament, sculpt its psyche, and influence its perspective. The Ukrainian language helped revive the nationalist sentiment and sustain a yearning for Ukraine's independence. With additional tribulations suffered under successive reigns of masters from abroad, an increasingly distinct Ukrainian identity emerged.

Unfortunately, the Ukrainian language was also persecuted under the Soviet system. The Kremlin realized that in the hands of a writer like Shevchenko, the Ukrainian language could very effectively promote and instill nationalist sentiments. Moscow did not merely want Ukraine under the Soviet shadow; it wanted a fully sovietized Ukraine. Moscow thus declared Russian Ukraine's second official lan-guage in 1928. The land's native language was promptly supplanted by Russian in all official and institutional settings. Both tsarist Russia and the USSR understood the identity the Ukrainian language could impart to the people of Ukraine, and both strove for its disuse and disappearance. Although Ukraine's capital city of Kiev counted only two secondary schools using Ukrainian as the official medium of instruction in 1991, the Ukrainian language and a Ukrainian culture survived.

A TORMENTED PATH TO INDEPENDENCE

From the dawn of Ukraine's recorded history until 1991, the land was steeped in accounts of uprooted captives, serfdom, exiles, and oppression. For centuries, foreign powers attempted either to subjugate Ukraine or to integrate it into their respective domains. None hesitated to apply harsh measures in order to secure such envisioned objectives. Historically, Ukraine was a playground for neighboring powers. Even under the most promising of circumstances for independence, Ukraine's leaders were obliged to choose one ally for protection against others. Circumstances first compelled Khmelnytsky in 1654 to choose from among the tsar of Russia, the king of Poland, the sultan of Turkey, and the khan of Crimea. He and his *rada* pledged Ukraine's fealty to the tsar of Russia. Efforts at Russification of Ukraine thereafter, and the suppression of Ukrainian nationalism, reduced the people of Ukraine to a fate more devastating than the serfdom experienced under the Poles. Ukraine's first opportunity ever to formalize its independent identity dissipated into the thin air of Russia's vast expanse.

Ukraine's second opportunity for independence came when the Bolsheviks deposed the tsar in 1917. Nevertheless, before the newly installed *rada* had a chance to begin work, Ukraine was obliged to choose one among four for an ally: Marshal Pilsudski's Poland, Lenin's Bolsheviks, the White Russians, or the German-Austrian alliance. Pilsudski envisioned a revival of the Polish-Lithuanian Commonwealth, with Ukraine as a vassal state. Lenin promised Ukrainian autonomy and equality with Russia. The White Russians sought the defeat of the Bolsheviks and the restoration of the feudal system, and the German-Austrian alliance sought to curtail the spread of the Red menace. Through political pressure and military threat, the Bolsheviks forced a contrived union between Russia and Ukraine, and seven decades of Communist rule began.

Reenacting feats of the tsarist government, executions and mass deportations of Ukrainians began under Stalin. Nationalists, dissident intellectuals, defiant peasants, and even passive resisters suffered from either extended exiles or unexplained disappearances. There were also substantial inflows of non-natives, arriving as part of a plan for ethnic integration and the weakening of the Ukrainian identity. The extensiveness and thoroughness with which Stalin crushed Ukraine led many Ukrainians to view Germany as their liberator when Hitler's forces marched past Ukraine and onto Moscow.

Moscow drafted Ukrainians into its armed forces to fight the Germans; untold numbers of Ukrainians voluntarily joined the German forces to fight the USSR's Communists. A number of fierce battles took place on the convenient battleground of Ukraine, far from either Berlin or Moscow. Many of these battles fought on Ukrainian soil pitched Soviet-drafted against German-inducted Ukrainian soldiers. All in all, Ukraine lost more than six million of its sons and daughters to the two foreign interests during World War II. When the war ended, Ukraine was not an inch closer to regaining its political independence than it had been before the war.

INDEPENDENCE, SECTARIANISM

It has been but a few years since Ukraine regained its independence, but this has been the longest period of independence Ukraine has ever known. Ukraine is not a nation united in perspective, nor is it a collage of dissipated ethnic or geographic communities. It is a nation with many commonalities among its people, but also with many differences among groups of special concerns: "Ukraine is not integrated in terms of ethnicity and culture, which is reflected in the result of the recent presidential election (July 1994). Western observers even say that Ukraine is doomed to an eventual division between the east and the west. They think that such a danger really exists" (Pirozhkov interview, 1994).

Ukraine hosts peoples of diverse ethnic and religious backgrounds. People in the western parts of Ukraine assimilated influences from the west during centuries past. They also resisted and fought against foreign authorities. They are "a resilient people who have demonstrated a peculiar ability to assimilate, in part, with the ruling nationality, while almost simultaneously resisting it" (Tremblay 1979: 39). When circumstances permitted, they were also the most vocal in demanding Ukraine's independence. That was true both in 1917 and in 1991. People in the eastern regions of the country, on the other hand, exhibit an affinity toward Russia. They assume a more pragmatic approach to governance and are less affected by political considerations. People in western Ukraine advocate widening the distance between Ukraine and Russia, including the economic relationship between the two; easterners accede to the legacies of seventy years of Soviet integration of Ukraine's economy, cautioning the impracticality of an abrupt divorce from everything past.

On another front, the Ukrainian language, which for centuries identified, unified, and rallied the consciousness of a suffering people under foreign occupation, carries differing significance for different groups of people in different parts of the country. Ukrainian is spoken almost universally in rural areas, especially in the western regions of the country. It is not widely used, though, in population centers. In central and western Ukraine, urban dwellers speak mostly Russian at their workplaces and revert to speaking Ukrainian at home. The western city of L'Viv is an exception; there, Ukrainian is widely spoken. In eastern regions, where Russian émigrés dominate, the Russian language eclipses Ukrainian in daily usage.

Another facet of Ukraine's regional heterogeneity is its dispersed religious groups. Roman Catholics, influenced by neighboring Poland, dominate the western portion of the country, while the Byzantine Orthodox faith is predominant in the east.

It is not likely that east will part with west. There is a sufficiently strong degree of cohesiveness between peoples of the east and the west in Ukraine, at least at the present. Boris Parakhousky, a researcher at Ukraine's National Academy of Sciences, notes:

There were also differences between the south and the north after the U.S. became independent. We should admit a similar situation in Ukraine. A new Abraham Lincoln may be needed (in Ukraine). However, historically the Ukrainian situation is better than that of the U. S. in the eighteenth century. Ukrainians are unique with a single historical past, with a common historical memory. The Ukrainian people suffered under different foreign powers, identifying themselves as a single people. (Parakhousky interview, 1994)

Nevertheless, discernable differences exist among different interest groups. Ukraine's unity and sovereignty in the long run depend on the success of its current economic reform. While the western Ukrainians sought independence for its own sake, the eastern Ukrainians voted for independence more due to economic considerations than to nationalist sentiment. They voted for a divorce from Moscow to spare themselves from the devastating economic conditions unfolding in the FSU.

Presuming lasting political cohesiveness among peoples of different regions, religious faiths, and ideologies in an infant democracy is premature. There have already been murmurings among select subgroups of easterners, suggesting a return to union with Russia. They consider the current economic conditions in Ukraine to be no better than those in Russia.

On the political front, efforts are needed to synchronize the differences among peoples of divergent ideological inclinations. Only a unified nation can effectually focus its energy on questing for *de facto* independence through democratic processes and economic stability and growth.

SOCIAL, CULTURAL MILIEU FOR ECONOMIC REFORM

Ukraine's fateful chronicle helped etch its people's predispositions. For centuries, the Ukrainians resisted civil authority to the extent circumstances would permit. Until 1991, civil authority personified foreign domination and oppression, and there was a perpetual adversarial relationship between the Ukrainian people and a perceived antagonist. Inherited background forces have been at work in Kiev's policy formulation processes since late 1991.

Politically active voices are still often locked in quasi-fossilized mental sets, desisting from empathizing with alternative views, resisting constructive compromises. In the past, "it has been the case, . . . that the (Ukrainian) peasant has been more capable of rebelling against a bad government than of creating a good government" (Chamberlin, 1944: 6–7). Though independent and peasants no more, Ukrainians are still engaged in veiled confrontations. Countless ideological battles are being fought; unyielding beliefs and contentious disputes have detracted from the strengthening of Ukraine's nascent democracy.

As a result of this combative political milieu, the economy has suffered. Ukraine has had six economic reform programs between August 1991 and January 1995. None has received broad support, and none has been extensively implemented.

The task at hand calls for creative alternatives to resolve conflicting views. Ukrainians need to fully realize that they are now masters of their own destiny, and that sensible cooperation contributes more to nation-building than does expending national energy on mutual subjugation of rival viewpoints. The Ukrainians must be made fully aware that Communist elements of the FSU still lie in wait seeking an opportunity to exploit Ukraine's historically bequeathed weaknesses. Historian Yaroslav Bilinsky made the following observation more than three decades ago, but it still rings true today:

It has been noticed that Soviet Ukrainians tend to be so preoccupied with abolishing the ills of the regime that little thought is given to what precisely should be put in its place. But as soon as the regime starts breaking apart, . . . the resentments are being aired in larger groups, rational and irrational alternatives are discussed, and various clandestine organizations start mushrooming, some of them with distinctly nationalist hues, (Bilinsky, 1964: 308)

Mikhail Gorbachev's call for *perestroika* and *glasnost* encouraged disenchanted Ukrainians to air their grievances against the Communist system and the FSU. It was easy and comforting then to level criticisms at Ukraine's masters in Moscow; no constructive and workable policy recommendations were needed. The Ukrainians wanted the system abolished, without a replacement within the framework of the FSU. The scenario has changed. Now that the old system has demised, new policies are needed. It is no longer sufficient to lament what was wrong; now policymakers and activists must direct their attention to doing what is right. No longer can Ukrainians merely blame Moscow for their economic difficulties; Ukraine must henceforth assume responsibility for its own actions. Already, the number of commentaries and criticims with "distinctly nationalist hues" have been on the rise, except "nationalist hues" this time applies to Ukrainian groupings in different parts of the country espousing divergent ideologies.

The future of Ukraine as an undivided and sovereign state to a large measure depends on the success of its current economic reform. The remainder of this volume presents and analyzes the most cogent facets of economic reform in the newly independent Ukraine. Recommendations about policy alternatives are offered in light of the nation's tormented past, with the hope that the future history of Ukraine will be one of a prosperous and independent nation.

2

Ukraine under the Soviet System

This chapter examines how seven decades of Soviet control affected the Ukrainian economy. Understanding the legacy of Communism permits an objective approach to recognizing Ukraine's contemporary problems. It also expedites the prescription of sensible and workable reform policies appropriate for Ukraine's unique situations.

UKRAINE'S IMPORTANCE TO THE SOVIETS

Moscow's sovietization of Ukraine, especially during the Stalin era (1928–1953) was methodical, ruthless, and exhaustive. The thoroughness with which the Kremlin politically subjugated and economically integrated Ukraine into the Soviet system was indicative of Ukraine's strategic importance to the USSR; the Bolsheviks could not likely have succeeded without Ukraine, for geographic, demographic, and economic reasons.

Ukraine borders a portion of Russia's southern frontier, directly south of the metropolises of Moscow and St. Petersburg. To the west and southwest it is bounded by Poland, what was Czechoslovakia, and Hungary. Historically, with a restive and assertive Germany barely beyond the confines of these countries and with other Western nations mistrustful of Moscow's designs, the Soviets needed Ukraine as a partial shield against the West. Furthermore, Ukraine's extensive shorelines on the Black Sea could provide the Soviets with ready access to international waters lapping the shores of southern Europe, the Middle East, and beyond. For all these reasons, the Bolsheviks needed Ukraine as part of their envisioned union of Soviet republics.

In addition to geographically strategic considerations, Moscow also needed Ukraine for demographic reasons. By 1917, Ukraine had a population comparable to that of France or Italy. Within the envisioned Union of the Soviet Socialist Republics,

Ukraine would be the second most populous republic. The USSR needed Ukraine for the same purposes that tsarist Russia had needed it—for drafting Ukrainian laborers and conscripting Ukrainian soldiers.

Finally, Soviet Russia needed Ukraine because of its rich agricultural land, abundant mineral deposits, and immense industrial potential. The vast expanse of Ukraine's thick, black topsoil has for centuries been the envy of Europe, and its rich mineral reserves held broad development potential for the USSR's future industries. The last consideration was particularly cogent in the late 1910s, since rich minerial reserves east of the Ural Mountains were either unknown or economically nonviable. Ukraine's Dnepropetrovsk region was one of tsarist Russia's three industrial centers in the late 1910s, the other two being Moscow and St. Petersburg. Communist Russia coveted continued supplies of material and human resources from Ukraine, much as the tsarist regime had.

LENIN'S PLEDGES

Ukraine's independence in 1917 was punctuated by domestic strife and foreign invasions. On the domestic front, the nationalists founded Ukraine's first autonomous government in Kiev, while the Ukrainian Communists set up theirs in the northeastern city of Kharkiv. On the external front, foreign powers, including the Germans, the Austrians, the Poles, the White Russians, and the Red Russians, vied for control of, or influence in, Ukraine. By the end of 1919, the Red Army controlled all of Ukraine's territories.

As an inducement for Ukraine's voluntary reunion with Moscow, Lenin pledged full equality between Russia and Ukraine. He also assured social and cultural autonomy for Ukraine in a proposed union of Socialist Republics. The Moscow-backed government in Ukraine adopted Lenin's invitation. Ukraine became a founding member of the USSR in 1922.

Ukraine did experience relative autonomy within the newly formed USSR during Lenin's brief administration (1918–1924). Ukrainization programs, including the active promotion of the Ukrainian language within the republic, gave the impression that Ukraine incurred no undue loss of autonomy consequent to its union with the other republics of the USSR.

The country's economy, however, experienced severe jolts after the Kremlin-backed Ukrainian government proclaimed the country a Soviet Republic. The Communists' economic policy was based on a command model normally adopted under wartime circumstances. Mobilized by revolutionary zeal and expressing their antagonism toward the establishment, industrial and urban laborers purged their enterprises of experienced managers and technical experts. The republic's industrial production, in particular its famed iron ore and coal industries, suffered precipitous decreases in output. The Bolsheviks' farm policy also brought critical declines in agricultural production, since Moscow had ordered all surplus grain not consumed by the farm population be surrendered to the state at a government-determined low purchasing price. Farmers' resentment expressed itself in reduced areas being sown during the subsequent planting seasons. The reduction in areas being farmed, combined with a severe drought in 1920, resulted in Ukrainian farmers and urban consumers coming face to face with severe grain shortages. Widespread famines followed, plunging an already tumultuous Ukrainian economy into yet a deeper abyss. Lenin had little room for maneuvering; he temporarily suspended the implementation of the mobilized command model. A revised strategy for dealing with Ukraine's industrial and agricultural production ensued. A more moderate and balanced approach to economic growth, as outlined in Lenin's New Economic Policy (NEP), made its appearance in 1921. This temporary absence of extensive intervention in Ukraine's economy was not due to Moscow's respect for Ukraine's autonomy; it was a period in which the Kremlin was not certain of the appropriate development path for the envisioned USSR economy. Unsure of the correct economic development path toward socialism, the young USSR, which consisted of four republics, Russia, Ukraine, Belorussia and Transcaucasia,[1] adhered to Lenin's NEP until 1927. At that time, therefore, Ukraine's economy sustained no significant structural aberrations or sectoral distortions.

STALIN'S DECADES (1922–1953)

Stalin succeeded Lenin in 1922, liquidated his political rivals, consolidated his power, and radically transformed the young USSR. Ukraine and its economy took a fateful turn for the worse for decades thereafter.

Stalin discontinued Lenin's NEP in 1927 and replaced it with his own plan for economic growth. He opted for accelerated growth through rapid industrialization. Rapid expansion in heavy industry, however, meant more than accelerated economic growth for Stalin; it could also provide the USSR with the necessary foundation for a military buildup. Ukraine figured centrally in that cause. Radical changes were swiftly introduced throughout Ukraine, modifying institutional, structural, and functional aspects of the republic's economy. All changes in Ukraine came within the framework of securing the fulfillment of policy objectives as outlined by the Kremlin. The remainder of this chapter presents the implementation and effects of Moscow's policy in Ukraine.

Full integration of Ukraine's productive forces into the Soviet system was a precondition for fulfilling Stalin's mandate. Harnessing Ukraine's rich agricultural potential, abundant mineral reserves, and productive human resources under the absolute control of decision makers in Moscow began on the political and cultural fronts. Moscow-sponsored political movements were calculated to impact the most fundamental facets of Ukraine's society, culture, and economy.

Sovietizing Ukraine required the liquidation of "enemies" of the socialist state. Any Ukrainian manifesting the least sign of resistance to Soviet rule was a candidate for liquidation. Aside from owners of capital assets, who were capitalists and therefore enemies of the proletariat, two groups posed potential impediments to Moscow's scheme in Ukraine. They were the native intelligentsia with nationalist tendencies, and the peasants with deep attachment to family farming. Both categories were slated for removal when the reign of terror began.

On the political front, staged trials of prominent public figures came in waves. These public figures were the Ukrainian Communists ideologically aligned with their comrades in Moscow. They were the same Ukrainian Communists who founded the Ukrainian Socialist Republic in Kharkiv in 1917. Moscow suspected that some of them might be entertaining the dream of maintaining a Ukrainian republic distinct and autonomous from the envisioned Union of Socialist Republics. All first-generation Ukrainian Communist leaders, therefore, were liquidated, under one pretext or another. The standard indictment against the accused was "bourgeois nationalism." Christian Rakovsky, the first prime minister of the Soviet-backed Ukrainian government in Kharkiv, was tried and sentenced to twenty years of imprisonment. Gregory Petrovsky, the president of Rakovsky's government, disappeared without a trace. Rather than undergoing the humiliation of a trial and certain execution, Mykola Skyrpnyk, Rakorsky's interior minister, committed suicide (Chamberlin, 1944: 53). Other political and cultural figures, as well as their successors, did not fare much better. Among other prominent Ukrainian Communist leaders who were tried and sentenced to death in the 1930s were Yuri Kotsiubinsky, a deputy prime minister, and Panas Lyubchenko and Vlas Chubar, both of whom were prime ministers.

Waves of mass arrests, trials, and deportations also befell leading Ukrainian thinkers and academicians. The most prominent among them was Myhailo Hrushevsky, Ukraine's best known historian and its first president.[2] Though Hrushevsky did not stand trial, he was exiled from Ukraine in 1930 and died four years later in Russia. The campaign continued throughout the decades, sovietizing and suppressing Ukrainian nationalism with violence and terror. Lev Hryhorovych Lukyanenko, a Communist party functionary in the western city of L'Viv, wrote as follows in his clandestinely circulated pamphlet titled "A Draft Programme of the UWPU (Ukrainian Workers' and Peasants' Party)":

The nationalities policy in the Ukraine throughout the entire period of the Soviet regime's existence was particularly criticized: mass accusations of nationalism against millions of Ukrainians and their physical extermination, including that of thousands of people active in the political, academic and cultural life of the Ukraine; the proscription of hundreds of Ukrainian poets, writers, historians, and people active in art and culture. (Quoted in Browne, 1971: 59)

Lukyanenko was arrested, tried, condemned, and executed. The reign of terror silenced all real or perceived opposition to the Soviets' political integration of

Ukraine. The vacated positions were filled by either younger members of the Communist Party whom Moscow mistrusted less, or by non-native appointees designated by Moscow.

In the social and cultural spheres, Russian was declared the second official language of Ukraine in 1928. It soon replaced Ukrainian in official, institutional, and media usages. Ukrainization programs, which had previously encouraged a revitalized Ukrainian culture and an enriched native environment, abruptly halted. Social and cultural activities, civic programs, and printed materials were closely scrutinized by Moscow's secret police for either covertly anti-Soviet or latently nationalist manifestations. Kremlin strategists were aware that Ukrainians had not forgotten the harsh treatment they had received from tsarist Russia. They realized that rebel tendencies ran deep in the Ukrainian blood since governmental authority in Ukraine historically meant foreign masters.

Silencing political opposition to Soviet integration and suppressing nationalist sentiments were comparatively easy, because removing political opposition and curtailing Ukrainian cultural programs in a totalitarian milieu rarely delays or derails the political agenda of those in power. Ukraine's subjects remained largely unaffected economically by political purges or cultural and social constraints.

Forced integration of Ukraine's economy into the Soviet system under Stalin nevertheless created a different scenario. Lenin had attempted state intervention in the economy's allocative mechanism, but failed, which prompted the introduction of his NEP. The NEP was a temporary concession to widespread resistance from Ukraine's economic subjects. Stalin's planned changes for Ukraine's economy were radical and extensive, affecting all economic subjects and altering all economic relationships in Ukraine. Since Ukraine was the most populous minority republic in the Union of Soviet Republics, the success of Moscow's economic integration of Ukraine was crucial.

Central planners were acutely aware that trust in or cooperation with civil authority was not part of the Ukrainian tradition. Passive resistance by Ukraine's masses could pose severe challenges to the credibility of Moscow's policy architects. Economic integration began with political subjugation of the republic.

SOVIETIZATION OF UKRAINE

The process of sovietizing Ukraine was simple, blunt, and brutal. Moscow first exercised tight control over the mass media: Ukraine was isolated, and the outside world was kept unaware of the goings-on in Ukraine. Regions of Ukraine were also isolated from each other; certain areas of Ukraine were prevented from learning of happenings in other areas. The state-controlled media disseminated only news and programs approved by the secret police, who served as the party's propaganda machine.

Moscow transformed Ukraine into a republic entirely dependent on its dictates. The transformation scheme, which was phased in rapidly, contained three broad objectives encompassing the political, cultural, and economic spheres: (1) there would be no Ukrainian government independent of the USSR government in Moscow; (2) there would be no Ukrainian programs promoting Ukrainian culture or tradition; and (3) there would be no Ukrainian economy distinct from the USSR economy.

The relative autonomy Ukraine had enjoyed until 1927 was discontinued. All important decisions concerning Ukraine were either made in or preapproved by Moscow. Officials in Ukraine were prevented from making decisions, even those concerning local issues arising from local concerns. Ukrainian officials only served as administrators of directives from Moscow, and there was no autonomous Ukrainian administration at any level.

To ensure the central government's absolute control over Ukraine, Moscow-appointed officials, overwhelmingly of Russian heritage, replaced Ukrainian nationals. The replacements took place first in major administrative positions in the republic, then in directorships of important industrial plants. The displaced Ukrainian administrators were either liquidated under trumped-up charges, or deported with their whole families to remote parts of the USSR, such as Siberia or regions far east of the Urals. Faithful execution of central directives was monitored through offices of the Communist Party Secretariat. Each party-founded office paralleled a government office or a state institution. Government offices and institutions in Ukraine, therefore, were inundated with non-native administrators appointed by Moscow, as well as with reliable Communist cadres who tracked the loyalty and performance of the Moscow-appointed administrators.

On the cultural front, programs or events with native contents were strictly censored, monitored, or curtailed. In their place, party-approved programs promulgating USSR values and ideology were actively promoted and forced upon Ukrainian citizens. Moscow required factory and construction workers, miners and professionals to view propaganda films and attend party-sponsored meetings. Party-sanctioned social events and cultural programs were aimed at diluting and neutralizing Ukrainian sentiments whenever and wherever feasible. The objective was to create future generations of Ukrainians who would regard themselves as Soviets rather than Ukrainians.

On the economic front, the forced integration of Ukraine's economy into the Soviet system was swift and unrelenting. Moscow interjected itself into Ukraine's industry and agriculture on every possible level beginning in the mid-1920s. On the industrial front, the Soviets expanded their control of plants in key industries first. The directors in pivotal establishments, such as coal mines and steel mills, iron foundries and machine-building plants, were party loyalists in favor of the USSR and supported the sovietizing of Ukraine's economy for the common cause of the USSR. The fate of their immediate predecessors was fresh in their minds. The fear of exile or imprisonment was sufficient incentive for the directors' faithful execution of orders. As a result, the new enterprise directors made more demands on Ukrainian subjects than was necessary, creating a safety margin for their own job security and personal safety. They implemented Moscow's directives, with minimal need for independent decision making. Fear, in combination with pragmatism, resulted in habitual shunning of decision-making responsibilities. By this time, Ukrainian industry was as much the object of Soviet control as was the Ukrainian administration and legislature. There was no longer any illusion of an autonomous Ukrainian economy.

The Ukrainian workers, whose support for a union between Ukraine and Russia was actively solicited by Lenin in 1919, had by the mid-1920s "been deprived of any of the rights which they might have imagined themselves possessed when they took over the plants. They were by now completely dependent for their conditions of work and for their employment on the whims of the plant managers who were themselves directly under the central authorities in Moscow" (Manning, 1953: 89). The workers had once considered themselves the leaders of the Bolshevik revolution. This romantic notion all but disappeared during the early Stalin years.

Integrating Ukraine's agricultural sector into the Soviet system proved to be more challenging to the Soviets than integrating industry had been. Moscow had envisioned collectivized farming, insisting that all farmers be members of either state farms or collectives. The Ukrainian farmers, however, had a deep attachment to the land they cultivated. Family farming was a way of life. Moscow had no patience with the Ukrainian farmers' "bourgeois" mentality and applied political and financial pressures on the wealthier farmers first. Exiling entire families of wealthy farmers was routine. Increased taxes and reduced grain prices were only two of the many economic leverages Moscow arbitrarily employed against peasants resisting collectivization. Through relentless liquidation and open intimidation, Moscow subjugated and forcibly integrated Ukraine's agriculture into the Soviet system in only a few years. Ukraine's farmers lost their land and their autonomy to the Soviets. Like factory workers, they became subjects of Moscow's directives.

Ukraine was no longer producing for Ukraine's needs. All economic decisions—and how much of which goods should be produced, as well as factor allocation and product distribution—were made in compliance with the dictates of Moscow. The Soviets had enacted a macro application of the dictum "from each according to his ability, and to each according to his need." From Ukraine, Moscow exacted what it wanted, and to Ukraine, Moscow allotted what it deemed sufficient.

A PLANNED ECONOMY

Soviet planning for Ukraine did not take Ukrainian interests into account. Moscow's only consideration was the role Ukraine could play in the Soviet economy. The planning process began with the Communist Party's Politburo in Moscow. The primary control agency for sovietizing Ukraine's economy was the USSR Central Planning Committee (CPC). Through the CPC's five-year plans, Ukraine became an integral part of the USSR's economy. The remainder of this chapter profiles Ukraine as a planned economy, a subjugated economy, and a dependent economy.

The Politburo's prerogative was determining the long, medium, and short-term objectives for the USSR economy. The CPC accordingly crafted the long, medium, and annual economic plans, with the fulfillment of Politburo-mandated objectives as the focus. The CPC's five-year plans were then submitted to the Politburo for evaluation, critique, and endorsement. Thereafter, the Politburo-endorsed five-year plan proceeded, pro forma, to the Communist Party's Central Committee for approval. The party-approved five-year plan was then submitted to the Supreme Soviet, the USSR parliament, for legislative sanction, gift-packaging the plan with some semblance of legitimacy and the approval procedures with some semblance of democratic process.

The CPC focused its planning blueprint on setting output targets. Recommendations concerning the levels and categories of investment, determinations of factor allocations among competing users and uses, and production quotas assigned to respective republics and plants all revolved around the fulfillment of the targets. Upon approval of a proposed plan, the CPC's detailed decisions were communicated to producing units in Ukraine, either through the appropriate ministries or agencies in Kiev or, in the case of all-Union factories, to the plant management itself.

Ukraine had its own CPC, but its primary function was not planning for Ukraine's economy. Instead, it coordinated the tasks assigned to the republic of Ukraine by Moscow's national CPC. The functioning of Ukraine's government on different levels was specifically tailored to implement orders, file petitions, make inquiries, and transmit reports.

Industrial plants and state or collective farms devised their own plans for fulfilling their respective production quotas. Factor supplies were allotted according to the plan, and the state automatically purchased all output from industrial plants and collectives at plan-determined prices. In the Soviet rationale, plan-determined factor and product prices eliminated the need for competitive purchasing and selling, allowing management to focus its effort on meeting production quotas. Fulfilling the quotas, especially during the earlier five-year plans, outweighed all other important considerations such as efficiency, value maximization, financing, and profit. Passive adherence to central directives rather than to creative economic activism assured personal safety and political standing.

The five year plans' overall thrust was accelerated growth in industry, in particular in heavy industry such as steel, coal, machine building, construction, chemicals, and power. Since Ukraine was still an agriculturally based economy in the late 1920s, the required rapid growth in capital formation in industry could materialize only from the agricultural sector. The emphasis in the late 1920s and early 1930s, therefore, centered on increasing pressure on Ukraine's farmers, forcing increased agricultural surpluses for planned industrial expansion.

Restrictive measures aimed at reducing consumption were incorporated into the five-year plans. Wages became a function of state budget instead of the worker's productivity. Since accelerated investment in heavy industry held priority over budget allocations, low budgets for wages and consumer goods industries became a permanent feature of the five-year plans. Further, even with depressed wages, the average worker could not expend his or her meager income since there was a lack of consumer goods on the market. Unused income became forced savings. The plan-crafted banking system was monopolist as well as monopsonist in financial transactions. Since the banks in Ukraine merely served as clearing houses for state-directed activities, there were no market-determined competitive rates for household savings. Forced household savings, kept by state banks at a depressed rate, were expected, planned, and allocated in advance to investment needs vis-à-vis the CPC directives. The CPC's five year plans thus promptly reduced Ukraine's once vital and dynamic economy into compliant submissiveness and abject passivity.

A SUBMERGED ECONOMY

The absorption of Ukraine's economy into the Soviet system aimed first and foremost at socializing the means of production, the elimination of private entrepreneurial activities, and the submission of Ukraine's will to Moscow's dictates. The forcible integration of Ukraine's agricultural and industrial sectors into the Soviet system is briefly outlined below.

By steadily increasing control over Ukraine's farm sector, Moscow persuaded private farmers to favor collective over family farming. Private ownership and individualism had no place in a rigidly controlled economic system. A combination of economic and political leverages was applied toward that objective. Confiscation of property from wealthier and middle-class farmers supplemented the earlier practices of raising taxes and reducing grain prices. Moscow disallowed the private sale of surplus grain by farmers, permitted only subsistence-level retention of grain by producers, and repeatedly raised the production quotas of grain imposed upon the farmers. The state also requisitioned more grain per private farmer than from his counterpart in a collective or state farm, further pressing private farmers into joining collectives. In addition, state and collective farms were granted priority claims over the state-distributed supply of scarce inputs.

The ever-growing need for surplus from Ukraine's farm sector obliged the planners to keep prices of requisitioned grain low. This made grain less valuable relative to other consumer goods and effectively reduced farmers' real incomes. The scheme was ideal for facilitating accelerated growth in capital formation. On the one hand, Moscow obtained grain from the Ukrainian farmers with few budget outlays. On the other hand, it kept the farmers' purchasing power for nonfarm products low. Investment in and production of consumer-goods industries thus could remain low, channeling surplus from the farm sector into increased savings for investment in heavy industry.

Moscow's claim on Ukraine's agricultural sector increased when the state changed its grain requisition formula halfway through the first five-year plan. The central planners increased the grain production quotas for farmers, regardless of actual or potential crop yield. The new mandate applied to private farmers resisting collectivization, as well as to collectives and state farms. CPC directives to farm producers included which farm cultivated how many *hectares* of what crop and how much of a given crop a collective or state farm had to deliver to the state by the end of which harvest season. The directives permitted no deviations therefrom. Detailed schemes were devised, forestalling passive resistance, pegging a farmer's share in a farm's output to his or her earned work points instead of to the number of hours worked. Work schedules prevented members of collectives or state farms from engaging in private entrepreneurial endeavors. The possibility of supplementary incomes, which peasants could previously earn by engaging in small-scale cottage industries or by manufacturing simple handicrafts, was likewise eliminated.

In addition, periodic campaigns were launched, obliging farmers to contribute to real or imagined causes, routinely draining savings that the farming households might have accumulated.

As a result, a large number of agricultural producers abandoned farming and drifted into urban centers in search of a less oppressive environment. This shift expeditiously increased the labor supply for the planned industrial expansion. Resentment from those remaining on farms was, on the other hand, expressed in the slaughtering of privately owned livestock, preventing it from falling into the hands of the state. Furthermore, anticipating eventual loss of assets to collectives, farm producers drastically curtailed investment and factor employment beginning in the late 1920s. Precipitous decreases in agricultural production followed, accentuating the Ukrainian farmers' passive resistance to Moscow's policy. Moscow, in response, once again modified its grain-requisition formula. Central planners now demanded that the targeted economic surplus from Ukraine's farm sector be forthcoming, regardless of investment levels or harvest conditions. Therefore, instead of retaining a given percentage of output for the farm family's consumption, the state exacted an assigned grain quantity from the farmer first, irrespective of whether any grain would be left for the farmer's household.

Concurrent with Moscow's increasing pressure on Ukrainian farmers was a severe drought in 1932. Though the drought was not as devastating as the one in 1921, the response from Moscow aggravated, rather than ameliorated, its effects. In 1921, Lenin permitted relief measures, alleviating the Ukrainian consumers' hardships. After the 1921 famine, he introduced the NEP, which tolerated private land holdings in rural regions and permitted select forms of private entrepreneurship in urban

—centers. In stark contrast, Stalin did not respond to the severe grain shortages in Ukraine in 1932. Since Ukraine's economy was thoroughly integrated into the USSR's economy and its system, Stalin demanded that the Ukrainians submit their will to Moscow in its totality. The 1932 drought was an opportunity for teaching the independent-minded Ukrainians a lesson. Moscow therefore insisted on collecting the assigned grain quota from the farmers. Door-to-door searches in rural areas resulted in the confiscation of the little grain the farmers had retained for their own consumption ; mass starvation followed. Conservative estimates by historians and demographers suggest that in less than two years, four to five million Ukrainians lost their lives because of the grain shortage. Stalin had virtually crushed Ukraine's private farming. After two successive five-year plans (1928–1938), no longer were there middle-class farmers, nor was there private ownership of land or family farming. All Ukrainian farmers became employees of the state, working either in state farms or collectives.

In sum, Ukraine no longer had an independent agricultural sector. It had farmers on state or collective farms, implementing directives from Moscow's CPC. The sole function of agricultural production in Ukraine was to contribute to the cause of the USSR.

Moscow's subjugation of Ukraine's industry was equally complete. Richly endowed with potential in the coal, iron, and steel industries, Ukraine provided an ideal setting for the establishment of new industries, as well as for the expansion of existing industries. Also, because of its location, it became a prime site for weapons plants. From the first five-year plan onward, the CPC kept the development of industry in Ukraine under the tightest of reins.

Moscow's industrial policy in Ukraine was twofold in principle: first, Moscow sought to expedite rapid growth in select industries in eastern and southeastern Ukraine, flooding industrial centers with nonnative workers for ethnic balance; and second, it fostered Ukraine's complete dependence on Moscow for both factor and product markets. CPC directives specified production tasks for industrial plants. Overfulfillment of production quotas was encouraged; whereas failure to meet assigned quotas could damage the professional career of administrators. Workers' wages were kept low, which reduced the demand for consumer goods. Their work habits, attitudes, and political dispositions were closely monitored by planted informers. Discontent could be brought forward only in the form of petition for change, never as criticism or protest. The petitions, however, were routinely dismissed. According to a contemporary account:

The crying need of the Ukrainians was for consumer goods. Odessa and Kharkiv (Kharkov) requested that they might be given the power to build textile mills to supply the needs of the local population. The request was denied. . . . The iron and steel cities requested that they might be given permission to build factories to complete the fabrication of certain delicate types of machinery. The request was refused because it was to be only in the Moscow area that such articles were to be made. (Manning, 1953: 133)

The policy-induced famine of 1932–1933 in Ukraine crushed the people's resistance. Overt resistance ceased in the farm community. The lesson was not lost on the industrial workers. For their personal safety, nonfarm workers quietly followed orders without betraying their personal sentiments. The fate of Ukraine's economy and its people sank to a low unprecedented in Ukraine's long history of subjugated serfdom.

A DEPENDENT ECONOMY

Ukraine's successful private farming disappeared by the early 1930s. In urban centers, inflexible directives replaced dynamic entrepreneurship. The Ukrainian economy no longer served Ukrainian society. Ukrainian subjects were no longer making independent decisions. From the first five-year plan onward, Moscow dictated the levels and direction of Ukraine's economic activities.

Substantial and cumulative investments in heavy industry took place in Ukraine in one five-year plan after another. The rapidly increasing productive capacity of priority industries such as military hardware, chemicals, and metallurgy, among others, necessitated the importation of essential inputs and machinery parts. Ukraine became increasingly dependent on Russia and Turkmenistan for oil and gas imports, and on Russia and the rest of the republics for machine parts and other essential inputs. It simultaneously became dependent on other republics of the USSR for basic consumer goods such as textile products, household appliances, and furniture, as well as for product markets. The massive quantities of industrial outputs from Ukraine's plants were in demand neither by Ukraine's consumers nor by its own industrial producers. Only Moscow's planned distribution channel could absorb all the industrial products originating from Ukraine. The central planners intended and succeeded to create an insurmountable interdependence between Ukraine and the rest of the USSR.

The longer Ukraine remained a part of the USSR, the greater its dependence on Moscow for factor and product markets became. As the Cold War dissipated in the mid-1980s, demand for Soviet-made military hardware, much of which was made in Ukraine, plummeted. Moscow remained the primary purchaser of increasingly unwanted final products from Ukraine's heavy industries, artificially maintaining the operation of many unwarranted plants within the Ukrainian territories. The CPC wastefully kept the otherwise potentially productive factors in Ukraine producing unmarketable products.

By the time Ukraine regained its independence in late 1991, it was still wholly dependent on the FSU for markets. The centralized command system thus left a structurally deformed Ukrainian economy picking up pieces that were no longer compatible with other pieces elsewhere in the FSU.

The effects of seventy years under the Soviet system is taking its toll on Ukraine's attempts at systemic transformation. Though Ukraine has been independent and autonomous since 1991, its economy remains structurally submerged and functionally bound to the largesse of the command system. Legacies from the command system pose realistic challenges to reform architects and decision makers alike. Unless historical lessons from the recent past are duly acknowledged and factored into the reform blueprint, avoidable social, economic, and political costs could mount, propelling disillusioned economic subjects to demand a return to the days of the USSR. Comprehending Ukraine's difficult reemergence from the shadows of its recent past, therefore, requires understanding the built-in impediments to reform. Only then can sensible and effective measures be prescribed for possible adoption and implementation. With that understanding in mind, the ensuing chapter analyzes the inherited economic dilemmas in Ukraine since perestroika.

NOTES

1. The Transcaucasian republic of 1922 comprised the land mass between the Black Sea and the Caspian Sea. The area was divided into the republics of Armenia, Azerbaijan, and Georgia in 1936.

2. Hrushevesky became Ukraine's first president when the Supreme Rada proclaimed Ukraine an independent state in 1917. Hrushevsky's government was distinct from the Moscow-backed government of Christian Rakovsky established in Kharkiv, also in 1917.

3

Economy upon Independence

This chapter presents an overview of Ukraine's economy between the mid-1980s and late 1991. It then analyzes the structural, institutional, and functional concerns of Ukraine's economy to the extent they may impede efforts at the nation's economic restructuring. The analysis helps shed light on the nature and extent of the obstacles that Ukraine currently encounters. The flaws in, and lessons to be learned from, Ukraine's current reform efforts can then be more readily recognized in the ensuing chapters.

INTRODUCTION

Each newly liberalized economy encounters a unique set of obstacles to systemic transformation. While many of the newly liberalized economies may quickly focus their energy on systemic reform, the Ukraine has been forced, because of its tragic history and its inexperience in independent governance, to search for its own identity while concurrently proceeding with reforms. For instance, there was still debate in Ukraine's Supreme Rada in 1991 over whether Ukraine was merely regaining its independence from the FSU or creating an entirely new state. Ukraine's political leaders since 1991, moreover, have instilled neither confidence nor optimism. As governments have changed, so have the emphasis and speed of reform programs. Partisan squabbling and poorly defined official roles have bewildered and exhausted the general public. Legislation, executive action, and bureaucratic initiative have been uncoordinated and, as a result, often inconsistent or contradictory. This lack of clearly defined purviews frustrates not only the political community but also lower-level administrators and industry decision makers. On another frontier, there are a small number of enterprising individuals, many of whom were closely connected to the Communist Party, who now capitalize on the many legal and institutional loopholes existing between the erstwhile Communist system and the nascent market system. They enrich themselves at the expense of society and of the nation's already impoverished masses; consequently, more people have begun questioning the appropriateness of the government's hasty introduction of a free-market system.

This hesitancy over economic liberalization has its roots in the post-Khruschev era. The Brezhnev administration (1964–1982) was a period of economic stagnation during which the high growth rates the Soviet Union enjoyed after World War II had dwindled. The swagger with which Nikita Khruschev (who was premier from 1953 to 1962) declared confidently to the West, "We will bury you!" had all but disappeared. In its place emerged a pallid but secure political and economic system: those who did not "rock the boat" would be guaranteed a livelihood. For the following thirty years, many Soviet politicians and citizens therefore strove to minimize insecurity, regardless of the cost to economic growth. Since the spirit of entrepreneurship in a market setting requires the management of risk, Ukrainians must now cope with a "risks-for-rewards" system, rather than a "passivity-for-rewards" system. The challenge of a market-based system has been difficult for most Ukrainians.

Worse, a growing number of Ukrainians question the wisdom of progressing to capitalism, as well as of declaring political independence from the FSU. As Peter Bielienkiy, of the Ukrainian Academy of Entrepreneurship and Management, put it: "If something goes wrong with the economy in France or in Germany, the people blame the government but not the independence of France or Germany. Here in Ukraine, many people say that it is Ukrainian independence that is to blame. . . . In any parliament of the world, there are no deputies (parliamentarians) who oppose the independence of their country. But we have such deputies" (Bielienkiy Interview, 1994).

Developing an internally consistent, operationally functional, and socially and politically agreeable reform agenda under such conditions becomes difficult. Ukraine's lack of tradition as an autonomous and sovereign state deprives many decision makers of the crucial reference points necessary for self-identification and self-assertion. It compromises their effectiveness in reaching acceptable accords over the appropriate policies and programs and adversely impacts the nation's attempts at effectuating an envisioned economic transformation.

ECONOMIC OVERVIEW: 1985–1991

More than two-fifths of Ukraine's labor force in 1990 was engaged in industrial production and nearly one-fifth in agriculture. That is, three-fifths of Ukraine's labor force was engaged in material production in 1991. Signs of stagnation became evident in the early 1980s, with slow growth and inflationary pressures mounting during the second half of the decade. But they were only symptoms of the deep-seated difficulties confronting Ukraine's economy. The roots of the problems Ukraine's economy faces today date back to the 1930s and 1940s.

Symptoms of the problems emerged as early as the 1950s, by which time the USSR's extensive development approach had already become inappropriate and ineffectual. Even official statistics suggested serious structural deformities and functional inefficiencies inherent in the system. Nevertheless, the combined forces of vested interests, bureaucratic inertia, and inexperience were an effective deterrent to meaningful attempts at reform in the 1960s through the 1980s. Thus, for decades, Ukraine's economy was frozen in a rigidly structured and operationally inefficient system. Politicians, much like citizens, had grown accustomed to avoiding risks during the Brezhnev and succeeding administrations. By the time Gorbachev emerged, the Ukrainian modi operandi seemed frozen in time.

Economic reform in Ukraine involves a systemic transformation. A significant segment of the economy, together with its associated activities, will be removed from the potentially viable parts, leaving fewer users competing for a share in the nation's scarce productive resources. The short- and medium-term tasks ahead will be trying and at times painful.

The performance of Ukraine's economy since the mid-1980s provides a generalized frame of reference for specific problem areas discussed later in this chapter. Table 3.1 provides an overview of select macro indicators of Ukraine's economy between 1985 and 1991.

Data in Table 3.1 present the Ukrainian economy as nearly stationary during the second half of the 1980s. Although industrial production grew by 2.7 percent in 1985, agricultural production decreased by 1 percent and national income grew by a mere 0.2 percent. Ukraine's growth in industrial production reached 4.2 percent in 1988, but agricultural production declined by nearly 1.5 percent (Director of Intelligence, 1992: 66). While decreases in agricultural production reflected real reductions in output, growth in industrial production indicated continued structural imbalances rather than meaningful gains in the production of goods in demand. Both industry and agriculture in Ukraine experienced decline in 1990, commencing a downward trend for the first half of the 1990s. Industrial production—which perennially symbolized the core of economic activities and vitality in a centralized economy—declined 0.1 percent in 1990. By then, even the core of the Soviet economy was no longer expanding. The fact that industrial production declined by 4.8 percent in 1991 strongly suggests that Ukraine needed a radically restructured economic system. The dissolution of the USSR's internal market only intensified this urgent need.

Table 3.1
Main Indicators of Ukraine's Economy, 1985, 1990, 1991

	1985	1990	1991
Gross Domestic Product (GDP)			
(At current prices, in billions			
of rubles)	128	165	295
as % of previous year	——	——	——
National Income (NI)			
(At current prices, in billions			
of rubles)	94	112	274
as % of previous year	100.2	96.4	86.6
Industrial Production			
(At 1989 constant prices, in billions			
of rubles)	140	162	154
as % of previous year	102.7	99.9	95.2
Agricultural Production			
(At 1989 constant prices, in billions			
of rubles)	47.1	49.0	42.5
as % of previous year	99.0	96.3	86.8

Source: Ministry of Statistics of Ukraine, 1994a: 4, 6

On other frontiers, Ukraine's agricultural production fell by 3.7 percent in 1990 while its national income declined by 3.6 percent. By the time Ukraine regained its independence a year later, agricultural production had fallen another 13.2 percent and national income had declined by an additional 13.4 percent. Since structural adjustments to Ukraine's economy had not yet commenced at that time, such decreases indicated systemic hemorrhages. As was stated above, the predicaments facing Ukraine's economy are deep-rooted. The remainder of this chapter examines some of the roots of those structural, functional, and institutional anomalies prevailing in Ukraine's economy.

SECTORAL IMBALANCES AND SEMI-FINISHED PRODUCTS

During the Soviet era, Moscow's central planners favored accelerated industrial expansion in Ukraine. Since sectoral imbalances persisted with the implementation of each of the USSR's eleven five-year plans, Ukraine's economy became a casualty of decades of planned imbalances. During that time, imbalances between the consumer-goods and producer-goods industries, as well as between industry and agriculture, steadily worsened. Within the industrial sector itself, imbalances existed between light and heavy industry, as well as between consumer-oriented heavy industry and the capital-intensive military-industrial complex. By the time Ukraine regained its independence, the bulk of outputs from its industrial sector could find markets only in the governments of neighboring republics, and even those markets were rapidly disappearing. Two comments may help project the magnitude and complexity of the problems confronting Ukraine's reform architects. The first was by academician Ivan Lukinov, Deputy Director of Ukraine's National Academy of Sciences:

When it comes to economic reform, Ukraine faces far more difficult problems than smaller countries and countries whose economic structures have been less deformed. Ukraine occupied a very important place in the former USSR. It was submitted to the former USSR's structures. A considerable share of the former USSR's military-industrial complex is imbedded in Ukraine's economy. The share was very high. For the Ukrainian industry as a whole, sectors or branches of the "A-group"—construction, metallurgy, and the military-industrial complex—accounted for 74 percent of total. Consumer demand could not be satisfied as a result, because domestic supply of consumer goods were not forthcoming. (Lukinov interview, 1994)

The second observation was made by Ukraine's former president Leonid Kravchuk:

Two aspects of the Soviet legacy deserve particular attention. . . . First, 90 percent of Ukraine's "domestic" product was not controlled by Ukraine itself, but by various ministries of the central Soviet government. This product was brought to 80 percent completion in Ukraine, and then sent [most often] to Russia for the final stages of production. A third of the USSR's military-industrial complex was situated in Ukraine, accounting for 2.5 million jobs. Second, it should be kept in mind that this product was not sold on any market, it was simply delivered. Once the Soviet system fell apart, the orders dried up, and Ukraine's economy plunged into crisis. (Quoted in *Ukrainian Weekly*, January 22, 1995: 3)

Both statements accentuate the predicament that confronts Ukraine's inherited industrial sector. As Kravchuk observes, most Ukrainian output was in the form of semifinished products destined for other plants, not for consumer markets. As dictated by the Marxist capital structure and by central planning administrators in Moscow, goods were produced step-by-step in a highly specialized, highly coordinated series of plants. Now that there is no longer a CPC directing this cumbersome process, and now that these plants are dispersed across fifteen different former Soviet Socialist Republics (SSRs), the chains of production have disintegrated and industrial production has declined.

Ukraine has inherited a capital stock that is virtually worthless to a market economy intent on economic efficiency. With its already strained financial resources, Ukraine cannot easily make its capital stock more adaptable to market situations. Furthermore, its producers were entirely isolated from the demands of the consumer market; they dealt only with monopsonistic contracts to other industrial operations. They are thus inexperienced in responding to consumer demands. Ukrainian industry once relied heavily on Moscow for distributing its goods, particularly military material; it obviously can no longer continue this pattern of reliance.[1]

Sectoral imbalances and semifinished products—together with their adverse effects on Ukraine's economic and social scenes—are only the beginning of a long litany of structural and institutional deformities that Ukraine has inherited from the USSR. Below is a brief analysis of a few others showing evidence of the depths from which Ukraine must extricate itself.

COLLAPSED COORDINATING MECHANISM

As recently as 1991, the coordinating mechanisms for Ukraine's preindependence economy were still based on the USSR'S planning system. Profits or losses were only remotely associated with efficiency and competitive performance. The market's information feedback system vis-à-vis supply and demand conditions was suppressed in order to facilitate centralized planning and control. Controlled wages and regulated prices on essential consumer goods and services effectively curtailed the consumers' purchasing power. The command economy lacked a functional mechanism that could objectively reflect relative resource scarcity and product values. State-determined factor costs and product values displaced the market's traditional function in resource allocation; as a result, allocative anomalies such as overproduction in heavy industry and underproduction of consumer goods became increasingly pernicious problems. Ukraine inherited an inflexible centralized system that had for decades inflicted high opportunity costs on the Soviet economy.

Even by 1991, six years after the beginning of perestroika, the Soviet system still lacked an objective feedback mechanism capable of signaling relative abundance or scarcity. Without a self-correcting mechanism, prices could not be adjusted to the changing demands of consumers. The only means through which repressed inflationary pressure was kept in check was the central planning committee's fiat. Extensive resource misallocation progressively reinforced existing price distortions in all aspects of Ukraine's economy. When it regained its independence in 1991, Ukraine possessed neither a mechanism that could effectively coordinate the nation's economic activities nor a workable solution to the economy's long repressed inflation. Decision makers in Kiev lacked practical experience in the market pricing system, experience in devising a flexible and adjustable price realignment schedule, and finesse in combining administrative regulation with market coordination during this transitional phase of economic restructuring. In addition, Ukraine still retains a core of administrators who coordinated the very policies that now need correction.

Because it has no ready functional substitute for the old coordinating mechanism, it suffers from continued distortions in economic relationships.

RESTRICTED COMMODITY CIRCULATION CHANNELS

The command economy restricted the market allocating function, as well as the economy's commodity circulation channels. Central planners during the Soviet era reduced the channels of economic relationships and limited the avenues of commodity circulation. A simplified flow of economic relationships helped expedite the command process; it also facilitated centralized supervision and control of activities by principal industrial and agricultural producers. Decades of centralized purchasing of outputs and centralized distribution of factors freed management from the responsibility of exercising judgment in price determination, factor employment, and product marketing. As a result, management grew indifferent toward quality control or value and cost considerations. Managers made decisions with planners' demands in mind, not with the concerns of consumers or of efficiency. Ukraine thus inherited an economy whose enterprise management had experience only with restricted commodity circulation channels and restrictive economic relationships.

DISTORTED OWNERSHIP PATTERN

Private ownership of the means of production ended with the completion of the second five-year plan in 1938. Suppression of this institution eliminated profit motivation as a natural agent for efficiency, resulting in decades of inefficiency and wastefulness. As recently as 1991, privately owned enterprises and farms remained in short supply. Although several years have passed since Ukraine declared its intent to introduce reform measures, its privatization policy still lacks internal consis- tency, external transparency, and logical soundness. Its existing property ownership pattern constitutes a serious impediment to reform endeavors. Until ownership rights have been equitably and efficaciously transferred from the state to the private sector, state enterprises will continue to drain the society's scarce resources, while the potentially productive inputs of the private sector remain dormant.

MONOPOLIES

During the early phases of the sovietization process, planners consolidated private industrial and agricultural producers into large, socialized producing units. Under the pretext of attaining economies of scale, the policy reduced economic linkages and simplified command planning. Horizontal and vertical integration expedited central control of production establishments.

Central planning policy produced two types of monopolies. One type of monopoly was created by planners, who dictated parts-production specialization by industrial establishments. Successive five-year plans reinforced the highly constrained functions of these producers, granting them the dubious distinction of possessing monopoly powers over parts of a final product, rendering industrial restructuring in Ukraine more complex than in other Eastern European economies. If the demand for any semifinished or final products along the production chain weakens or dissipates, so does the salvage value of the highly specialized capital assets and labor force. This capital structure leaves minimal slack and no flexibility in either product reorientation or organizational restructuring.

The second type of monopoly Ukraine has inherited are establishments that exercise genuine monopoly power over select markets within the economy. Though still state owned, they are administratively independent and enjoy operational autonomy from the state. These establishments may now freely administer prices in a captive market. Many farm input suppliers, select metallurgical and chemical producers, and most manufacturers of consumer goods are producers of outputs in marketable forms that have a demand in the domestic economy. In the absence of clearly defined antimonopoly legislation, an operative antimonopoly agency, or a functional judicial system in the economic sphere, these monopolies exploit the flawed market structure at the expense of the already fatigued consumers.

SINGLE-TIER BANKING

Ukraine did not possess a two-tier banking system when it regained its political independence in 1991. Commercial banks or alternative financial institutions did not exist. For facilitating central planning through a simplified command structure, for state control of financial flows, and for reduced linkages in economic relationships, banking operation on a private and competitive basis was suppressed during the Soviet era. Banks within Ukraine were merely branch banks in the USSR banking system. The system comprised the central bank and five special-purpose banks,[2] all state owned. Ukraine thus inherited a banking system that could neither effectively mobilize nor efficiently allocate financial resources.

Ukraine still lacks a functional two-tier banking system, a network of complementary financial institutions, or institutional foundations for money and capital markets. The Bank of Ukraine, the nation's central bank, does not possess the authority to independently formulate the nation's monetary policy. Old habits—with the government exercising effective control over the nation's vital institutions—persist under the new economic environment, effectively impeding the process of meaningful reform. Parliament's unwillingness to grant *de facto* autonomy to the

Bank of Ukraine denies the actualization of the monetary policy's inherent potency. Furthermore, the slow development of a substantive private banking sector retards the evolution of a link between the real and the financial flows of the economy. While Ukraine's economy drifts aimlessly due to decision makers' indecisiveness, potentially effective instruments and institutions lay idly by, compounding escalating opportunity costs.

LEGAL TENDER

When Ukraine declared its independence from the USSR, the sole legal tender in circulation was the ruble, presently known as the Russian ruble. Ukraine had no control over its money supply; the Bank of Ukraine was not authorized to issue legal tender. When Moscow accelerated its poorly devised price liberalization program in late 1991 and early 1992, consumers' purchasing power in both Russia and Ukraine plummeted. Prompt unloading of ruble holdings by enterprises and consumers in all republics of the FSU sent the nominal ruble supply soaring, further fueling inflation and ruble depreciation. Inflation rates outpaced increases in the ruble supply, simultaneously creating an acute shortage of rubles in circulation. Moscow continued printing rubles to meet Russia's own needs for paper money without also supplying neighboring republics with enough currency for their transaction needs. As the nominal ruble supply soared, so did the price level. Purchasers from neighboring Confederation of Independent States (CIS) countries poured into Ukraine, soaking up marketable commodities for which prices were still under state control. Ukraine was thus subjected to adverse consequences of reform programs in Russia. Ukrainian holders of Russian rubles lost the currency's original value and were circuitously subsidizing the Bank of Moscow and consumers in neighboring CIS economies. Because it did not have its own legal tender upon independence, Ukraine was prevented from initiating an independent monetary policy from the onset.

LIMITED EXTERNAL MARKET

Ukraine was dependent on the republics of the USSR, especially on Russia, for factor and product markets. The dissolution of the USSR ushered in a new era of trade relationships; all the former SSRs are seeking expanded export bases. All are also progressively aligning export prices with world market prices. In practice, this means that Ukraine must pay near-world or world market prices for imports from republics of the FSU. Although in theory the prices of Ukraine's exports to CIS member countries could also rise to near-world market levels, the development of financial conditions in republics of the FSU has been such that few, if any, are able to maintain levels of past demand from each other. Demand for Ukraine's exports by CIS members, therefore, even from Ukraine's primary sector, has met with serious decreases. That, in turn, has seriously compromised Ukraine's ability to maintain its

Table 3.2

Ukraine's External Trade: Total and Select Industries, 1989–1991 (millions of rubles)

	1989		1990		1991	
	Export	**Import**	**Export**	**Import**	**Export**	**Import**
Total	48,062	54,540	45,606	54,059	—	-----
Foreign	7,595	14,569	7,287	15,071	—	—
(&)	15.8	26.7	16.0	27.9	—	—
Interrepublic	40,467	39,971	38,319	38,989	49,410	45,390
Oil & Gas						
Total	863	4,381	639	3,875	—	—
Foreign	495	61	301	78	—	—
(%)	57.4	1.4	47.1	2.0	—	—
Interrepublic	368	4,321	337	3,797	—	—
(%)	42.6	98.6	52.9	98.0	—	—
Machine Building						
Total	18,164	18,046	17,881	18,745	—	—
Foreign	2,251	3,846	2,381	5,025	—	—
(%)	12.4	21.3	13.3	26.8	—	—
Interrepublic	15,913	14,200	15,500	13,720	—	—
(%)	87.6	78.7	86.7	73.2	—	—

Source: World Bank, 1992: 402–403; World Bank, 1993: Table 3.1

traditional import levels, idling the productive potentials of domestic factors and curtailing export potentials. Table 3.2 exemplifies how much Ukraine's export position has weakened since independence.

Table 3.2 suggests that as late as 1991, Ukraine still had only limited access to foreign markets outside of the FSU. In 1989, for instance, 84.2 percent of Ukraine's exports were destined for markets of the FSU. Further, the non-FSU markets were either former members of the COMECON organization or third world economies. That is, Ukraine's export market had no niches in the developed markets of the Western economies, and most of the value product from Ukraine's exportable commodities originated from primary productive activities rather than from the manufacturing or service-oriented sectors. Paralleling Ukraine's dependence on the FSU for output markets was its dependence on other republics of the FSU for factor or parts supplies. As may be noted in the import data in Table 3.2, nearly three-quarters of Ukraine's imports in 1989 originated from interrepublic sources. The permanency and degree of Ukraine's dependence on the FSU for exchanges may be seen in the 1990 import-export data in Table 3.2. In 1990, Ukraine continued to import to and export from FSU members at roughly the same rates it had in 1989. In spite of its military-industrial complexes, Ukraine's export markets for military hardware contracted and dissipated once the USSR disbanded. Ukraine has neither the financial resources nor the technical expertise for restructuring its industry from unwanted productive activities into manufacturing consumer goods for the domestic and world markets. The restructuring of Ukraine's external sector, therefore, faces nearly insurmountable obstacles, at least in the short term. There are many complex problems Ukraine must address. A select few are outlined below.

First is the Ukraine's export position, which steadily weakened toward the end of the 1980s. Ukraine registered a trade surplus of 6.3 billion rubles against other republics of the FSU in 1988 (Lukinov, 1993: 2). The surplus dwindled to 496 million a year later (see Table 3.2). By 1990, Ukraine's imports from other republics of the FSU exceeded its exports by 670 million rubles. Though the interrepublic trade deficit for 1990 was small, the trend toward a trade deficit was significant. The trend reflects both Ukraine's declining ability to sell its products, even in other republics of the FSU, and its inability to proportionately mitigate its needs for interrepublic imports. There has been an inverse relationship between economic liberalization in the FSU and Ukraine's export position. The more liberalized the economies of the FSU republics have become, the lower their demand for Ukraine's exports. On the import side of the equation, however, Ukraine's need for interrepublic imports has remained nearly unchanged. A reversal in this condition does not promise to be forthcoming.

Second is Ukraine's external sector, which experienced slight decreases in trade volume between 1989 and 1990. Its export total declined by 2.5 billion rubles between 1989 and 1990, whereas its import total decreased by only .48 billion. The decreases in interrepublic trade between 1989 and 1990 were more pronounced.

Ukraine's interrepublic exports fell by more than 2.1 billion rubles, while its imports declined by less than 1 billion rubles. Although trade with foreign markets outside of the republics of the FSU remained stable for 1991, trade within the FSU market plummeted. As noted in Table 3.2, Ukraine exported 38.3 billion rubles worth of goods to other FSU members and imported 39.0 billion in 1990. By 1991, Ukraine's interrepublic export was valued at 49.4 billion rubles and import at 45.4 billion. This appears to be an exceptional increase until one considers that consumer prices rose 83 percent during the same interval. Obviously, interrepublic turnover declined dramatically during the final year of the USSR's existence. This was a foreboding sign for Ukraine's foreign trade sector for the following years.

Third is that Ukraine's exports of military hardware and semifinished products from heavy industries collapsed following the disintegration of the USSR. As seen in Table 3.2, 37.8 percent of Ukraine's total exports in 1989 were listed under the machine building category. Within that category of exports, 87.6 percent was destined for interrepublic markets. Although a more detailed categorization of such exports was never made public, it was public knowledge that a high proportion of Ukraine's "machine building" exports consisted of military hardware and components thereof. That is, Ukraine inherited an economy whose export sector depended heavily on military products for which demand had slackened dramatically. The loss in potential export value was substantial in this newly independent economy in which foreign earnings are crucial for economic reform. The future of Ukraine's export sector thus hinges closely on its success in restructuring a significant segment of its inherited military-industrial complex into the manufacture of exportable consumer goods.

Fourth is Ukraine's imports of oil and gas, which in 1989 accounted for 8 percent of that year's total import values. More than 98.6 percent of the imported oil and gas originated from interrepublic markets. The 1990 share decreased to 7.2 percent of the total, of which 98.0 percent came from interrepublic sources. Plainly stated, Ukraine depends almost exclusively on Russia and Turkmenistan for its oil and gas imports. The perils of such dependence were concealed under the cover of centralized planning in an increasingly unstable union of republics. Ukraine's dependence on Russia and the central Asian republics of the FSU was not an issue during the Soviet era; however, it is now a compelling concern. The energy-intensive industries that the FSU built in Ukraine will remain dependent on imported oil and gas. As a consequence, there will be reduced levels of production from many of the industrial plants in Ukraine. The expected decrease in energy needs, however, will be proportionately less than the combined declines in industrial production. In the equation of payment balances, Ukraine may expect continued substantial outflows for energy imports and less significant inflows for value products resulting from the consumption of imported energy. In brief, Ukraine's existing industrial structure will drain hard currency reserves in the coming years.

These are only a few of the predicaments that Ukraine inherited from the FSU in 1991. Under various forms or shapes, they will be discussed as reform priorities in the following chapters. Before proceeding to a discussion of the framework for reform in the next chapter, however, a brief commentary on the appropriate reform approach in Ukraine is in order. Severe criticisms have been leveled against the nation's reform attempts. Recommendations abound, many of which suggest "shock therapy." The ensuing commentary addresses this specific recommendation.

A PRELIMINARY COMMENT

Major international organizations and Western governments expected that Ukraine would lead the way among CIS members in successfully making the transition from a centralized economy to a market economy, for Ukraine has highly educated intellectuals, a skilled labor force, a rich resource base, vast expanses of fertile land, and a favorable geographic location. Next to those of the Baltic states, its population was among the most vocal in advocating independence from the USSR. Ukraine appeared as one of the CIS countries most eager for a quick divorce from the Soviet system. After several years of disappointing economic performance, the call has arisen for a radical approach to systemic transformation in Ukraine. The call emanates primarily from select economic advisors from abroad. These advisors prescribe a shock therapy approach for Ukraine's economy, maintaining that the success story in Poland can be duplicated in Ukraine. A comparison between Poland and Ukraine, however, may not be valid. Poland is often cited as having achieved the speediest recovery among the Eastern European economies, with the fastest growth rates in foreign trade and foreign investment. Its apparent success has been attributed to shock therapy. Treat Ukraine with a similar shock, so the rationale goes, and the Ukrainian economy's performance will yield similarly encouraging results. This apparently sound while objectively flawed line of reasoning, if applied, would be harmful to the Ukrainian people's aspiration for permanent independence. It could also provide an impetus for the resurgence of Communist or socialist ideology among segments of Ukraine's mixed population. The principal reasons why a shock therapy—similar to the one Poland was subjected to in 1989—should be avoided in Ukraine are outlined below.

Poland was an independent nation, culturally affiliated and psychologically aligned with the Western European nations. The Polish nationals had more contact with the West, even during the Communist decades, than the Ukrainians experienced under the Soviets. The Polish people have cultural attributes facilitating entrepreneurial, adaptive, and creative responses not only for survival but also for economic gain. The Polish economy was inefficient under the centralized system, yet at least it had its own distribution system. Right after the liberalization of Poland's political and economic policies, many of its prewar commercial ties and relationships with the

West were reestablished, while new avenues and approaches to Western markets were vigorously explored by Polish entrepreneurs.

In addition, and perhaps more importantly, the so-called shock therapy approach was not maintained at shock levels. Economic subjects, among others, indeed did receive shocks following the price liberalization policy, the subsidy withdrawal policy, and the enterprise autonomy policy. However, the Polish government showed reluctance to enforce capitalist principles of market relationships. For instance, a large segment of the urban population, most of whom were occupants of state-owned housing units, refused to pay rent to the state, for the shock from price liberalization had left them destitute. Refusing payment of the ever increasing rental charges also signaled their open defiance against the Polish government's adoption of shock therapy. No dwelling units were repossessed by the government as capitalist practices would have dictated. Furthermore, tax evasion was widespread. Unpaid taxes were siphoned off by innovative managers and citizens. While the state incurred budget deficits owing to lower than expected tax revenues, enterprising tax evaders channeled unlawful savings into profitable ventures domestically or abroad. There were plant closings, yet demand for and sales of armaments in marketable forms remained firm, especially in the markets of the third world countries. While many firms helplessly awaited bankruptcy, others sold state assets from enterprises and converted profits into productive investments for personal accounts.

The [Polish] people at large ignored the shock policy wherever they could. They were tacitly permitted to be left to their own devises for entrepreneurial ventures. Both the government and the enterprises led a live-and-let-live existence, permitting a gradual and steady rise of the middle class.

The shock therapy was not fully enforced. The Polish scenario has had more existing factors cushioning the much publicized shock than the Westerners realize. There was a shock, but not a full one. (Askanas interview, 1994)

Unlike Poland, Ukraine had not been an independent state. Even the Baltic states, forced into a union with the FSU for nearly fifty years, had a longer experience with independence than did Ukraine. Ukraine had no independent economic life. For centuries it had been subjected to the economic gains and political expediency of the tsarist and Soviet governments. The people of Ukraine were captives to Soviet propaganda. For seven decades, the Ukrainian economy was thoroughly integrated into the USSR system. Distancing Ukraine's economy from its recent past, including the ways of thinking its people were accustomed to, their work habits, their economic behavior, and their established institutional structures, among others, is a more complex and painstaking process than the transformation of other newly liberalized economies of the region. A shock therapy approach to systemic transformation in Ukraine could drive the less certain Ukrainians into the expected, or even anticipated, "bear hug" of the former Communist ideology. Even the enterprising Poles have not been exempt from such an alternative. Despite Poland's being advertised as a success story of a radical approach to economic restructuring, the Polish voters restored the former Communists to parliament in the general elections in December 1993, and as recently as early 1995, the parliament approved the appointment of a former Communist to the position of the premiership. Ballots in the newly liberalized economies, including Ukraine, tellingly map the Eastern European consumers' indifference curve. Prudence needs to take precedence over theoretical gymnastics. Ukraine has a population of fifty-two million, and the success or failure of Ukraine's efforts at economic reform is of crucial importance to political stability and economic well-being of the region.

NOTES

1. In 1990, 74 percent of Ukraine's industry was engaged in the production of non-consumer goods, and 90 percent of the industrial producers were under the direct control of Moscow's ministries. This means that 67 percent (90 percent of 74) of industrial establishments in Ukraine produced nonconsumer goods and were under the direct control of Moscow. Since a number of industrial plants producing consumer goods in Ukraine also came under the direct jurisdiction of ministries in Moscow, the 67 percent is a conservative estimate. More than 67 percent of Ukraine's existing industries thus were controlled by USSR ministries and depended on USSR budgetary allocations. When Ukraine established independence, the allocations once received from Moscow ceased. As Kravchuk notes, a staggering two and one-half million Ukrainians will soon become unemployed as a result of the end of Soviet military-industrial contracting.

2. The five special-purpose banks were the Agricultural Bank, the Industry and Construction Bank, the Savings Bank, the Foreign Trade Bank, and the Housing and Social Development Bank.

4

Framework for Reform

The unique conditions in Ukraine challenge the wisdom of the mechanical application of reform theories developed from experiences of mature capitalist economies. Ukraine's unique history, its uncommon experience under the Soviets, and its singularly flawed economic structure defy a mechanical transfer of reform lessons, even from the economies of other recently liberalized states. Solutions to Ukraine's economic anomalies must be designed from and applied to its unique conditions.

INTRODUCTION

Removing obstacles to systemic transformation is not an end in itself. It is a means to an end. The end encompasses a collection of objectives for which reform finds justification. Some criteria validating attainment of objectives are quantifiable; others are more qualitative in nature. The quantitative criteria include the following: improved efficiency in production, distribution, and consumption; growth as measured in increased factor productivity and increased earnings; and distributional equity, along with a stable and secure environment for producers and consumers, savers, and investors. The qualitative criteria, on the other hand, reflect the economy's progressiveness, its flexibility with and adaptability to change, and its freedom in entering into or withdrawing from economic relationships, as well as the availability of economic opportunities to decision makers.

The overall purpose for reform is improved economic efficiency leading to an enhanced quality of life. The consequences of policy measures directed at the attainment of these objectives are either objectively quantifiable or intuitively discernable. The relative merits of reform policies and programs, therefore, may be adequately measured or evaluated. Priorities for attaining given measures in each of the objectives may nevertheless vary from one economy to another, and, within the same economy, from one period or phase of developmental adjustment to another. While growth may significantly outweigh other criteria in one society at a given time period, it may rank secondary in importance to, or even much lower than, stability, security, and equity in another society, especially one which has only recently emerged from centuries of suppression and lack of independence. Furthermore, the same economy at different times, and different economies at the same time, may face vastly divergent constraints as well as opportunities. Appropriate approaches toward attaining desired objectives in given economies under distinct and unique circumstances, therefore, must be separately examined and differentially devised.

Ukraine's economic conditions upon regaining independence were distinctly unique, unlike those in any other economy in the FSU. Whereas the general framework for restructuring Ukraine's economy may be similar in many respects to that used in other newly liberalized states, approaches toward realizing the desired objectives should vary in accordance with the unique conditions prevailing in Ukraine. A synoptic analysis of these prevailing conditions can help delineate the appropriate parameters for restructuring Ukraine's economy. Workable and sensible reform measures in Ukraine may, as a result, be more logically deduced.

Ukrainians enjoyed no economic freedom, no flexibility, and minimal economic opportunity during the seven decades under the Soviets. The centralized planning system bred apathy toward efficiency and fostered an environment in which productivity was low. Low income, matching low productivity, completed the circle for a contrived equilibrium in the consumer goods sphere. Plainly stated, Ukrainian consumers' budget lines were kept markedly below where they should have or could have been. The recent political and economic liberalization has drawn attention to the need for economic reform.

A tempting solution is simultaneous outward advancement of both the budget line and the indifference curve at any cost. While focusing on the eventual attainment of reform objectives, reform proponents unfamiliar with local conditions and sentiments need to acquaint themselves with the values cherished by the people, for it is consumer preferences that, in the final analysis, constitute Ukraine's social indifference map. Whereas consumer preferences change over time, it is their current values that chart the shape, as well as the position of, the indifference curve. Highly valued among Ukraine's producers and consumers, at least under given conditions, are economic stability, economic security, and a relatively equitable distribution of the society's economic opportunities and value product. The relative importance that Ukrainian consumers will place on each of these conditions in the future may, and most likely will, change. For now, however, after decades of material deprivation, these are the sole values remaining which Ukraine's economic subjects may retain. These values, therefore, should in no way be regarded lightly when formulating reform programs. Reform architects should respect and protect these values to the extent that it is realistically feasible to do so, preventing well-intentioned reform programs from becoming instruments of disillusionment over the promises of the market system.

Priorities assigned to the most basic values by residents of the West may differ significantly from those in Ukraine at its present state of uncertainty. Factory owners in developed countries, for instance, may indulge in the luxury of engaging in less certain and more speculative ventures. Income or earnings fluctuations have long been accepted as partial cost for, or as due returns to, investment decisions. Although the players may be impoverished or enriched in the process, legal protection and a social safety net shield them from utter destitution in case of failure. Therefore, in economically more developed and secure settings, the importance assigned to prospective gains is high, while the importance assigned to stability and security is relatively low. Social indifference curves in the West can vary markedly from those in newly liberalized and newly independent economies like Ukraine. That is, Ukraine's residents attach a higher value to economic stability and security than do their counterparts in developed market economies. Without stability and security, Ukraine's residents have little left to fall back on. The nominal social safety net for the masses is nearly nonexistent, as there has been no genuine safety for Ukrainians. In devising and proposing reform programs, therefore, it is imperative that reform proponents be in tune with the value system of the persons for whose improved well-being reform finds ultimate justification.

A painless, costless reform agenda does not exist. All reform programs entail deferred satisfaction, while exacting major sacrifices. Nevertheless, the responsibility of reform designers and advisors is to identify the reform programs that are the most cost-effective, the cost including the hardships Ukraine's economic subjects must bear in the process. Cost effectiveness within that context must dictate the minimization of avoidable disruptions, unnecessary dislocations, chaos, uncertainty, and instability. In light of the preliminary considerations outlined above, conditions in Ukraine will be more realistically grasped hereafter in order to evaluate the relative merits of alternative reform strategies.

This chapter delineates the framework for economic reform in Ukraine. It comprises four parts: (1) reform priorities; (2) political environment for reform; (3) legal foundation; and (4) reform prospects and recent performance.

REFORM PRIORITIES

Reform in Ukraine, as expressed in summary terms, must aim at improving the economy's structure, functioning, and performance. These facets overlap and are closely interconnected. They include price liberalization, foreign trade, foreign investments, the development of financial institutions and a social safety net, and general fiscal reform. Reform priorities are only briefly mentioned here relative to policy or program needs. Detailed analyses of major reform programs will be presented in the chapters that follow.

PRICE LIBERALIZATION

Among known economic systems, the market system, though having innate flaws, remains the most efficient in resource allocation. As the command system has failed, Ukraine's economic reformers intend to replace the inherited central planning system with the market system. The introduction of market mechanisms and the development of market forces thus constitute the reform's centerpiece. Markets are established institutions formed through interacting forces in the marketplace. Market forces influence and shape the markets' respective sizes, structures, forms, and relative competitiveness. Interacting market forces express themselves through free pricing's allocative adjustment processes. To promote the free flow of information embodied in the rapidly transmitted signals reflected in price fluctuations, Ukraine's reform agenda must aim at the orderly removal of barriers impeding the objective reflection of relative scarcity and abundance. Price liberalization thus constitutes one of the reform priorities.

Liberalizing prices in Ukraine is imperative. A word of caution, however, is in order. Ill-conceived and hastily implemented price liberalization programs, as evidenced in other newly liberalized economies, can cause avoidable macro dislocations, induce widespread destabilization, and subject the masses to the total loss of their lifelong savings. The program for freeing previously controlled prices needs to take into account the importance that Ukraine's residents assign to stability and security.

PRIVATIZATION

Efficient resource allocation through the market's pricing mechanism safeguards the minimization of opportunity costs, the maximization of surplus to consumers, and the accruing of profits to investors and producers. The investors and producers labor for their own accounts. They should be the legal owners of accrued profits and wealth. In other words, it is necessary that constitutional and legal guarantees for private ownership of wealth and the means of production be in place alongside the proper functioning of the market's pricing mechanism. The reform agenda in Ukraine, therefore, must incorporate the legalization of private ownership rights and the transfer of property ownership from the state to the private sector. Privatization constitutes another cornerstone for Ukraine's reform agenda.

FOREIGN TRADE

In addition to price liberalization and privatization of state properties, reformulating the nation's foreign trade strategy constitutes another priority for restructuring Ukraine's economy. Ukraine's preponderant dependence on the FSU for factor and product markets, as outlined in the previous chapter, highlights the urgent need to restructure its external sector.

Reform of Ukraine's foreign trade policy must recognize Ukraine's unique trade and economic environment in the recent past. Ukraine's approach to trade reform may and should differ from that adopted by other formerly centralized economies. For instance, foreign trade reform in Poland, in the Czech Republic, in the Baltic states, or in Hungary has meant liberalized foreign trade practices and a reorientation of trade relationships. That is, in addition to liberal foreign trade legislation, these economies all strive toward redirecting their import-export orientation from the East to the West. Other than Poland, which has a population of nearly 38 million, the other newly liberalized economies are small relative to Ukraine. Most of them also had trade relationships with the West before being pressed into the COMECON organization or being integrated into the CIS. Their initial phases of trade reorientation were trying. However, after enduring and surmounting initial impediments, foreign trade reorientation became easier, more natural, and more rewarding. Foreign trade reform in Ukraine may, in the long run, achieve the same economic results as elsewhere in the region. Yet, as will be explained in Chapter 8, drastic foreign trade reorientation in Ukraine, at least in the near future, is not recommended. Suffice it to say that foreign trade ranks high among reform priorities in Ukraine.

FOREIGN INVESTMENT

Having inherited highly specialized productive assets of minimal salvage value, Ukraine is urgently in need of foreign investment for economic restructuring, especially for its industrial sector. Ukraine's agricultural and extractive sectors may reorganize and restructure without as extensive an injection of foreign capital and technology. This is feasible owing primarily to the nature of these sectors and the productive assets they require. This, however, does not apply to Ukraine's industrial sector, which suffers from severely distorted and extensively deformed structural aberrations.

Ukraine's existing industrial enterprises, which belonged to the most prominent sector of the economy while Ukraine was under the Soviets, are not capable of producing competitive goods readily marketable abroad or in strong demand domestically. Outlets for many industrial enterprises' semifinished products or parts have been interrupted or severed. The quality of products from most of Ukraine's industrial producers also prevents them from seriously competing on the international market. Nearly all industrial enterprises in Ukraine need reorganization. Most are in need of improving the quality of their product and reconfiguring their product mix. Moreover, all sorely need investment capital for asset replacement and upgrading. The majority of industrial enterprises in Ukraine could directly benefit from foreign investment. Foreign investment may be in the form of imported technology, financial inflows, capital equipment, or the introduction of management techniques and marketing expertise. Even with massive foreign investments, Ukraine's industrial restructuring may take a decade or longer before sectoral compatibility can be established. Without it, Ukraine's industrial sector faces continued deterioration and likely disintegration. In addition to enacting progressive foreign trade laws, decision makers need to actively foster an environment conducive to foreign investment.

FINANCIAL INSTITUTIONS

Upon independence, Ukraine had no financial institutions other than branch banks of the FSU. Money markets and capital markets did not exist. Money served only as a medium of exchange. The command system prevented financial institutions from fulfilling their potentially efficacious function of mobilizing and allocating the economy's financial resources. Furthermore, money was relegated to a passive accounting role devoid of meaningful potency. The reform agenda, therefore, must incorporate policies and programs to activate the role played by Ukraine's financial institutions and financial resources.

Among the needed measures are the creation of a central bank, the guarantee of the bank's autonomous operation, and the privatization and commercialization of all state banks not part of the Bank of Ukraine.

The need for creating a central bank is self-evident. Aside from legally creating the bank and guaranteeing its independent status, the parliament and government must also refrain from interfering in the bank's decision-making processes. In countries such as the Czech Republic and Hungary, legal guarantees of the central bank's independence have been sufficient assurance that it is independent in principle and in practice. This has not been so in Ukraine. An independent Ukraine inherited a parliament made up of members of the former Communist *nomenklatura*, who customarily ruled the people and lorded over institutions. These individuals are still steeped in traditional Soviet practices and cherish many of the same old values. Their inherited mentality lingers, having the tendency to express itself in legislative or administrative decisions. Nominally, the leftist-dominated parliament accorded the Bank of Ukraine the status of being the nation's central bank, independent from the parliament and the government. In practice, however, the parliament dictates the bank's major policies, especially in the realms of credit and money-supply policies. Separation of rational decision-making processes from political considerations necessitates the central bank's being *de facto* independent and free from parliament's interference. Only thus can the nation's monetary authority conduct a rational monetary policy free of political interference. Only thus can the policy's latent potency be fully actualized to help restructure and develop Ukraine's economy.

For effectuating a freer market-directed flow of financial resources, banking reform must also rank the privatization and commercialization of noncentral state banks high among its priorities. Banking reform should oblige bank management to execute transactions solely on the basis of sound business practices, help convert passive money holdings into active investment creating efficiency and productivity in the sphere of real flows, and strengthen the effectiveness of the central bank's monetary policy, including its credit policy and money supply decisions. The maturation of the private banking sector can also, in time, provide the framework and impetus for developing other special-purpose financial institutions.

In sum, a two-tier banking system and a monetary policy that is free from parliament's interference can significantly help dismantle the structural rigidities of the recent past and help restore sectoral balances to the economy.

FISCAL REFORM

In tandem with reforming the nation's financial system, fiscal reform must aim simultaneously at fiscal discipline, macro stabilization, a rationalized tax structure, effective revenue collections, and responsible public spending. Such concurrent realization of objectives is difficult even in stable, developed market economies; thus it will be most trying in Ukraine. Yet failure to amend fiscal practices might nudge Ukraine's economy over the edge, into bankruptcy.

Reform architects in Ukraine are faced with difficult tasks in this sphere. They must introduce a market-oriented, market-based fiscal system while remaining socially responsible. Many predicaments must be faced. For instance, not only is the industrial sector no longer a secure source of tax revenues, it still looks to the state for subsidies. Meanwhile, the inherited tax collection system has collapsed, with barter and unreported exchanges accounting for nearly half of all transactions. Tax evasion and tax default thus run parallel with the need for increased state expenditures on social programs.   There are no ready solutions to unfamiliar problems.   The temptation is to disregard fiscal discipline and fiscal responsibility in favor of short-term, Band-Aid solutions to systemic and structural problems. The consequence could be lethal, since budget deficits fuel inflationary pressure, destabilize public confidence, and seriously compromise the effectiveness of other reform programs. Indifference to extreme economic hardships, on the other hand, must be avoided as well, for such indifference could easily lead people to the erroneous conclusion that the Communist system is superior to the free-market system. In brief, the need for fiscal reform poses many practical problems, promising many nearly insurmountable obstacles along the way. It not only ranks among reform priorities, it demands the most serious of reform attention.

SOCIAL SAFETY NET

Under the socialized command system, Ukrainians lived with shortages. Few lived in luxury, although none lived in abject poverty. In that sense, there was relative equality. Because the socialized system collapsed under its own weight without the replacement market system in place, there is a need for a social safety net to cushion millions of wage earners, pensioners, and consumers from a free fall from the relative security of the past.

As in most newly liberalized economies, large numbers of disguised unemployed become statistics of open unemployment. The number of people falling through the cracks of social and economic upheavals rise with the general public's loss of life-long savings through hyperinflation, with plummeting purchasing power of those on fixed incomes, and with a steadily growing sense of uncertainty and insecurity. While other newly liberalized economies encounter many serious obstacles to economic restructuring, Ukraine faces more, and reform designers and policy advisors may expect a greater need for a social safety net in Ukraine than elsewhere. A well-knit social safety net necessarily places severe constraints on a cash-poor state budget. The costly new social programs would swell the state budget, exacerbate the deficit, and fuel inflation. Inadequate social programs, on the other hand, may cause social unrest and a shift in ideological allegiance among the people. This risk is more real in Ukraine than elsewhere, considering the background forces at play in Ukraine's social and political arenas upon independence. This reform priority demands a delicate balance between purely economic considerations in the short term versus the social-political and long-term economic well-being of the newly independent Ukraine.

Not infrequently, under the pretext of exercising fiscal responsibility and expenditure controls, some experts from abroad urge upon the host economy a balanced budget at all costs. Such advice may be acceptable, for instance, in the two republics of former Czechoslovakia, because the prevailing social, political, and economic conditions in what was Czechoslovakia can endure the anticipated hardships without a rising sentiment in favor of a return to a centralized system. Social and economic conditions are less favorable in Poland, and they are unfavorable in Ukraine. Ukraine can ill afford foregoing a reasonably well-knit social safety net in the name of fiscal responsibility, particularly during this critical phase of political and economic transition. Relatively small financial savings in the short run may result in high political opportunity costs in the long term. Objective social and political factors in Ukraine dictate the necessity of an adequate social safety net.

The above section enumerated select reform priorities that decision makers need to consider for Ukraine's reform agenda. However, in reforming and transforming Ukraine's inherited centralized command system into a private-sector based and market-driven economy, new game rules must be established and rendered operative. The timely definition and creation of the necessary legal foundation for economic reform are the responsibility and prerogative of Ukraine's parliament. Compared with other newly liberalized economies in which legislative reform has preceded or proceeded alongside economic restructuring, Ukraine's political system and political environment are such that the needed legal foundation has not been forthcoming. The brief presentation below of Ukraine's current political environment anticipates the discussion of the need for a legal foundation during systemic transformation.

POLITICAL ENVIRONMENT

The political environment most conducive to economic reform may vary from one economy to another. For instance, Italy and France weathered political upheavals and frequent government changes after World War II. Both emerged with relative success in economic reconstruction and development. The former West Germany owed much of its postwar growth to Chancellor Konrad Adenauer, who directed the country's economy with an iron fist. South Korea had minimal democracy under its dictatorial president Syngman Rhee, yet its economy recovered and progressed rapidly during his presidency. Only in retrospect, it seems, may valuable lessons be drawn concerning the ideal political milieu a given nation should have for economic development or for economic restructuring.

Ukraine needs more than political stability, democratic processes, and the absence of internal or external military threats. It needs competent decision makers who, among other qualifications, also possess a clear vision, practical wisdom, political determination, and grassroots support. Ukraine needs political forces that will set aside partisan differences over approaches to economic restructuring. Ukraine's economic reform agenda needs constructive and coherent inputs and support from the nation's diverse political ideologies and forces. This, however, is in the realm of the ideal. Even under such ideal conditions, economic reform in Ukraine can still expect unanticipated detours and results that fall short of the mark. Theoretically, therefore, Ukraine can ill afford a political scenario which is less than ideal.

Nevertheless, political reality in Ukraine since independence has been far from ideal. At the grassroots level, people in the western regions of Ukraine observe and analyze the political sentiments of people in the eastern regions of Ukraine with suspicion, for the latter favor closer ties with Russia. People in eastern regions, meanwhile, wearily denounce strong nationalist feelings of those in the western regions who favor distancing Ukraine from Russia and maintaining closer political ties with the West. Both easterners and westerners view people in Crimea to the south as possible secessionists toying with the notion of declaring independence from Ukraine.

Ukraine has had two parliaments and seven governments since regaining independence in 1991. Before the 1994 general elections, the former president, Leonid Kravchuk, favored Ukraine's greater independence from Russia, but wavered among the reform priorities proposed by successive governments under his presidency. He lacked the decisiveness and finesse to steer Ukraine into a new economic path as an independent state. The former parliament, the majority of whose deputies were holdovers from the Communist era, criticized and disagreed with each reform proposal and did not accept any one of the seven economic reform programs introduced by successive governments under Kravchuk. Ukraine has thus never adopted a comprehensive, coherent, and consistent reform program. Its economy and economic reform have aimlessly drifted and are ever closer to the brink of total collapse.

In the new parliament elected in 1994, there are fifteen political parties and nine political factions. The parliament is still under the majority control of leftists represented by the former Communist Party, the Socialist Party, and the Agrarian Party, and former Communist deputies still comprise the largest single bloc in the legislature. Many of the deputies lean left in their ideological orientation, yet are not Communists. Essentially they are socialistic in ideological orientation, yet do not crave a return to a Communist-style regime. Most of the leftist deputies do not have the breadth in political experience to engage other ideologies. They have drifted in a doctrinal vacuum since the collapse of the USSR, feel insecure, and are deeply immersed in coping with swift and abrupt changes. A convenient modus operandi has been to criticize, though not necessarily with malice or ill will, the weaker elements in reform proposals and delay decisions for action. The parliament, thus blocked, has been ineffective in advancing alternative reform proposals or in improving upon the ones pending in the legislature. Endless delays in orderly reform contribute to a sustained downward slide of Ukraine's economy. Public opinion places very little trust in public officials, voicing increasing doubts over the merits of a market system. The general public has seen disjointed reform measures being introduced, while experiencing nothing but hardships with no end in sight.

For his part, former president Kravchuk has admitted there were "past errors" during his presidency. However, he has not accepted personal responsibility for the errors. Instead, he has pointed to the uniquely precarious condition Ukraine's economy was in by the time Ukraine regained its independence. Kravchuk's reason for indecisiveness and inaction during his presidency was Ukraine's lack of preparedness for independence. His explanation has been echoed, in part, by Ukraine's first deputy speaker, Olexandre Trachenko:

Neither the parliament, nor the president, nor the government had a model ready for Ukraine as a sovereign state. We had two choices: to be well off and dependent [on Russia], or to be uncertain and independent. The parliament chose the latter. If a model for gradual secession from the [FSU's] integrated system had been elaborated beforehand, then Ukraine would not have to undergo such a breakdown in the economy. (Trachenko interview, 1994)

Liberally interpreted, Kravchuk and Trachenko's explanation may be distilled into the following: if Ukraine's economy had been less integrated into the Soviet system, and if plans for a phased disengagement from the system could have been in place beforehand, then Ukraine's economy would not have suffered the dislocation and disintegration to the degree it has thus far sustained. However, being less well prepared or unprepared for independence cannot explain the government's indecisiveness or inaction after independence became a reality. Furthermore, the possession of a blueprint for gradual political disengagement from the FSU could not guarantee its implementation in Ukraine's political setting. That is, even if a phased disintegration of the totalitarian system was politically conceivable, Ukraine's politicians would still have probably been as indecisive and unprepared in moving economic reform forward. Ukraine has had neither the tradition nor the experience of formulating and implementing independent economic policies. As a result, its haphazard attempts at reform seem more deleterious than constructive.

On June 26, 1994, voters elected a new parliament, and they elected Leonid Kuchma as president. Kuchma had served as the prime minister under Kravchuk between October 1992 and September 1993. During that period the Supreme Rada granted Kuchma extraordinary authority for implementing reform measures. Kuchma wielded considerable influence in both the executive and legislative branches of the government. However, his initial reform measures alarmed the parliament's conservative left, who six months later refused renewal of the extraordinary authority vested in him. Kuchma relinquished the post of prime minister in September 1993, only months after submitting his administration's reform agenda to the Supreme Rada. As a presidential candidate in 1994, he centered his campaign themes on closer ties with Russia, orderly market-oriented reform, and national unity. Although he trailed Kravchuk during the first round of the presidential election,[1] Kuchma won 52.4 percent of the electoral votes during the runoff election.

Two significant indicators emerged in Ukraine's 1994 presidential election. First, the majority of voters who backed Kravchuk during the December 1991 presidential election favored Kuchma during the 1994 election. Moreover, those who seriously distrusted Kravchuk during the December 1991 election, primarily because of his past close ties with the Kremlin, voted overwhelmingly in favor of him during the 1994 election. Second, it was evident that a significant polarization of sentiments among Ukraine's population had occurred during the few years since independence.

Behind the small overall majority of the winner [Kuchma], there are significant regional preferences. Leonid Kravchuk won in 13 electoral districts out of 27, which form a compact tract of territory that in the former Soviet Union was called the South-Western economic region. Here, for every vote given to Leonid Kuchma, Leonid Kravchuk received 2.89 votes. On the other hand, in the former Donetsk-Dnieper and Southern economic region, for every vote cast for Leonid Kravchuk, Leonid Kuchma received 2.86 [votes]. (Kvaniuk, 1994: 3)

In short, the industrial east and south voted overwhelmingly in favor of Kuchma during the 1994 presidential election, voting for orderly reform, although recognizing the unavoidable need for a closer economic relationship with the republic of Russia. Regions to the west, however, especially areas with closer cultural ties to Poland and Western countries, gave their strong support to Kravchuk in the 1994 election. That is, despite the dismal performance in economic reform during Kravchuk's two and a half years as Ukraine's first democratically elected president, western Ukrainians still trusted him and voted for him because he favored distance between Ukraine and Russia. As a whole, Ukrainians in the eastern and southern regions, at least via their electoral privileges, manifested their preference for genuine economic reform over asserting national independence. Those in the western regions, on the other hand, believed national identity and distance from centuries of involvement with Russia more important than economic issues.

Polarization of sentiments aside, political democracy and social order have prevailed in Ukraine, which now has a new president intent on implementing reform measures. Kuchma has openly and repeatedly pointed out the mistakes of past administrations, outlining the path that Ukraine must take in effectuating economic restructuring. He apparently possesses the political will for a more resolute approach to reform, yet genuine attempts at moving reform forward, it seems, have only begun. Parliament, however, is divided into factions and is deeply unsure of the territories within the market system. Kuchma follows his own counsel. Delivering his "Along the Road of Radical Economic Reform" speech to the Supreme Rada on October 11, 1994, demanding resolute commitment to reform, Kuchma demonstrated his intent on being the driver, whether the Supreme Rada rode with him or not. Nearly a week later, he won a rare concession from the parliament: "After nearly nine hours of debate, a vote of 231–54 cleared the way for free market reforms previously blocked by Communist lawmakers, and allowed Ukraine to free prices, reduce state subsidies, overhaul the tax system, and push ahead with privatization, including private land ownership" (*Ukrainian Weekly,*1995, No. 52: 4).

Nevertheless, six months elapsed, and no definitive legislation on these issues materialized. The new president, intent on moving economic reform forward, appeared to be a hostage of a parliament dominated by deputies of unsure convictions and insecure identities.

When Kuchma was prime minister for eleven months in 1992–1993, he was ob-structed by parliament and resigned from his position. As president, he repeatedly and publicly vowed his reform program would not fall victim to parliamentary inaction as before. Kuchma believes that, given prevailing conditions in Ukraine, political reform must antecede or at least accompany economic reform. Enhanced presidential powers are the only remaining hope for moving Ukraine's reform program forward. Kuchma's proposal for defining the division of governmental powers—with strong authority for the office of the president—received no initial objection from the Supreme Rada. While the proposal was undergoing review by a parliamentary committee in early 1995, however, leftist elements in the parliament and on regional and local levels actively and openly campaigned against it. The irony is that it had always been the leftist-controlled parliament that had derailed all reform proposals in the past.

The immediate future of Ukraine's political development remains uncertain. The near future of Ukraine's economic reform and economic performance therefore is equally uncertain. The Supreme Rada will eventually move forward with reform legislation, though at a significantly slower pace than justifiable or salutary. One certitude along the economic frontier is that whether the Supreme Rada will actively assist or passively retard the president's initiatives for reform, Ukraine's economy is still quite a distance from having effectuated substantive and constructive reform measures. On the presumption that eventual legislative cooperation will be given to the president, the following section briefly examines Ukraine's need for a legal foundation in its attempts at a systemic transformation.

LEGAL FOUNDATION

During the Soviet decades, the state owned the means of production, the state planned economic relationships, and the state directed economic activities. Ukraine is in between the collapsed command system and the pending new market system. The most basic of inherited institutions and relationships must undergo fundamental changes.

First, on the most fundamental level, constitutional reform must guarantee personal property and ownership rights. The legal foundation for the transference of state ownership rights to the private sector rests on such constitutional guarantees. Restitution, corporatization, and privatization are among the possible facets of the ownership-rights transformation process. Constitutional guarantee of private ownership rights is a basic prerequisite of the market system.

Second, the state's planning apparatus and operation must be replaced by market mechanisms developed for the coordination of pricing relationships. Other than the state's principal responsibilities in realms such as contract enforcement and monopoly regulations, economic relationships should be entered into, maintained, and adjusted according to objective forces in the market. So that such relationships possess legally binding rights, privileges, and obligations, Ukraine's legislature has the prerogative, as well as the responsibility, to enact economic laws delineating the parameters of such relationships during the various stages of systemic transformation.

Thirdly, reform needs to create and foster an environment in which market forces constitute the primary mover of economic activities. So that people may fully understand the rules of the game and freely engage in activities within the confines of the law, a host of consistent and transparent economic laws are needed. Thus laws governing property ownership, private contracts, labor relations, external trade, domestic and foreign investments, anticompetitive forces and bankruptcy, among others, need to be in place as the foundation for people entering into economic relationships.

Between late 1991 and mid-1994, Ukraine's first parliament passed more than 402 laws, 128 resolutions, and countless amendments to the newly enacted laws; it gave the impression of being productive. Nevertheless, there was a discernable lack of cohesiveness among the new laws pertaining directly to economic issues. The laws were prolific on generalities and short on specifics, frequently requiring many amendments, clarifications, and revisions. "The government, including the parliament, was practically behaving like a fire corps. It extinguishes one fire here, and then rushes off for another somewhere else. There was no consistency. There was no continuity. There was no comprehensive grasp over economic reform issues" (Pirozhkov interview, 1994).

On a more concrete level, people lack certainty over how specific provisions of a given law might read six months hence. Because of lack of legislative discipline, gaping legal loopholes multiply. Even the courts and lawyers are ill equipped for interpreting new laws and adjudicating economic issues. Prospective foreign investors and traders hesitate and feel insecure about making substantive commitments. Meanwhile, as old disciplines fall into disuse and appropriate new rules or laws remain conspicuously absent, enterprising profiteers take advantage of the situation at the expense of a helpless and hapless general public.

A lot of decisions in the field of monetary and import-export policy were adopted with the results considered beforehand. They were intended to enrich certain persons and coterie . . . The aggravation of the situation may be beneficial for some deputies, state and local administrators. It is a great chance for them to establish themselves in a good way. Ultimately, it's a harmful and suicidal policy but they won't let the chance of a lifetime slip. (*Ukrainian National Information Service*, 1994: 14)

Many of the newly rich were members of the *nomenklatura*. Having maintained past connections, they now define windows of opportunities. Murky legal waters can serve their personal interests. Positioning Ukraine's reform on track, therefore, requires establishing a sound legal foundation without further delays or excuses.

REFORM PROSPECTS AND RECENT PERFORMANCE

In a three-year period from the beginning of 1991 to the end of 1993, Ukraine's GNP declined by 24.8 percent, its national product fell by 39.4 percent, industrial production by 17.8 percent, consumer goods production by 29.1 percent, and agricultural production by 21.8 percent. GNP during the first six months of 1994 was 36 percent less than in the comparable period in 1993 (Kuchma, 1994: 3–5). Obsolete capital assets face accelerating depreciation while capital accumulation has come to a virtual halt. The state's budget for 1992 accounted for 61.7 percent of the year's national income, increasing to 73.2 percent in 1993 and to 85 percent in 1994. Ukraine has the highest income tax rate in the world, reaching 90 percent for individuals earning more than U.S. $150 a month. Barter accounted for an estimated 50 to 60 percent of all exchange activities in 1994, compounding the already difficult tasks of revenue collection. Furthermore, the state has been collecting less than 50 percent of the expected tax revenue in recent years, intensifying the existing budgetary crisis.

Ukraine's inflation rate ranked the highest in the world in 1993, and in 1994, unemployment in the state sector reached a record 33 percent (*Ukrainian Weekly*, January 8, 1995: 2). Reluctant to openly discharge surplus labor and to fall behind in meeting wage payment obligations, enterprise directors increasingly resort to a reduced work week, forced unpaid vacations, maintaining interenterprise payments in arrears, exchanging promissory notes with those who willingly accept them, and selling enterprise assets that are supposedly still owned by the state. More than 80 percent of hard currency earnings by Ukraine's residents remain unreported, and between 80 to 90 percent of their hard currency deposits are kept in financial institutions abroad. Industry has barely begun restructuring and adapting to the changing environment. Economic potentials remain potentials, while rapidly aging, obsolescent capital assets continue to depreciate and to fall into disuse. Ukraine's overall economic conditions have gone from a state of inherited inefficiency to an unwarranted crisis of neglect and mismanagement. Instead of charting, adopting, and executing a reform agenda uniquely suited to the nation's existing conditions, Ukraine's leaders have permitted the economy to drift and slip.

In the five years since independence, disjointed reform processes in Ukraine have netted mostly negative results. President Kuchma will increase his pressure on the parliament for rule by administrative decree. If necessary, he will resort to national referenda on crucial issues. The likelihood is that political reform will accompany Kuchma's call for economic restructuring. In the words of Victor Nebozhenko, Ukraine's leading researcher in the field of social issues, economic reform without concurrent political reform is a near impossibility: "To start making any progress Ukraine has to reform the political system first. The economic reforms are impossible without that. Only decisive actions will stop the drifting towards the catastrophe and chaos. . . . The future of the country will be determined by those politicians who will mange to work out the acceptable political model for Ukraine" (quoted in *Ukrainian National Information Service*, 1994: 40).

Finally, in the long run, the likely scenario is that the legislative branch of the government will make compromises to the executive branch, and for good reason. All indications in mid-1995 point to continued economic decline, worsening social stagnation, and predictable political impasses. Pressure for decisive action will mount from both the domestic front and international forums. Despite the anticipated worsening of economic conditions and the continued erosion of consumer purchasing power, the dismal results of several years of nonreform and partial reform will force Ukraine's decision makers to face choosing between two equally unpleasant alternatives: systematic and systemic reform, exacting high political and social cost; or total collapse of Ukraine's economy, and anarchy. Despite the people's inborn docility, rising social tensions will be correlated to declining economic conditions. The Supreme Rada will come to its senses, yielding more power to the president in matters pertaining to economic reform. Public pressure on the parliament's deputies will ease as a result, while public dissatisfaction will temporarily shift to blaming the executive branch of the government for sustained economic hardships. As reform progresses via administrative initiatives, the memory of secure and stable decades under the Soviets will become a mirage in a setting of steadily increasing hardships. Ukraine's economic performance will bottom out, stabilize briefly at the underside, and slowly begin an upward climb. Ukrainians will, in time, become increasingly more educated as to the relative merits of divergent economic systems. They will recognize that the painful experiences between late 1991 and the inception of a genuine reform program were due more to nonreform, partial reform, political ineptitude, and malice on the part of vested interests and profiteers than on inherent ills of the market system. As the economy stabilizes and recovers, the merits of the new system will take root in the people's value system. The influence of socialist ideology will correspondingly fade.

Kuchma's reform agenda has a better chance of being implemented than any previous reform proposals had. Kuchma was granted extraordinary powers by the Supreme Rada during his brief tenure as prime minister of Ukraine, the sole former prime minister to be granted such powers. Kuchma's brief tenure as prime minister brought measurable discomfort to many deputies of the first parliament (1991–1994), who customarily had the final say in matters such as new economic institutions. They encouraged Kuchma's departure from office by refusing an extension of the extraordinary power initially granted to him. However, the political scene has changed since then. The new parliament, though still under the majority control of the leftward leaning factions, also includes center-right, right, and nonaligned deputies. Because the country lacks a tradition of public trust in and respect for civil authority, and faces continual deterioration of economic conditions, the parliament will yield to Kuchma's demand for enhanced presidential power in economic matters. As Ukraine's economy edges closer to the brink of collapse, the deputies have more at stake if Kuchma's demands are not met. The prognosis is that Kuchma's reform agenda will be the cornerstone, the real beginning, of a systemic transformation in Ukraine.

The ensuing chapters will examine Ukraine's major reform policies to date.

NOTE

1. Leonid Kravchuk, Ukraine's first president after independence, received 37.7 percent of the electoral votes during the first round of the presidential election held on June 26, 1994; Leonid Kuchma received 31.3 percent; and the balance were distributed among five other major candidates. Since no candidate received more than a simple majority, a runoff election between Kravchuk and Kuchma was held on July 9, 1994. Kuchma emerged as the winner, with only a slender edge over Kravchuk.

5

Price Liberalization

There have been numerous governments since Ukraine regained its independence in 1991,[1] and more economic reform programs than administrations during that time. Although the different proposed reform programs contained distinctive reform emphases, there was a common thread running through all of them: the liberalization of economic relationships and the marketization of economic activities. Four reform areas that appeared in all the proposed programs are: (1) price liberalization and stabilization, (2) enterprise reorganization and privatization of state assets, (3) a new foreign investment policy, and (4) liberalized foreign trade.

This chapter examines price liberalization and stabilization policies in Ukraine, and comprises six sections. The first section examines the justification for price liberalization in Ukraine. The second summarizes government policies and actions concerning price deregulation. Consequences to price liberalization—including discussions of prices, wages, real incomes, and monopolies—constitute the third segment of this chapter. The fourth part evaluates the government's stabilization policies. The fifth segment discusses major factors affecting inflation and price stability. The chapter's final section outlines policy errors and highlights lessons to be learned therefrom.

RATIONALE FOR PRICE DEREGULATION

Price liberalization policy extends beyond the freeing of prices in product markets. It applies to the freeing of prices in factor markets as well. Concurrent with price liberalization is the need for reduced state financing of economic activities and relationships in a timely manner, for it was the state's direct intervention in the marketplace in the past that encouraged pervasive distortions and imbalances.

The Soviet planners deliberately suppressed the free-market pricing mechanism, overemphasizing the industrial and military sectors at the expense of agriculture and consumer goods industries. They created economic distortions in the process. A liberal market economy does not permit the persistence of such distortions; markets reflect comparative abundances and scarcities and allocate resources in an efficient fashion.

In a free-market system, points along the demand function reflect marginal value product of the respective units to the consumers. In a single-product situation, utility maximization dictates that the consumer equate marginal value product with free-market-determined product price. The consumer reaps a surplus and thus would willingly pay more for the goods he receives than he actually does pay. Likewise, the producer reaps a profit, more for his product than the cost of production. In a free market, both consumers and producers enjoy surpluses.

The free market encourages allocative efficiency and provides incentives for cost efficiency. Market forces oblige producers to continuously improve efficiency if they are to remain competitive. Improved efficiency results in lower production costs. Lowered production costs, combined with sustained market competitiveness, ensure competitive prices. Such prices increase the level of consumption and contribute to consumer surplus and social well-being. While profits accrue to investors and producers, enhanced surplus assures simultaneous redistribution of benefits to consumers, many of whom are also savers and therefore investors. Meanwhile, the steadily increasing consumer surplus is also an alternative expression of income redistribution in the form of extending economic benefit to consumers. The economy concurrently expands, growing more dynamic. The simplified cycle of the market's primary functions—production, distribution, and consumption—is completed and begins anew. Aside from the need for internalizing the hitherto unspecified external diseconomies, there are no undue distortions, imbalances, or waste of the society's resources.

Therein lie the merits of the free-market system. The relevant question in effectuating price liberalization in Ukraine is not whether, but how, the process should be carried out. Answers to the question reside in grasping the underlying causes of the need for price liberalization in Ukraine.

This free market system has been purposefully suppressed in Ukraine by the command system during the past seven decades. A brief explication of the causes and methods of market suppression will help us formulate a price liberalization policy for Ukraine that is rational, feasible, and appropriate, for it is toward the attainment of the market system's benefits that the economic system in Ukraine needs to evolve.

Suppression of the market mechanism in Ukraine under the USSR command system facilitated state control of market activities and relationships. Socializing all the means of production was an avenue to the elimination of market-based and market-driven economic activities. Once the process was complete, namely when the private ownership was abolished, plan regulation replaced market coordination. All productive efforts were concentrated on the fulfillment of production targets, on self-sufficiency rather than on exchange for profit. The enhancement of surplus value to consumers was absent from consideration, a consequence of the Marxian insistence that the only kind of surplus value is "stolen" profit.

The other central function of the market system—resource allocation through the pricing mechanism—ceased reflecting objective values to consumers and costs to producers, maintaining state-determined equilibrium, and requiring plan-decreed factor and product prices to deviate from realistic abundance and scarcity conditions. As planning objectives placed disproportionate emphasis on accelerated industrial-ization and militarization, plan-determined prices on industrial goods and military hardware steadily rose through successive five-year plans. Unrealistic interest charges, or interest-free credits to capital accumulation in heavy industry, resulted in sustained inventory accumulation in these sectors and in the depletion of resource availability to other productive spheres.

Wages in heavy industry rose proportionately faster than wages in other sectors of the economy, regardless of whether profits or losses resulted from these productive endeavors. Meanwhile, planners assigned secondary importance to consumer goods industries, including Ukraine's promising agricultural sector. Budget allocation for investment in consumer goods industries was held below what was appropriate. State-determined central purchasing prices for consumer goods were also kept low, collecting surplus value for the state budget. Wages in nonprimary industries, includ-ing those in the agricultural sector, likewise remained low. The state thus maintained an artificial equilibrium in the production sphere by budgeting a subsistence-level income for the average consumer, suppressing the average consumer's purchasing power in the face of an inadequate supply of consumer goods. The infrequently adjusted wages necessitated an artificially maintained pricing system which then gave the appearance of price stability and relative supply adequacy.

Distortions in resource allocation and imbalances in product mix emerged even during the early years of the Soviet era. In response to severe shortages, rationing coupons replaced the market's function in product distribution, suppressing effective demand for goods upon which consumers assigned high product value. In time, successive five-year plans intensified and institutionalized the built-in distortions and imbalances, causing increasingly greater deviation of production from opportunity costs and of product prices from objective value produced. Plan-designated prices deviated further from economic reality, increasingly impairing the pricing system's transmission of correct signals concerning relative abundance and scarcity. Despite periodic calls for reform and occasional price and wage adjustments, cumulative imbalances over the decades continued to reinforce existing distortions. For decades, therefore, planned prices prevented inflationary pressure from exhibiting its effects, concealing the widening distance between the real and the plan-determined costs and values.

The planned pricing system did not correct these imbalances, nor did it neutralize inflationary forces. The planned pricing system only postponed the manifestation of inflationary pressures built up over the decades. Policymakers do not argue about whether price controls should be lifted. They argue about whether price liberalization policies call for controlled gradualism or a complete and sudden abolition of controlled prices. The following section examines Ukraine's price reform in recent years.

GOVERNMENT POLICY AND PRACTICES

Price liberalization is the cornerstone of systemic transformation. Decision makers may or may not be convinced of its long-term merits, yet all agree that price deregulation is necessary because planned pricing brings wastefulness, inefficiency, and imbalances. That Ukraine continued circulating the Russian ruble after independence made Ukraine a passive and unwilling participant in Russia's hasty attempts at price liberalization. According to the *Plan for Urgent Economic Reforms* issued by Ukraine's Cabinet of Ministers in February 1992, Ukraine's "prices should be liberalized simultaneously with the freeing of prices in Russia" (Cabinet of Ministers, 1992a: sect. 2.2, para. 3). This statement suggests that Ukraine had no schedule of its own for deregulating prices. Other sections of the *Plan for Urgent Economic Reforms,* as well as of *The Programme of Economic Reforms and Policy in Ukraine* also authored by the Cabinet of Ministers in 1992, alluded to what would remain under state control in the short run rather than explicitly stating what sectors could, or would, be subject to deregulation in the future. General, noncommittal statements dominated these documents, leaving no clearly defined parameters for realistic implementation of price reform proposals.

In another reform proposal by then–Prime Minister Kuchma, more emphasis was placed on raising the state's purchasing prices for agricultural produce and on price parity between farm and nonfarm products than on price liberalization itself (Cabinet of Ministers, 1993: 81–82). Finally, Kuchma, in his 1994 presidential address entitled "Along the Road of Radical Economic Reform," merely suggested that price-setting policy would be "implemented through the government regulated and controlled gradual liberalization of prices. Its pace will depend on the actual economic and social situation" (Kuchma, 1994: 2, sect. 1). However, at the time of Kuchma's address, only a select few prices on consumer goods and services were still under government regulation. Price determination in most productive spheres was already beyond the state's control. His proposed gradualism policy in late 1994, therefore, was no longer relevant. By then, hyperinflation had already ravaged consumers and savers for three consecutive years. As the Ministry of Economy reported, by early 1995 "the worst of the price increases may be over for the citizens of Ukraine" (*Ukrainian Weekly,* February 5, 1995: No. 6: 1).

Owing to the plan-crafted structural integration of the two republics during the Soviet decades, Russia's unilateral price deregulation in 1991 drew an unprepared Ukraine into spiraling inflation as well. What Moscow initiated prior to and until that time directly affected Ukraine. After the dissolution of the USSR, Russia accelerated its own pace of price deregulation. Ukraine could not have pursued an independent price liberalization policy at that time, even if it had a program and a schedule ready for implementation, because the ruble was still the sole legal tender in all the republics of the FSU. Moreover, Ukraine had no effective border control to prevent the free flow of goods into or out of the country; therefore, consumer goods prices in Ukraine were reactive to increases in Russia and in neighboring CIS countries. Russia removed state control over a wide range of industrial and consumer goods beginning in January 1992, prompting Ukrainian Prime Minister V. Fokin to state in his administration's reform policy that price liberalization in Ukraine must parallel those efforts in Russia.

Initially, consumer goods whose prices remained under state control were energy, housing, transportation, and basic food items. The fact that prices on these items remained controlled did not mean they remained unchanged; it meant that prices on these goods and services would increase, under the state's supervision. As a result, the inflation rate for the first four months of 1992 soared to 1,000 percent (the inflation rate had been only 4.2 percent in 1990) (Frydman, 1993: 89). By then, two-thirds of the average consumer's purchasing volume went toward basic household supplies. Price increases on regulated commodities continued throughout subsequent administrations, while prices of items no longer under the state's control skyrocketed. The inflationary pressure, long suppressed under the Soviet Union, vented most of its steam in a matter of four years, between early 1991 and late 1995.

Since prices of most industrial products—except those originating from monopolistic producers—as well as those of agricultural inputs, were freed, consumers and producers were dealt severe shocks. The government attempted to cushion these hardships with occasional increases in wages paid and prices offered to factor employers. The state budget also granted partial compensation to savers for loss of their lifelong savings. Nevertheless, partial indexation of wages, savings, and farm product purchasing prices could not save people from sinking into destitution. According to a United Nations report, "approximately 40 percent of the population could be considered as below the poverty line well before the dismantling of central planning began to accelerate. This situation must have worsened considerably already in 1991 and again following the price liberalization of January 1992" (Secretariat of the Economic Commission for Europe, Geneva, 1992: 149).

The high poverty rate that Ukraine endured even before the price liberalization program began can be attributed to both low standards of living and earlier measures aimed at the partial release of inflationary pressure by Moscow in the late 1980s. That the "situation must have worsened considerably already in 1991, and again following the price liberalization of January 1992" was an understatement; the deterioration of economic conditions in Ukraine after 1991 was rapid.

While he was still prime minister of Ukraine in May 1993, Kuchma declared that "our economy is in [a] catastrophic condition . . . [and that] inflation is an illustration not only of the poor condition of the economy, but also of the weak state power or weak political wisdom" (Lukinov, 1993: 10). Yet, despite Kuchma's statement, successive administrations continued rapid price increases on controlled items. The devastating effects prompted Kuchma, who was now the president of Ukraine, to address the Supreme Rada on October 11, 1994 in these words:

Previous experience has shown that the abrupt liberalization of prices is unwise. In the absence of market institutions and requisite competitive environment, this approach is counterproductive, and has a negative influence on both productivity and the social climate. For this reason, our price-setting policy will be implemented through the government regulated and controlled gradual liberalization of prices. Its pace will depend on the actual economic and social situation. (Kuchma, 1994: 22)

Nonetheless, a month after Kuchma's speech, the Ukrainian government initiated a new wave of price increases on controlled items. It announced yet another round of increases scheduled for February 1, 1995. The price of bread, for example, would rise by 150 percent while the price of public transportation in Kiev would rise by 367 percent (*Ukrainian Weekly*, February 5, 1995, No. 6: 1). Such abrupt price increases for basic goods and services would have been considered radical by any measure in developed market economies, making unclear what Kuchma meant when he stated that "gradual liberalization of prices" was henceforth to be the government's policy.

Rapid and relentless rounds of price increases on controlled items eventually brought about the Supreme Rada's intervention. On February 9, 1995, the legislature prohibited the administration from implementing the scheduled price increases unless wages also rose by an unspecified amount. Forecasts for 1995, however, still placed the projected price increases for the year at 300 percent (OMRI *Daily Digest*, January 24, 1995; February 10, 1995). In brief, despite Prime Minister Kuchma's statement in May 1993, price liberalization policy continues its rapid course under President Kuchma in 1995. By the end of 1995, prices on almost all consumer goods will have been liberalized.

PRICES, WAGES, INCOMES

Price increases in the USSR as a whole were modest until 1990. In the five years between 1986 and 1990, the annual retail price index rose by 2.0, 1.3, 0.6, 2.0, and 4.8 percent, respectively. Wages for the corresponding period rose by 2.9, 3.7, 8.3, 9.4, and 10.0 percent, respectively (International Monetary Fund, 1990: 49). Real incomes and real household savings thus rose for most Soviet citizens during this period. It was 1991 that marked the beginning of a swift decline in living standards for most Ukrainians. The inflation rate for 1993 was 83.5 percent.

Table 5.1
Consumer Price Index, December 1991–July 1994
(Dec. 1990 = 100 for all three indices)

	Dec. 1991	Dec. 1992	Dec. 1993	July 1994
Goods and Services	390	8,190	840,130	2,268,351
Food	431	7,723	940,507	–
Nonfood	378	7,987	894,624	–

Sources: Ministry of Statistics, 1994d: 97; Kuchma, 1994: 7

Table 5.1 presents an overview of consumer price indices between December 1991 and July 1994. It was during that period that consumer purchasing power sustained the most severe shocks. The data bear out several noteworthy trends:

First, inflation had become a problem even before the price liberalization program went into effect; consumer prices roughly quadrupled during 1991, the year before the price liberalization program officially began.

Second, the fact that the prices of nonfood items rose more slowly than the prices of food items reflects the weak demand Ukrainians have expressed for nonfood items. The average Ukrainian was spending nearly his entire income on food during the worst inflationary periods. Prices of most household food items—excluding restaurant meals and imported foods, which had been deregulated—remained under the state's control in 1992.

Because under the Soviet system, food production and distribution were more heavily subsidized than were nonfood consumer goods, distortions in the food sector were greater. Prices in the food sector therefore must rise even more than prices in other sectors to more accurately reflect relative marginal value product.

As a result of these aggravating conditions, food prices climbed by 1,692 percent in 1992. When compared with the 350 percent increase in the price of oil incurred in the United States between October 1973 and October 1974, the devastating effects of which are well-known, the effects of a 1,692 percent increase in food prices in Ukraine within a one year period need no further elaboration. The price adjustment process for food and other commodities or services still under the state's control may persist for an extended period of time.

Third, while the controlled upward price adjustment of food has been unrelenting, controlled price increases in services and energy consumption have been comparatively mild. Consumption and production in the energy sector, however, were also excessively subsidized during the Soviet era. Consumers may thus expect more pronounced price increases in these spheres once food price increases level off.

Fourth, the 170 percent increase in consumer prices for the first seven months of 1994 provides a reason for cautious optimism. While such an inflation rate is unacceptable in a developed economy, the dramatic *disinflation* indicates that the worst of the price increases could be over. Some caveats are in order, however: Ukrainian consumers had not reached the base of their downward plunge in living standards as of mid-1995.

Using January 1992, the commencement of price liberalization, as the benchmark, prices of consumer goods and services increased by 5,816 times in two and a half years—that is, a product that sold for one *karbovantsi (kbv)* at the beginning of 1992 was selling, on average, for 5,816 *kbv* by the end of July in 1994. The deceleration of the price level during the first half of 1994 may be cause for encouragement to economic advisors and reform architects, yet not for the average consumers: their living standard has continued its free fall, though at a slower rate than before.

Problems stemming from rapid price increases assume countless forms and exhibit their adverse effects in many ways. Undesirable income redistribution, unrealistic and unmanageable rates of interest, rising trade imbalances, capital flight, and savings disincentives are only a few such anomalies. The ensuing discussion analyzes the adverse effects of Ukraine's hyperinflation on wages and income.

A disproportionate amount of scarce national energy, better aimed at reconstructive programs, has instead been used to battle the adverse effects of inflation. Ukraine's legislature and administration had no prior experience in coping with the social and economic ills that are consequent to hyperinflation. Their policy measures and decisions became passive and defensive. They were capable only of crisis management and spent precious time and energy on wage-indexation, farm-purchasing, and savings-loss policies. Though periodic increases of nominal wages, savings compensation, and state purchasing prices of select products did take place, consumers' living standards nevertheless continued to plummet. Table 5.2 demonstrates the manner in which real wages have not kept up with inflation.

Clearly, wages have not kept up with prices; real wages by late 1994 averaged only one-fourth what they had been thirty-four months earlier. Prices rose more than 10,000-fold after the price liberalization program began. Though the numbers make the plight of the Ukrainian economy painfully apparent, three observations warrant further detail. These regard income indexation, fluctuations in purchasing power, and losses in real income.

Nominal Wages

The average nominal wage by the end of January 1992, the month in which the deregulation program began, surpassed the average nominal wage for December 1991 by 90 percent. Since prices more than tripled during that first month of liberalization, consumers purchasing power was nearly halved in only one month's time. Shocked, the government hastily indexed the wages of workers, most of whom were state employees. However, once the ill-conceived price liberalization program was set in motion, much of the decision makers' energy was then devoted to damage control.

Table 5.2
Monthly Nominal Wages, CPI, Real Wages (December 1991–November 1994)

	(1) Average Wages	(2) CPI	(3) Real Wages	(4) Average Wages	(5) CPI	(6) Real Wages	(7) Average Wages	(8) CPI	(9) Real Wages
1991									
December	100	100	1.00						
1992									
January	190	352	0.54						
February	212	433	0.49						
March	237	478	0.50						
April	352	543	0.65						
May	410	667	0.61						
June	627	787	0.80						
July	618	1,004	0.62						
August	655	1,159	0.57						
September	883	1,332	0.66						
October	1.001	1,670	0.60						
November	1,299	2,048	0.63						
December	2,304	2,830	0.81	100	100	1.00			
1993									
January	1,742	4,901	0.36	76	173	0.44			
February	2,209	6,313	0.35	96	223	0.43			
March	2,649	7,708	0.34	115	272	0.42			
April	2,945	9,527	0.31	128	337	0.38			
May	3,493	12,156	0.29	152	430	0.35			
June	6,689	20,872	0.32	290	738	0.39			
July	8,268	28,720	0.29	359	1,015	0.35			
August	9,268	34,953	0.27	402	1,235	0.33			
September	22,615	63,020	0.36	981	2,227	0.44			
October	27,567	104,676	0.26	1,196	3,699	0.32			
November	35,259	152,094	0.23	1,530	5,375	0.28			
December	91,003	290,195	0.31	3,948	10,255	0.38	100	100	100
1994									
January	87,636	345,912	0.25	3,801	12,224	0.31	96	119	0.81
February	87,285	389,497	0.22	3,786	13,764	0.28	96	134	0.71
March	97,148	411,698	0.24	4,214	14,549	0.29	107	142	0.75
April	101,423	435,989	0.23	4,400	15,407	0.29	111	150	0.74
May	108,218	458,660	0.24	4,694	16,208	0.29	119	158	0.75
June	119,798	476,548	0.25	5,197	16,840	0.31	132	164	0.80
July	127,105	486,555	0.26	5,514	17,194	0.32	140	168	0.83
August	132,062	499,206	0.26	5,729	17,614	0.32	145	172	0.84
September	140,382	535,648	0.26	6,090	18,929	0.32	154	185	0.84
October	217,171	656,704	0.33	9,421	23,207	0.41	239	226	1.05
November	290,358	1,132,158	0.26	12,878	40,009	0.32	326	390	0..84

Source: Ministry of Economy, 1994c: 19

Nominal wages rose at a phenomenal rate during the three-year period presented in Table 5.2. As may be observed under column 1 in Table 5.2, the increases were most conspicuous for the months of December 1992 (in which wages rose, on average, by 77.4 percent), December of 1993 (in which they rose, on average, by 158 percent), and September through November of 1994. Never before in history had any government attempted increases in nominal wages so rapidly. In thirty-five months, wages stood at 2,903.58 times their December 1991 level.

The costs of rising wages mirrored the consumers' loss of confidence in the nation's new legal tender (also referred to as the Ukrainian coupons), bloated state budgets, and sustained inflationary pressure. Since budget-financed wage indexation necessarily compromises the effectiveness of attempts at curbing inflation, a valid question presents itself: why not slow down price increases in areas still under state control until more favorable market conditions evolve? Such a policy could release decision makers from expending excessive energy on coping with the dilemma of inflation and wage indexation, as well as reduce the growth in budget deficits and slow down the momentum of the inflationary spiral. Only expert advisors to the Ukrainian government and the public officials themselves can satisfactorily answer these questions.

Purchasing Power

As has been discussed, stability and security, though contrived and inefficient under the centralized command system, are two attributes that people in Ukraine highly cherish. The fact that stability often came at the cost of economic growth during the final three decades of the Soviet Union demonstrates how highly Soviet citizens and planners valued economic certainty. Stagnation seems like a setback only to those familiar with consistent progress. Soaring price levels, however, demolished the remotest semblance of security. Hasty implementation of price liberalization stripped wage earners, savers, and persons on fixed incomes of their protective shield against economic uncertainty. The hasty implementation of price liberalization did not merely breed economic insecurity; it also paralyzed the already poorly functioning components of the inherited system and the embryonic components of the replacement system.

Another element closely associated with economic security is economic stability. The volatility of real wages, as evidenced in columns 3, 6, and 9 of Table 5.2, occurred as a result of poorly organized, poorly scheduled indexation; between September and October of 1994, for example, wages were adjusted upward some 50 percent, causing a temporary rise in the average consumer's purchasing power by roughly 25 percent. By November, however, prices soared in response to the increased demand, while real wage levels reverted to their September levels. This pattern of a downward slide in real wages, accompanied by occasional upward adjustments, left wage earners at the mercy of external forces. Unregulated industries and the government-raised prices of both freed and controlled goods and services inflicted extensive losses on Ukraine's people. It was only when an unscheduled wage indexation of unplanned magnitude was effectuated that real wages temporarily recovered some of the lost ground. Stability thus became a relic of the past. In summary, Ukraine's hasty approach to price liberalization deprived Ukrainian wage earners and consumers of their only remaining shields against economic depravity.

Real Incomes

The third detrimental effect the hastily implemented price liberalization program had on wage earners, savers, and persons on fixed incomes was the drastic losses in real incomes. The evidence presented under the CPI columns in Table 5.2 leads to two ready conclusions.

First, despite compensatory indexation for savings, the loss to which savers have been subjected is extreme. If a rational and appropriate price liberalization program had been carefully articulated and implemented, the accumulated financial resources of the population could have played a vital role in Ukraine's economic restructuring. Lifelong savings, and thus purchasing power, for tens of millions of people, were dissipated, effectuating an unhealthy redistribution of wealth not conducive to economic recovery.

Second, those who depended exclusively on their monthly income for subsistence witnessed a steady decline in their purchasing power, even for bare essentials. As noted earlier, the government took ineffectual steps in compensating wage earners for their loss in real wages, particularly in 1991. Despite soaring budget deficits and phenomenal increases in government expenditures between 1992 and 1995, the less frequent and less substantive nominal wage increases in 1993 and 1994 reflected the government's rapidly declining ability to budget for wage compensation. Even with government intervention via wage indexation, the average worker lost more than two-thirds of his/her real wages within a twenty-four month period between December 1992 and November 1994 (Table 5.2, column 6). From December 1991 to November 1994, real purchasing power declined by 74 percent. A recent study released by the United Nations reports that "since 1991, living standards have fallen by 80 percent" (*Ukrainian Weekly*, March 19, 1995, No. 12: 1).

[There has been] a drop in the standard of living that has no peace-time precedent. In fact, the middle class which forms the basis of any modern society has been completely destroyed in Ukraine. Already by October 1993 the minimal consumer budget [needs] exceeded the average salary in the state sector of the economy by 38%, and the minimum salary by a factor of 17. The purchasing power of a fixed income in relation to a range of basic necessities dropped 15-25 times compared to March 1991. There is absolutely no motivation to work. (National Institute for Strategic Studies, 1994: 22)

Ukraine's ill-prepared approach to price liberalization caused people incomprehensible hardships which could have been mitigated. Before evaluating the rationale of Ukraine's price liberalization policy, the following section first presents the government's stabilization policy, illustrating the Ukrainian government's lack of preparedness in effectuating a systemic transformation of its economy.

PRICE STABILIZATION POLICY

As discussed in the section above on prices, wages, and incomes, the primary force behind Ukraine's open inflation in recent years has been the rapid increases in prices of goods and services that have remained under state control, and price increases over the majority of commodities no longer regulated by the state have not contributed as significantly to the escalating consumer price indices. Hyperinflation in Ukraine has been caused primarily by government-sanctioned price increases of items still under its control. More specifically, state-authorized price increases in food, energy, housing, and basic services have contributed most to the soaring consumer price indices. As previously noted, by 1991, nearly two-thirds of an average consumer's disposable monthly income was expended on food and other essentials and demand for nonessentials was weak. When the price liberalization program began, in January 1992, consumers expended nearly all of their disposable income on food and other basic essentials. Weak demand, or the absence of effective demand, for industrial products or semifinished products not intended for retail-level consumption prevented producers from raising prices. Price increases from these industries did not contribute to hyperinflation. Price stabilization policy, therefore, should be first and foremost directed at government actions having a bearing on the price of consumer goods items.

The Ukrainian decision makers have debated, deliberating over the need for an urgent price stabilization policy. They have continuously issued vague, noncommittal statements regarding the urgency of stabilization, yet have offered no specific, coherent proposals for a stabilization policy. Occasional impromptu decrees over recentralization of price controls and temporary price freezes have been short-lived. Below is a composite picture of the different governments' formal statements on price stabilization policy, with their actions regarding the restoration and maintenance of stable prices.

In *The Programme of Economic Reforms and Policy in Ukraine,* approved by Ukraine's council of ministers in early 1992, the price stabilization policy is stated as follows: "To avoid uncontrollable price increases, their control by the state will be realized mainly through the economic levers, through implementation of tax, fiscal, credit, monetary and customs policy, as well as through the instrument of fixing prices for the output of enterprises-monopolists" (Cabinet of Ministers, 1992b: 6). The primary instruments for price stabilization, therefore, were price control and profit ceilings for monopolistic producers, a progressive tax structure, fiscal discipline, tight monetary and credit policies, and customs controls over flows of traded goods. The main themes of the above policy statement were echoed in reform programs of other administrations.

Prime Minister Vitold Fokin's *Plan for Urgent Economic Reforms* of February 1992, then–Prime Minister Leonid Kuchma's *Plan of Action* of July 1993, followed by President Kuchma's *Along the Road of Radical Economic Reform* of October 1994 dedicated more space to generalities about antimonopoly policies, wage/pension indexation, and assessing blame for poor antitrust and wage-indexation programs to previous administrations than workable solutions. Since the price liberalization program began in January 1992 and continuing through late 1995, Ukrainians have heard rhetoric without experiencing substantive action that would stabilize runaway price increases.

The initial round of price deregulation beginning in January 1992 covered items affecting two-thirds of the consumers' expenditures; prices of select consumer goods increased between 500 and 1,000 percent in a matter of days. "Under pressure from the parliament, the government reasserted control over prices of additional goods, including dairy products and sausages. Food prices were nevertheless further decontrolled during the summer of 1992" (Frydman, 1993: 88–89).

When Kuchma assumed the office of Prime Minister in 1992, one of his administration's primary objectives was price stabilization. His November 18, 1992 speech to the Supreme Rada described the economic situation in Ukraine as critical. Kuchma attributed Ukraine's current crisis to his predecessor Vitold Fokin's poor administration. Kuchma declared his own objective of reducing inflation to an annual rate of between 6 and 10 percent by the end of 1993 (Ministry of Economy, 1993b: 4). Instead of the economy being stabilized by the end of 1993, price increases in Ukraine reached the hyperinflation threshold. Though Kuchma's administration received rule-by-decree authority from the Supreme Rada for six months, the Kuchma administration failed. When Kuchma resigned from the office of prime minister in September 1993, Ukraine's economy had descended to far deeper levels of chaos than when he first assumed office in October 1992. Because Kuchma's extraordinary power could not stabilize prices effectively, uncertainty grew, and with the administration's inaction came further instability. Every administration since independence has contributed significantly to the price instability in Ukraine, some through their inaction in the face of crisis situations, others through acting on ill-advised decisions. For instance, "on 6 December (1993), the Cabinet liberalized prices on a variety of goods, including meat and dairy products, and raised prices on goods whose prices remain administered by the state, including utilities. The result was an average of 300% inflation for all goods in one day" (Brzezinski and Zienchuk 1993: 2). The successive administrations' lack of experience and common sense, coupled with imprudent fiscal, monetary, and credit policies, fanned the already rampant inflationary flames.

Though inflation in the post-Soviet era was expected as a consequence of decades of sectoral imbalances, inefficient subsidies, and twisted priorities, government policies during the last four years have also contributed to inflation. In short, there has been no coherent or consistent price stabilization program in Ukraine, only disjointed and ineffectual government actions. Meanwhile, the deleterious effects of inflation ravage the Ukrainian economy, creating further distortions, depleting savings, and weakening the nascent national currency and financial institutions. With no short-term solutions in sight, consumers must wait until the cumulative effects of inflation finally subside before any semblance of rationality can return.

The following section examines the basic principles of inflation and price stability. This discussion will indicate the faults inherent in the policies attempted by Ukrainian officials thus far.

EQUILIBRIUM AND STABILITY

Inflation in Ukraine was precipitated by the sudden release of price distortions repressed during the Soviet decades. Successive administrations' failures in formulating a coherent, workable reform program, combined with their unsound fiscal and monetary practices, have exacerbated the problem. Even now that this inflationary pressure has been nearly vented, new pressures will mount owing to inherited structural imbalances. The already battered Ukrainian economy may, therefore, expect persistent price instability for several more years. The following section examines in greater detail the immediate causes of, and long-term remedies for, inflation in Ukraine.

The single factor most responsible for the buildup of inflationary pressure during past decades was the Soviet's centralized command system. Central planning led to structural rigidities, sectoral imbalances, and institutionalized price distortions. Deregulating state controlled prices without due preparation initiated the inflationary sprial; supply inelasticities, monopolies, budget deficits, uncontrolled money supplies, irrational credit policies, factor immobility, low savings rates, and the lack of market-oriented managerial talents all contributed to the inflationary spiral.

Ukrainian inflation has been a cost-push, as opposed to a demand-pull, strain. One example of supply-side adversity demonstrates this.

In 1991, agricultural input prices increased twice. In conjunction with input cost increases were the prices for agricultural products. In 1992, a series of uncontrolled price increases began. From December 1991 to [December] 1992, the prices for agricultural inputs increased more than 100 times. In 1993, prices for agricultural inputs increased a further 60 times. The state was trying to compensate [farmers for] the uncontrolled rise in input prices by repeated increases in [product] purchasing prices. The state is the main purchaser of agricultural products. This was the state's way of maintaining price parity [between farm and nonfarm products] and control. (Paskhaver interview, 1994)

The initial round of rapid price increases in the farm sector originated from soaring energy costs and from monopolistic suppliers of essential factors. In meeting rising costs of imported oil from Russia, the state promptly began withdrawing subsidized consumption of energy. Energy costs charged to agricultural producers swiftly mounted, while farm input suppliers, freed from state planning and regulation, simultaneously raised the prices of their products. Prices rose in response to the rising producer costs. The state, meanwhile, raised the consumer prices of farm products, recouping a portion of the higher purchasing prices paid to the farmers and withdrawing part of the perennial subsidies budgeted for food consumption.

In the process, all major players in the cycle of economic activities became victims of rampant inflation. Farm producers lost because the prices the government offered for farm products were not increased as much or as often as the prices the government offered for nonagricultural products. Consumers lost because price increases outpaced by far their infrequent and modest wage and pension increases. Industrial users of farm-supplied inputs lost because inflation severely curtailed consumers' effective demand for their products while factor costs rapidly mounted. Even suppliers of farm inputs did not gain significantly in the process because of progressive taxation, eroded real value of earnings owing to hyperinflation, rapidly mounting costs of inputs employed in their own production processes, upward wage adjustments, and world-market prices for capital replacements. Finally, the state lost as well. Though nominal revenues rose, the real value of revenue kept falling due to inflation. Rapid losses in industrial production and GNP resulted in drastic decreases in taxable revenue. Widespread tax evasion and growth in barter and shadow-economy transactions contributed to the persistent revenue shortfalls. The state was at times collecting only approximately 50 percent of projected revenue, while demands on the budget continued to rise. The budget deficit grew. The state borrowed from the state bank as a means of maintaining social calm. Depressed sectors of the economy demanded easier credit and tax relief from the state. Economic instability deepened; the government struggled against insolvency in the face of growing demands for a share of the state budget pie. Once inflation started, the mere expectation of inflation kept pushing prices and wages upward.

Inflation rates will subside either when demand weakens or when supply expands. In the former case, consumers' demand even for household necessities will become elastic and thus artificially stable; in the latter, supply elasticities increase as the economy shakes off its short-run inability and expands its aggregate supply.

Though the second scenario is certainly the more attractive of the two, the first scenario may soon materialize. The overwhelming majority of wage earners, savers, and consumers are already expending almost all of their purchasing power on essentials. Demand for nonessentials has become so weak that producers are discouraged from raising prices, especially as the state continues withdrawal of consumption subsidies. The need for such goods has already been reduced to the nearly perfectly inelastic level.[2] The effective demand for them, however, depends on whether the essentials are food, energy, or other basic items.

Since most Ukrainians have access to small plots of farm land, they can resort to small agricultural production, circumventing the state-controlled price structure. They can also reduce their consumption of meat and other "luxury items," maintaining only the most basic level of consumption of essential food products. If they do so, price elasticity of demand on temporarily dispensable items such as meat products will increase, reducing the level of their consumption. A contrived equilibrium situation in those markets will ensue. Demand for income-elastic goods will increase only when gains in real wages are made, or when supply inelasticities vanish.

The consumption of nonfood essentials, on the other hand, depends on government policy. True "shock therapy" requires the state to prevent consumers from receiving goods without paying for them; if the government does not actively prevent "freeloading," the quantity demanded will exceed the market-dictated quantity to be supplied. This is true, for instance, of energy goods. If Ukraine takes the path selected by the Lithuanians, a contrived equilibrium will ensue, however the equilibrium position will indicate a significantly lowered standard of living until conditions improve. If Ukraine chooses the Polish/Hungarian option, and does not deny the continued supply of nonfood essentials to consumers, their real incomes will still fall owing to sustained inflation in non–government supplied essentials. Even then, this still implies a nonequilibrium position, because consumption levels would exceed the levels of real value productivity. It should be stressed that if the true measure of standard of living is value product, then the Ukrainians cannot improve their overall economic welfare through such a policy.

The second scenario, that in which supply elasticities will increase in response to healthy market development, will arise only sometime after Ukraine's economy has reached its trough. During the Soviet decades, both the supply and demand functions may be described as having been nearly perfectly inelastic owing to rigid production and consumption planning. That is, both supply and demand functions were nearly perpendicular to the base axis, with demand exceeding supply by varying quantities for diverse commodities. Perennial shortages of consumer goods became the norm; subsidies to producers and to consumers kept both the costs of production and product prices artificially low, yielding an artificial appearance of price stability without a genuine equilibrium.

In post-Soviet Ukraine, the supply curve remains inelastic, and demand for essentials has been very inelastic. The combination of inelastic supply and inelastic demand creates a scenario in which small changes in output yield very large changes in price levels; prices are thus highly unstable. Stable and competitive prices will come about only when supply elasticities increase.

Creating a more elastic supply function requires an increase in investment activity. The state is trapped: leaders could impose a policy for stimulating investment through such measures as tax credits and easy monetary policy. However, there is precious little room in the budget for such expenditure. If such a policy is not implemented, economic growth and, as a consequence, government revenue will not expand. The government cannot easily afford to implement such a policy, yet neither can it afford not to implement it. Ukraine's fledgling entrepreneurial class might willingly finance investment. However, it is not likely that such individuals will invest in consumer goods industries since speculative and commercial investment offer much higher rates of return. Though some domestic financial resources in the private sector are available, contributions will be insignificant to either price stability or economic recovery.

In the short run, therefore, price stability will materialize mainly because of slackened demand. In the near future, when repressed inflation from the past has exhausted its steam, slow recovery may be expected. Once a stable position has been reached, however impoverished it leaves the nation, a process of slow economic growth can begin, with aggregate supply gradually shifting downward and to the right. Only then will supply elasticities meaningfully increase, bringing stability for factor costs and product prices.

The primary concerns for Ukraine's economy now are containing the adverse effects of hyperinflation and preventing the development of new inflationary forces. The nation needs a sound, well-articulated reform agenda; policies must attempt to maximize the efficacy of a host of constructive programs. Only in this manner can Ukraine's economy stabilize and recover, its people rebuild, and a stable market scenario emerge. Ukraine's reform is not nearly this structurally sound; the final section of this chapter briefly identifies errors in and lessons to be learned from Ukraine's price liberalization program.

ERRORS AND LESSONS

The first fundamental flaw in Ukraine's price liberalization program began with one basic erroneous assumption: that practices and policies used in developed market economies could be transplanted into a radically different setting and still yield the desired effects without undue dislocations. Equilibrium prices in developed economies are arrived at upon the interactions of competitive market forces. Behind such forces are a network of legal, organizational, financial, technical, managerial, and marketing institutions that continuously coordinate and fortify each other's roles in a functional market. All essential ingredients in the proper functioning of a system are present in a developed economy's market setting.

These elements were entirely absent from Ukraine's infrastructure; there were neither market institutions nor market forces that could facilitate the abruptly deregulated prices for methodical realization of envisioned results without incurring uncontrollable dislocations. The advice given to, and the pressures placed upon,

Ukrainian decision makers contributed to the unfavorable developments that have swept Ukraine's economy into chaos. Policymakers must now minimize any further damage brought on by unsound price liberalization policy.

A second error associated with the premature implementation of the price liberalization program in Ukraine was its timing. That Ukraine had regained political independence did not mean that Ukraine was economically independent from the rest of the FSU. Ukraine continued using the Russian ruble as its exclusive legal tender until November 1992. The spillover effects of inflation from Russia on Ukraine's economy are well documented. Yet, Ukraine had initiated price liberalization some eleven months earlier. Between January and November 1992, Ukraine possessed no effective means of containing the adverse effects of galloping inflation in Russia. Ukraine should have tended to the introduction of its independent currency before deregulating prices.

The third mistake lay in Ukrainian decision makers' ineffective examination of the reform results in Poland. Economic "shock therapy" not only created undue dislocations, it also rekindled socialist and Communist sympathies, as capitalism was presented as a brutal and counterproductive system. An orderly systemic transformation would have been a wiser choice. Ukraine's decision makers should also have recognized that its economy depended heavily on markets in the republics of the FSU and in former COMECON nations. Since the rapid disintegration and collapse of many of these markets was inevitable, Ukraine's reform architects should have expected extensive disturbances in the external sector. The decision makers could have placed earlier emphasis on devising a stabilization policy rather than adding destabilization forces via a flawed price liberalization program.

Fourth, applying radical resolutions to deep-seated problems requires the inclusion of workable control mechanisms that would effectively halt or decelerate the process when and if needed. The following statement, published in the United Nations *Economic Survey of Europe*, requires little elaboration:

Most stabilization programmes applied in eastern Europe were based on the conviction that rapid price liberalization was a pre-condition for further reform steps. It was assumed that the size of the initial adjustment was not a major concern in the light of the urgency of restoring equilibrium on product markets. The experience gained so far, however, may necessitate a correction of this view: the release of pent-up pressures resulted in much higher-than-planned increases in prices, and this generated difficulties not only for the population but also for the orderly continuation of the entire transformation process. (Secretariat of the Economic Commission for Europe, Geneva, 1992: 95)

This conclusion was no mystery to economists, who had long understood the dangers of a hastily implemented price liberalization policy. A price stabilization program, therefore, could have been established before a price liberalization program was set in motion. Obviously, Ukraine had no such program. Price increases have been "much higher-than-planned." They have far exceeded the decision makers' worst fears. There has been no "orderly continuation of the entire transformation process."

The fifth error is that, after seven decades of rigid controls, the instant and near total abrogation of the state's role in economic coordination and management was likely to produce impulsive rather than responsible decisions by the average enterprise management. Unbridled price increases, selling of state-owned enterprise assets, and debt accumulation are only a few of the opportunistic decisions that have taken place on the enterprise level. Erosion of the economy's vitality has resulted, rendering the reform process even more trying. One research finding validates the assertion that in an economy newly liberalized from decades of rigid controls, the state should not arbitrarily relinquish its role in the name of reform:

The government must develop a strict program for state control of the economy, first and foremost in the state sector because for a time the state, which is the ultimate owner, practically removed itself from the administration of its property. Nowhere in the world, for example, do state industrial managers set their own and their workers' salaries and decide what proportion of income should be accounted for by capital depreciation or consumed. Salaries—in other words expenditure—and not profits became the main incentive for business. (National Institute for Strategic Studies, 1994: 24)

The role of the government in coordinating economic activities should indeed decrease over time. However, for government to abruptly vacate its traditional function when enterprise management still lacks experience in rational product pricing is socially irresponsible and economically unsound. Industrial economies, with the world's highest standards of living, all have government agencies that actively regulate, legislate, and even control the production of select goods and services.

Sixth, Ukraine has not yet created an effective antitrust legislation and administration. Administrative bureaucrats can have as much bearing on the outcome of a policy initiative as the three traditional branches of government can have. Though the Supreme Rada has passed comprehensive antitrust reform measures, the nation does not possess an agency equipped with trained personnel and adequate resources for policing monopolistic practices. Though state determination of prices is inefficient, widespread monopolistic pricing by plan-created monopolies causes even greater economic and social harm. Hasty price deregulation without effective antimonopoly measures, therefore, adds another dimension to the adverse consequences that could have been mitigated or circumvented.

Seventh, price liberalization after nearly seventy years of strict regulation must be accompanied by well-designed macro policies for stabilization purposes. More specifically, a tight yet socially responsible budgetary policy must be closely coordinated with a prudent course of monetary action. The Ukrainian parliament and governments pursued monetary and fiscal policies that were not conducive to stabilization. Instead, the decision makers repeatedly violated the most basic of economic principles by resorting to irresponsible monetary and credit policies and by accumulating phenomenal budget deficits. The lack of a comprehensive and internally consistent set of reform programs further compounded the already unmanageable consequences of a poorly conceived price liberalization program, plunging Ukraine's economy into undue chaos and disorder.

Ukraine must learn from these seven errors. Four lessons it can learn from them are described below.

First, there is much danger in implementing radical reform policies, particularly those whose effects cannot be reversed, under unstable political conditions. Ukraine's Supreme Rada declared independence from the FSU in August 1991; the Supreme Rada had for years been dominated by deputies of the former Communist party. The declaration of independence was motivated more by political expediency than by a burning desire for independence. The deputies representing different ideologies within the Supreme Rada did not articulate a clear political consensus. The successive governments also lacked continuity in policy approaches and consistency in their implementation. Moreover, there was more acrimony and disagreement between the legislative and executive branches of government than a meeting of minds and will. Although antagonistic, neither branch had the political strength or force to alter the reform approaches favored by the other. Under such conditions, the arbitrary or hasty introduction of radical reform measures should be avoided, especially where safeguards are lacking. Adverse consequences from such policies can cause even greater dissention among decision makers, further delaying an orderly process of systemic transformation.

Second, in marketizing economic activities in the newly liberalized economies, especially in rapidly deregulating price, it is imperative that the new institutions be viable before the previous ones are replaced or dismantled. This minimizes avoidable macro dislocations, reduces social tension, and moderates long-term economic costs. Before liberalizing prices that had long been under state regulation, decision makers must first decide that industries will be viable and competitive under the new economic order. Subsidies from such industries should gradually be withdrawn, and investment encouraged. For those industries that hold no promise in the long run, a well-designed social safety net needs to be promptly put into place. In Ukraine, both decision makers and the population at large consider unemployment a greater social ill than sustaining nonviable productive efforts. The absence of an adequate social safety net delays the inevitable cessation of productive activities in these establishments, draining society's already meager financial resources. The social safety net must, therefore, include effective job retraining and placement programs, as well as temporary income subsidies for those whose jobs will be eliminated by the emerging market forces. This type of policy helps preserve social calm, minimizes opportunity costs, and reduces the long-term loss of potential productivity.

Third, before executing a fast-paced price liberalization program, the government must establish a responsible and rational fiscal and monetary strategy. That is, a well-designed reform agenda would not permit surreptitious, extemporaneous decisions in the fiscal and monetary domains that would strengthen inflationary forces.

Finally, experiences in developed market economies have long established that the consequences of galloping inflation or hyperinflation are more destructive and containment more difficult than other economic afflictions. Therefore, the relative merits and demerits of a rapid price liberalization policy should be carefully weighed when necessary stabilization and controlling mechanisms are absent. Economic advisors should avoid recommending and decision makers should avoid forcing square pegs into round holes.

NOTES

1. During an interview in Kiev in August 1994, academician Ivan Loukinov, Director of the Institute of Economics at Ukraine's National Academy of Sciences, told the author that there were three governments and eight reform programs in Ukraine between August 1991 and August 1994. In contrast, Boris Parakhousky, Director of the Department of Welfare Studies at Ukraine's National Institute for Strategic Studies, told the author there were five governments and from five to eight reform programs during the same time period.

2. According to a 1995 United Nations report on social development, "the average daily calorie intake (in Ukraine) has declined from 3,517 cal per capita in 1989 to 3,151 in 1992 and 2,860 in 1993, a fall of 23 percent" (*Ukrainian Weekly*, March 18, 1995, No. 12: 1). And as the data in Table 5.2 indicated, the consumer's real wages/ income kept falling after 1993. That is, the average consumer's caloric intake in 1994 and 1995 represented a steady decline from the 1993 level, resulting in close to zero price elasticity of demand for consumer essentials.

6

Enterprise Reorganization:
Legal Foundation

Eighteenth-century champions of western liberalism favored government institutions whose design expedited the capitalist system and that provided for basic human freedoms, ownership rights, and property protection, as well as market prices determined by competitive forces. These institutions and corresponding government policies were not sought merely for their intrinsic ideological worth; the economic rationale behind capitalism promises allocative and productive efficiency and the maximization of benefits to society. Now that Ukraine has stepped toward a market economy, its legal institutions must be developed.

A legal foundation was never present in the USSR. The Soviet government discouraged individual initiative by nationalizing all means of production, compromised allocative efficiency by determining all levels and prices of output by decree, and discouraged incentives for the introduction of new technologies, new management techniques, and new entrepreneurs by disallowing many personal freedoms. The consequent costs were massive.

That ideological policies carry so much significance cannot be overlooked. Western traditions are somewhat alien to Eastern Europe. The spirit of Western "classical" liberalism took root in Britain and France and spread to America; however, it did not affect the largely hierarchical, feudal Russian and Slavic worlds of the eighteenth and nineteenth centuries. The earliest proponents of legally-sanctioned freedoms, except for Adam Smith, did not have economic gains in mind; rather, they had tired of feudalism, monarchy, and class-based hierarchy. The proposition that all men are created equal caught on much more readily in the postfeudal West than in the largely hierarchical East. In Ukraine, as in much of the FSU and former second world countries, reforms such as property ownership, price liberalization, and human freedom are seen as mere means to economic ends, while Westerners view these as ends in themselves.

This chapter discusses the current slate of problems and legal reforms with regard to ownership rights, economic restructuring, and antitrust, and recommends a framework for economic restructuring.

STATE ENTERPRISE

Under the Soviet system, all means of production belonged to the state. The state owned, managed, used, and disposed of centralized properties in accordance with planned dictates. Ukraine was controlled by Moscow bureaucrats. Their insistence on industrial and military growth filled Ukraine with giant industrial complexes and transport systems. As a result of Ukraine's strategic importance, most of these enterprises fell under the direct jurisdiction and budget of Moscow's national ministries, and reported directly to these ministries. By the end of the Soviet era, more than 90 percent of the industry of Ukraine fell entirely outside the jurisdiction of Ukrainian ministries.

Upon independence, however, the control over these industries quickly changed hands. Ukraine gained ownership and administrative control of its enterprises; the nation, in accordance with its decentralization policy, then distributed control of the enterprises to its newly appropriated state ministries. Though these ministries still nominally control the bulk of the enterprises, they lack the administrative skill, technical knowledge, financial wherewithal, and manpower for successful administration of industry. In line with the policy of liberalizing the economy, the ministries have granted the enterprise managers control over day-to-day operations.

Managers, however, are largely unaccustomed to such unfettered autonomy. They must now learn for themselves the procedures for securing inputs, pricing, and marketing. More importantly, managers must learn to cope with a reality despised by the Soviet bureaucracy: risk. Risk is a phenomenon of nature; man cannot avoid it entirely without forgoing economic growth. The Soviets, however, squashed uncertainty whenever possible, whether in politics or in economics, with grave economic consequences. Six entirely new or newly aggravated sources of risk bear further mention.

First, financial claims must be managed responsibly, a difficult task even in an economy with stable prices. In the USSR, debt was haphazardly shifted from enterprises to the central budget. Incorrect and irresponsible management of debt now could result in insolvency and bankruptcy. Financial intermediaries perform a role similar to that of security officers: they take on risks so that society does not have to. Ukraine, however, does not have the firmly rooted financial system that developed industrial nations do. Risk is thus not easily diversified and dispersed.

Second, the withdrawal of state subsidies makes any operation less secure. Westerners have for years recognized what economists call the Averch-Johnson effect: the tendency of state-regulated firms to overcapitalize and become less than fully active. Sudden exposure to all the pressure of competition creates much distress among management.

Third, the interdependence of the Soivet capital structure creates supply-side uncertainty. Very little production in Ukraine went directly to finished products during the Soviet era. If any intermediate production step fails, the next enterprise in the chain of production is likely to fail because the latter's supply of inputs depended upon the former's output.

Fourth, demand-side uncertainty is aggravated by the unstable economies in most of the nations that purchase Ukrainian products. Nearly three-quarters of Ukraine's exports are destined for other FSU nations, but demand for these exports can decline rapidly.

Fifth, the "interim" status most enterprises currently find themselves in leads to more questions than answers. No one knows when or if they will be sold, to whom they will be sold, and so forth.

Finally, control over hiring and firing leads to labor unrest and to questions about what the optimal level of labor employment is. Attempts to reorganize an enterprise by using a rational, scientific approach cannot succeed in the face of labor disputes. Labor begins to doubt management's motives and management questions labor's preparedness for real reform.

The consequences of these risks are also important. If management expends energy on damage control and survival, it has less energy to expend on comprehensive restructuring of the enterprise. In an effort to remain solvent, enterprises often sell state-owned property. As decapitalization for survival becomes more widespread, the productive capactiy of the nation is compromised.

Since management does not own the property it administers, its approach to decision making is likely to differ from the approach it might take if it owned the factors it employed. Merely leasing out state-owned capital, a common strategy for Ukraine's privatization authority, is thus not as effective as true privatization. Privatization is essential in eliciting supply responsiveness from producers, in stabilizing product prices, and in promoting industry competitiveness. Ownership transformation is crucial to administrative responsibility and efficiency concerns.

A BRIEF HISTORY OF OWNERSHIP AND ENTERPRISE REFORMS

The USSR, in its constitution, disallowed private-sector ownership the means of production. Enterprise directors exercised management rights, but did not own any of the properties they managed.   Not until 1989 and 1990, when fundamental changes were introduced, were various forms of property ownership permitted. Legislation passed between 1987 and 1990 paved the way for private ownership and private control of what had been the exclusive domain of the public sector.

ON JOINT VENTURES

The Foreign Investment Law of 1987 was the first law to permit ownership of any kind of productive resource by an entity other than the state. The law lacked clarity and coherence, was marked by ambiguity, and was finalized more through trial and error than through coherent reasoning (Iachini, 1991: 112).

This new law rendered joint ventures exempt from the state's central planning and left them responsible for procuring their own factor supplies and marketing their own products. Foreign investors were permitted to own up to half of an enterprise. These ventures had to export a major portion of their product since factors of production were readily available only in exchange for hard currency. As a result, the law did little to affect foreign capital inflow between 1987 and 1990. The law, however, paved the way for expanded ownership rights.

ON LEASING

The Law on Leasing, passed in November of 1989, permitted the formation of worker-collective leasing organizations, provided that two-thirds of the workers give consent. Unless an enterprise may not be leased to a workers' collective for national interest or for security reasons, the worker organization was permitted to enter into an agreement with the appropriate authority for leasing arrangements. Either a department of the enterprise or the entire enterprise could be leased. The law allowed the enterprise management to exercise control over assets of and incomes from the leased property. Workers were permitted to invest in and receive dividends from the enterprise's operations. Most significantly, the lessee was also permitted to purchase and be the legal owner of the leased property (Raikhmilovic, 1991: 105). For the first time, fully private ownership of the factors of production was possible.

ON LAND

The Law on Land of February 28, 1990 granted republics and autonomous regions the authority to enact land-leasing legislation appropriate to local conditions. Legislative bodies could lease land to Soviet citizens, cooperative farms, domestic or joint ventures, institutions, and organizations (Amodio, 1991a: 118). The February 28, 1990 Law on Land was primarily intended as a prelude to agricultural reform and to the promulgation of private enterprises.

ON PROPERTY OWNERSHIP

The revised 1977 constitution gave citizens the right to own freely distributed housing units. Very few citizens, however, could secure these units; the average waiting period was fifteen years for five square meters (about fifty square feet) per occupant. Only through inside contacts could a citizen more readily secure a housing unit in this fashion. The property law of March 1990 granted citizens the right to buy, sell, or lease housing units without administrative interference. This new law explicitly granted property ownership rights to diverse juridical entities within USSR. Properties the Soviet Union once self-righteously described as belonging to "all the people," but that were, in fact, controlled entirely by the state, came under the direct jurisdiction and ownership of republics, autonomous regions, or municipalities. As a result, enterprise managers received more control over properties they administered. Ownership rights under this new law extended to state, collective, and foreign legal entities. The law allowed autonomous regions and collectives to own land. Foreign ownership was permitted in accordance with the Foreign Investment Law of 1987. Collective ownership was permitted in the form of "leased enterprises, collective enterprises, co-operatives, joint-stock companies, firms and partnerships, business associations, social organizations, and legal entities" (Amodio, 1991b: 115). For the first time, Soviet citizens and institutions had the right to incorporate themselves into legal entities and exercise ownership rights over state or privately accumulated properties. Under the provisions of this new law, enterprises were permitted to possess, use, and dispose of their property in accordance with the provisions of the law, including after-tax profits (Skredov, 1991: 95–96). The law granted operational autonomy to enterprise management. It was thus a gesture of decentralization, consigning decision-making authority over the use of properties and products to management. For prospective foreign investors, this new law reaffirmed the legal ownership rights of foreign interests, including buildings and other structures constructed for an enterprise's operation.

ON ECONOMIC RELATIONS BETWEEN THE USSR AND THE FEDERAL AND AUTONOMOUS REPUBLICS

The ownership rights of republics and autonomous regions delineated in the property law of March 1990 were strengthened by the April 1990 law on economic relationships between Moscow and the republics or autonomous regions. The new law reaffirmed the ownership rights of the republics and autonomous regions over the land and natural resources within their respective territories by permitting lower levels of government to draft their own legislation concerning the land they controlled. The law also transferred significant decision-making authority to lower-level governments, including authority over local and foreign investment, construction, currency reserves, and even the establishment of independent foreign economic relations policies.

ON ENTERPRISES

The June 4, 1990 Law on Enterprises is an extension the of 1987 Law on State Enterprises and the June 4, 1990 Law on Property Ownership. The law permitted enterprises to issue shares and to trade those shares on stock markets, authorized the establishment of diverse forms of businesses, including family and individual ventures, and allowed enterprises to form into associations. Although the provisions of the law most directly affected technical aspects of enterprise organization, they extended the confines of permissible economic activity by guaranteeing all economic entities the right to use and dispose of their properties.

DECREE ON FOREIGN INVESTMENT

Legislative action was not the only means through which reform was enacted. Decrees by the president or by the council of ministers carried the force of law under the Soviet system. The October 26, 1990 presidential decree on foreign investment granted foreign investors the possibility of being sole owners of business enterprises within the USSR. Foreign investors could hold majority or even complete ownership of business enterprises. Foreign interests enjoyed the same privileges and were held to the same obligations as domestic enterprises, and enjoyed the right of profit repatriation. Except for land, which could be leased but not owned, foreign investors exercised full jurisdiction over their share of the management, use, and disposal of their property.

The above laws and the decree on property ownership, business enterprises, and land leasing came into effect shortly before Ukraine declared its independence in August 1991. The single legislative act which carried the greatest significance for Ukraine was the April 9, 1990 law governing economic relationships between the USSR and the respective republics and autonomous regions. This vital law enabled Ukraine to reorganize economic relationships within its own territories.

UKRAINE'S ENTERPRISE REFORM

By the time Ukraine regained its independence in August 1991, property rights for the previously USSR-owned enterprises and institutions in Ukraine were appropriated by the Ukrainian state. A series of legislative reforms passed in 1991 and 1992 dramatically affected the decision-making climate in Ukraine. The centralized command system that had been institutionalized by Stalin was finally dismantled, and authority and ownership rights were dispersed.

Ukrainian laws displaced and replaced Soviet laws in regulating enterprise structure, operation, and conduct. Ukraine's Law on Business Enterprise and its Law on Enterprises in the Ukrainian SSR, both passed in 1991, during the waning moments of the Socviet Union, are still the basic laws governing private and state enterprises within Ukraine. These two laws, together with four other crucial reform laws of 1991–1992 are summarized and briefly analyzed in this section.

Law on Business Enterprise

The Law on Business Enterprise guarantees the freedom of private business enterprises and entrepreneurial activities in any organizational form chosen by entrepreneurs and under any form of ownership as delineated by Ukraine's Law on Property (Law on Business Enterprise, 1991: sect. 1, arts. 2, 6). The principle applies to foreign investments legally registered in Ukraine as well. The law does forbid individuals in military service, the courts, the state security service, and the internal affairs department, among others, from engaging in entrepreneurial activities. Entrepreneurs are free to determine the type of economic activity to engage in, to recruit labor and procure needed factors, and to dispose of profits, including shares of foreign exchange proceeds (ibid: sect. 1, art. 5). Mmanagement's obligation to hired workers is determined by a contract detailing working conditions, social and medical benefits, and wage and social security payments (ibid: sect. 2, art. 9). The state guarantees private businesses property rights and equal rights, irrespective of organizational forms.

In an effort to create favorable conditions for the development of a business environment, the state may, under given conditions, transfer state properties to entrepreneurs, provide technical and material supplies, and even grant subsidies, tax privileges, or easier access to credit (ibid: sect. 3, arts. 12, 14). Foreign entrepreneurs enjoy the same rights and privileges and are bound to the same restrictions and obligations as the managers of domestic enterprises.

Although the law came into force while Ukraine was still a republic of the USSR, it was liberal in tone and progressive in perspective. Ukraine's Law on Business Enterprise laid the legal foundation for the development of private entrepreneurship.

Law on Enterprises

The Law on Enterprises, introduced two weeks after the Law on Business Enterprise, provides a general framework for the creation, operation, and liquidation of business enterprises. The law defines types and organizational forms of business establishments, and delineates businesses' rights and obligations in conducting business activities. The enterprise is defined as an economic statutory subject, having the rights of a legal person in pursuit of profit. Enterprises can exist as individual endeavors in which the individual engages his/her own resources and labor, as family enterprises, with or without hired labor, or as collectives or joint ventures, with or without foreign capital participation. Except for business enterprises that are initiated and/or operated by private citizens, publicly owned enterprises fall under the jurisdiction of municipal, district, or state authorities.

The law defines the maximum size of a small business: for industry and construction, a small business can have no more than 200 employees; for scientific endeavors, the number is 100; for other productive industries, it is 50; and for the service sector, it is 25. Associations and conglomerations are permitted, provided such activities do not counter the spirit of safeguarding market competitiveness (Law on Enterprise in the Ukrainian SSR, 1991: sect. 1, art. 3).

Some of the most liberal provisions of the law deal with enterprise properties. While private entrepreneurs possess full rights over the use and disposal of their properties, the law grants state enterprises nearly the same discretionary latitude in property management and control.

State property which is allotted to enterprise of public sector shall belong to it on the basis of complete economical authority.

Enterprises, unless otherwise required by [enterprise] statute, shall be entitled to sell and to transfer to other enterprises, organizations and institutions, to exchange, to lease, to grant in temporary use or on credit buildings, installations, equipment, means of transport stock, raw materials and other material values, and to write them off the balance.

Enterprises shall be entitled, unless otherwise required, to sell, to transfer without paying, to exchange, to lease to private persons capital goods and other material values except those values which can not be their property according to enactments of the Ukrainian SSR. Transfer without paying and granting of material values to private persons shall be carried out with the consent of owner [the state] organ authorized by him [it] except the cases provided by legislation of the Ukrainian SSR. (ibid: sect. 3, arts. 3, 5, 6)

These provisions granted firms unreserved enterprise autonomy, freeing management from state planning mechanisms. The laws effectuated a transitional phase for enterprise management, paving the way for the eventual privatization of state-owned enterprises.

Mindful of the state's traditional interest in labor, the law details labor and management relationships, granting labor the right to be consulted in important matters. In a state enterprise of fifty or more employees, labor leadership must be consulted when enterprise managers are appointed, when changes in enterprise charter are contemplated, and if other notable organizational changes are under discussion (ibid: sect. 4, art. 3). All in all, the Law on Enterprises complements the Law on Business Enterprise, and elaborates on the rights, privileges, and obligations of enterprises. Other than having specific provisions safeguarding workers' positions in the reorganized economic setting, Ukraine's laws on enterprises are consistent with those of developed market economies. In theory, therefore, Ukraine's economic laws mark a clear departure from the past in the areas of enterprise organization and management.

Law on Economic Partnerships

The Law on Economic Partnerships was Ukraine's first major piece of post-independence legislation on enterprises. The law specifies categories of voluntarily-formed economic partnerships in pursuit of profit. They include: "joint stock corporations, limited liability partnerships, partnerships with additional liability, unlimited partnerships, [and] partnerships *in commendam*" (Law on Economic Partnership, 1991: part 1,· art. 1). The law specifies the process for forming partnerships, enumerates the rights and obligations of partners, including liabilities, specifies ownership rights for different types of properties, and outlines auditing and accounting procedures.

A joint stock company "has a charter fund subdivided into a specific number of stocks of equal face value and is liable for obligations only with the property of the partnership" (ibid: part 2, ch. 1, art. 24). The company may be publicly or privately held; a privately held joint stock company has the right to reorganize and become a public joint stock company if the partners so decide. The only instance in which the company is prohibited from issuing stock is if the intent of such stock is for covering economic losses. Under specified conditions, the company may either increase or decrease the charter-sanctioned authorized capital (ibid: part 2, ch. 1, arts. 38, 39). General meetings of stockholders constitute the highest authority of the company; shareholders elect board members and members of the internal audit commission at these meetings.

Partnerships are confronted with one of four types of liability: limited, additional, unlimited, and *in commendam*. Limited liability confines the partners' liability to the amount of their respective investments in the company. Additional liability expands responsibility to part or all of the partners' properties outside of the company. Articles of the company's incorporation must specify the limit of each partner's liability in advance. In unlimited liability partnerships, partners must jointly bear the responsibility of meeting financial obligations to the extent of all their properties (ibid: part 2, ch. 3, art. 50; part 3, art. 65; part 4, art. 66). Finally, partnerships *in commendam* are those in which both limited and unlimited partnerships may be present. In these cases, all partners are jointly liable for the venture's debts; unlimited partners are liable to the extent of their properties both in and outside of the company, while limited partners are liable only to the extent of the investments they have made in the company (ibid: part 5, art. 75).

Built upon the foundation of the Law on Business Enterprise and the Law on Enterprises in the Ukrainian SSR, the Law on Economic Partnerships is another step toward the promotion of growth in the private sector, and toward a reduced role for the public sector in the nation's economic activities. The above three laws, though not excluding state enterprises, concern themselves mostly with the establishment and operation of private businesses. The remainder of this section examines economic laws pertaining exclusively to the reorganization and management of state enterprises and/or properties.

ON LEASING

Leasing of state enterprises and organizations is an important facet of the privatization process, but it is an interim step; the process involves temporarily transferring the state's productive assets from the public to the private sector. The Law on the Leasing of Property of State Enterprises and Organizations defines legal entities that are qualified to lease, establishes the relationship between the lessor and the lessee, outlines the rights and obligations of both parties, specifies objects subject to leasing, and stipulates the conditions for either suspension or termination of a lease. On the basis of this law, the Council of Ministers and the State Property Fund exercise jurisdiction over the leasing process.

The lessee can be an organization formed by workers in an enterprise, a productive unit within an enterprise, a domestic or foreign legal entity, an international organization, or a group of stateless persons residing in Ukraine. All eligible lessees may initiate the leasing arrangement, but leasing organizations formed by workers' collectives have the preemptive right over other prospective lessees with respect to the enterprise or a division thereof (Law of Ukraine on the Leasing of Property of State Enteprises and Organizations, 1992 [referred to as Law on Leasing]: art. 9, para. 6). If the prospective lessee is not the workers' collective within the enterprise and if the workers do not wish to leave administration of the enterprise to outsiders, then the workers' collective must inform the prospective lessee of its intentions no later than three days before filing a formal petition of its own. A lease arrangement can be authorized by a simple majority of the workers within an enterprise or within a division thereof. If the entire enterprise is being leased, the state becomes the lessor; if a division of an enterprise is being leased, then the enterprise is the lessor.

A general meeting of the participants in the leasing arrangement or their representatives elects the management and ratifies the organization's charter. The appointed management drafts a leasing agreement, which must specify the object of leasing, including an inventory and the estimated value of the leased properties, the proposed lease payment, the conditions for the return of the leased properties, and "the procedure for the use of the depreciation monies" (ibid: art. 11). The object for lease is "valued at its reconstruction [replacement] cost, in accordance to the methodology approved by the Cabinet or Ministers of Ukraine and the State Property Fund of Ukraine" (ibid: art. 14). The phrase "depreciation monies" refers to the amount of depreciated capital assets. Though the law itself does not specify this, the provision implies that agreements should contain methods of reinvestment or recapitalization.

The elected management submits the leasing application to the appropriate lessor, which must review and make a determination within a thirty-day period. In case of a refusal or delay by the petitioned party, the prospective lessee has recourse either to the court or to an arbitration agency. An agreement, unless otherwise specified, instantly transfers all the leased properties from the lessor to the lessee. Mutual rights and obligations become binding for the duration of the agreement. The lessee then registers itself as a legal entity with the proper authority, completing the process of the leasing arrangement.

Though widespread leasing does not promote the same kind of efficiency that full private ownership does, it does assist in decentralization, and encourages independent decision-making. Ukraine's leasing laws are therefore an institutional step in the right direction.

CORPORATIZATION

Except for state enterprises already designated for privatization, all firms that are more than 50 percent state owned must reorganize themselves into joint stock companies. According to the Decree of the Cabinet of Ministers on Corporatization of 1992, enterprises that had not been singled out for privatization and whose assets were valued at between 20 and 1,500 million *kbv* as of May 1, 1992 were ordered to reorganize themselves into open joint stock companies (Decree of the Cabinet of Ministers of Ukraine on Corporatization of State-Owned Enterprises, 1992). Corporatization was intended to be the first stage of enterprise reorganization, a prerequisite to privatization. The State Property Fund and regional privatization authorities exercise authority over the reorganization process.

The management of an enterprise is entrusted with the task of forming a commission for corporatization no later than one month from the date the decree goes into effect. The commission should have at least three members and may be composed of representatives from the privatization authority, the enterprise, the bank servicing the enterprise, and member(s) of the council of deputies. The commission should submit to the State Property Fund an estimate of the property's value, a charter for the newly transformed open joint stock company, and a draft plan for privatization. The state privatization authority then reviews and acts upon the submitted documents within ten days. Upon approval of the charter, the value estimates, and the privatization plan, management registers the enterprise as a transformed, open joint stock company. The new legal entity then inherits all the rights and obligations from the previously unincorporated state enterprise. The decree set July 1, 1993 as the target date for completion of the transformation process.

MONOPOLIES

Ukraine's Law on Containing Monopolism and Preventing Unfair Competition was enacted on February 18, 1992. It defines monopoly and unfair competition, creates an antimonopoly agency, and delineates the agency's authority and responsibilities. Because Soviet economic planning created highly monopolistic market structures, establishing a legal basis for curtailing monopolistic conduct is an integral part of economic restructuring in Ukraine.

The law defines a monopoly as an economic entity controlling 35 percent or more of a given market in a given geographic region. The term also applies to a consortium of business entities if its members conspire to reduce market competition via collusive activities.

The antimonopoly authority may label an economic entity monopolistic if its market share is less than 35 percent, but it is capable of curtailing competitive forces to a significant degree. Restriction of production, price discrimination through separation of markets, and imposing unfair conditions on factor suppliers or product distributors are all considered monopolistic activities. A business enterprise that violates the rights of a competitor, disseminates false information, or obtains trade secrets in an effort to undermine or reduce competition is also subject to prosecution under this law. All forms of monopolistic power and activity are subject to supervision and sanction by the antimonopoly authority.

The Supreme Rada establishes the Antimonopoly Committee of Ukraine. Within the parameters defined by the law, the Committee and its regional administrations exercise the following authorities:

1. defining and identifying monopolies and monopolistic enterprises within their respective regions and districts;
2. ordering the vertical or horizontal divestiture or partitioning of a monopolist or a monopolistic business enterprise;
3. nullifing collusive agreements concluded by participants in their effort to restrict competition;
3. issuing cease and desist orders to the offending parties;
4. reorganizing or liquidating monopolistic enterprises where feasible and when advisable;
5. limiting the acquisition of controlling shares by an economic entity, if such shares may result in establishing the entity in a monopolistic position;
6. recommending to revoke licenses and permits of foreign concerns if their business conduct violates provisions of the antimonopoly law;
7. subpoenaing information from and, if found guilty, impose fines on suspected monopolistic activities. (Law on Containing Monopolism and Preventing Unfair Competition, 1992: sect. 4, arts. 11, 13; sect. 5, arts. 19, 20)

In a separate decree, also issued on February 18, 1992, the Supreme Rada ordered the Council of Ministers to submit an antimonopoly program by March 15, 1992. The program was to be based on provisions of this law. The decree further directed the council to submit recommendations to the Supreme Rada by April 15, 1992 for review if incongruity or conflicts existed between the current laws and the newly enacted anti monopoly law. By that date, the Council of Ministers was also to have ensured that all past and future council decrees and normative acts issued by ministries and departments were in full compliance with the provisions of the anti-monopoly law.

The above laws and decreee constitute the basic legislative acts to date on ownership rights and enterprise reform in Ukraine. They provide the legal basis and authorized parameters for improving industrial structure and function. Before delving into an evaluation of the legislative and administrative attempts at comprehensive restructuring, one additional point concerning the legislative-administrative gap needs to be considered.

The antimonopoly law and the decree implementing the law, both issued on February 18, 1992, granted the Council of Ministers twenty-five days to submit an antimonopoly program to the Supreme Rada. The legislators gave the Council of Ministers fifty-six days, from February 18 to April 15, 1992, to resolve conflicts between prior laws and the new antimonopoly law.

Ukraine had, by February 1992, experienced only six months of independence. Most of its legal foundations and all its industry were still rooted in the highly centralized command structure of the FSU. Soviet-era planning had created scores of monopolies and a baffling array of desultory legislation. That the administration was expected to resolve seventy years of inefficiency in only eight weeks reflects the Supreme Rada's unrealistic approach to reform and suggests that these politicians, largely remnants of the Supreme Soviet, do not fully understand the magnitude of the reforms that are needed. A passage from the decree confirms this suspicion: "According to established procedure, the Cabinet of Ministers shall eliminate the organs and structures of branch management of the economy at all levels, as well as all associations formed on the basis of ministries and departments, except for such natural monopolies as communications [telephone, telegraph, post office], railroads, pipelines, and air transportation" (Supreme Rada's Decree on Implementing the Law on Containing Monopolism, 1992: art. 4, para. 2).

To eliminate all monopolistic "organs and structures" in Ukraine's vast bureaucracy is not readily realizable. There exists an enormous gap between Ukraine's ability to legislate and its ability to successfully administer its own legislation. Merely passing laws that appear to be as strict as those in the West will do little to eliminate monopoly unless the laws are administered by a body with adequate staffing, internal judicial autonomy, and precedent on which to act.

AN EVALUATION

Common defects emerge in Ukraine's legislative acts and decrees. These include inconsistency, lack of dedication to promoting justice and equality, and the persistence of the fiat mentality. Inconsistencies among laws—and, in extreme cases, within laws themselves—have plagued Ukrainian legislation since independence.

One of the most detrimental incongruities involves ownership of and accountability for leased property. According to the Law on Leasing, the lessee enjoys full rights over the leased property "equal to the protection of property rights provided by the civil legislation" (Law on Leasing,1992: art. 30, para. 1). However, the same law states that: "The leasing of property does not change the property rights over the property. The organization of lessees in accordance with the Law of Ukraine on Property has property rights over the production manufactured with the leased property, over other properties acquired by enterprises, economic societies, etc., founded by them; and also have property rights over the income [profits] received by the lessee" (ibid: art. 25, para. 1, 2).

Article 30 of the law suggests that property ownership rights shift from lessor to lessee upon the commencement of a leasing contract. Article 25, however, refutes this, maintaining that ownership itself does not change hands upon leasing. It cannot be underestimated that firms behave very differently when operating with their own capital stock; the legal ownership status of capital thus carries widespread consequences for decision-makers in enterprise management positions. The Law on Enterprises further confuses the matter: "Enterprises, unless otherwise required by [enterprise] statute, shall be entitled to sell and to transfer to other enterprises, organizations and institutions, to exchange, to lease, . . . buildings, installations, equipment " (Law on Enterprise in the Ukrainian SSR, 1991: sect. 3, art. 5).

Enterprises now appear to have the right to lease out or sell off property that legally belongs to the state. Not only does this make little legal sense, but it also enables enterprises to deplete the nation's capital base without replacing it. Worse, neither lessor nor lessee knows the full extent of his/her responsibility. Justice is difficult to obtain when nobody fully understands the extent of his/her own accountability.

Another pattern specific to Ukrianian reform is a lack of dedication to promoting justice. Laws favor certain groups and the already privileged at the expense of others. Gaping loopholes compromise the effectiveness of many reforms. Institutionalized connections from the Communist era persist in independent Ukraine. The majority of decision makers, both in the government and on the enterprise level, are former members of the privileged *nomenklatura* class. Decisions are therefore frequently made and agreements reached on the basis of past and existing connections.

Cross-subsidization among branches of an enterprise was not uncommon in the Soviet Union. Since some enterprise divisions are more profitable, adaptive, and progressive than others, the leasing of select divisions of enterprises can render the rest of the firm non-viable. Enterprise downsizing should precede privatization. Nonproductive or non-viable portions of an enterprise should be trimmed off before leasing arrangements between the entire slimmed-down enterprise and the state are permitted. If this step is not taken, those with the most information about a firm can claim for themselves the most productive portions of the enterprise, leaving the rest of the firm in shambles. Thus one or a few can benefit at the expense of the rest of the firm and the rest of society.

Another example of such inequity appears in the Law on Leasing, which declares that: "The conditions set forth in the leasing agreement remain valid for the entire period of the agreement, even in cases when after its signing, done in agreement with this law, rules which worsen the position of the lessee are set by new legislation" (Law on Leasing, 1992: art. 11, para. 3). This provision allows those with inside connections to take advantage of sweetened leasing deals. The state is left with no legal recourse to correct such a privileged lease. Worse, the provision prevents lease payment schedules from being indexed for inflation. Since all leases are effected in *karbovantsi*, the temporary Ukrianian currency, enterprises that lease can simply watch their debts wither away at high inflation rates. Thus, firms can lease state property at very low real cost. The state and its subjects lose out on much-needed revenue.

Similarly, "workers are also given the option to purchase their enterprise at any time within three years of the beginning of the lease period, and the price is fixed at the value of the enterprise at the beginning of the lease" (Frydman, 1993: 101). Given the high rate of inflation, the state has for all practical purposes freely given away its properties to worker collectives that lease the enterprise.

These developments exacerbate the already massive wealth redistribution that inflation has produced, creating unprecedented and extensive inequities. Allocative inefficiency produced by state ownership and monopoly is worsened by inflation. All these maladies reward and punish citizens not according to whether they can meet any market test, but according to whether they happen to be debtors or creditors, privileged or not privileged.

Another discernible pattern of behavior in Ukraine can be seen in the recurring use of government issued fiat. The fiat mentality, which is rooted in the Soviet bureaucrats' belief that wealth and prosperity can be created by government decree, dominates the parliament. Many of Ukraine's economic laws and administrative decrees thus take the form of public pronouncements, full of rhetoric, optimism, and occasionally sound policy suggestions, but often lacking substance. For instance, the Council of Ministers' 1992 decree on corporatization set July 1, 1993 as the date for the completion of enterprise reorganization. Yet, a presidential decree on June 15, 1993 reordered "the transformation of state enterprises into state joint stock companies which, in their turn, will be completely or partially privatized in the future. . . . This process is scheduled to be finished by the end of 1994" (Pavlikovskaya, 1993: 1). The Council of Minsters' decree of mid-1992 clearly did not yield the desired results. Another decree was needed to postpone the process.

The policy as declared was obviously not feasible. Ukraine does not have enough experienced bank personnel, deputies of state, regional councils, or privatization officials to assist the enterprise commission.[1] Financial intermediaries do not possess the financial resources needed for transformation. Management has little experience in estimating the net worth of an enterprise; and inflation has rendered even the best-devised estimates worthless. The list of administrative difficulties that various groups encounter is virtually endless, as even nations like Britain and the United States have learned. To attempt to reconcile all these problematic areas with a single declaration defies the sensibilities of those accustomed to modern government.

Ukraine's reforms, despite their glaring inconsistencies, redistributive effects, and lack of administrative and institutional support, have, at the very least, created some legal basis for the emergence of an autonomous private sector. The Ukrianians have taken a small and uncertain step toward freeing economic relationships and mar-ketizing economic activity, but it has been a step in the right direction.

NOTES

1. The enterprise commission or committee consists of a number of representatives from management and the workers' council. The size of the commission may vary, depending on the size of a given enterprise. The commission is a deliberative body that makes recommendations to the enterprise management and workers over issues such as enterprise restructuring and leasing decisions and arrangements.

7

Privatization

Ukraine has gone through a series of privatization laws, amendments, and government decrees that would baffle the most learned economist. As the country slowly drags itself through the first stages of privatization, contradictory regulations and policy reversals are stifling the little progress that has been made. Powerful national interests are blocking privatization, as are local political squabbles and widespread fear of the hardships of the free market. (Rudekavych, 1994: 6)

The proven inefficiency of state coordination of economic activities and of public ownership necessitates managerial decentralization and transfer of property rights from the state to the private sector. Both microeconomic theory and historical evidence show that the "invisible hand" of the private sector allocates and utilizes resources much more efficiently than does the "heavy hand" of central planning. This is particularly true of Ukraine, where the public sector has inherited a discarded relic from an inflexibly centralized and rigidly controlled command system.

Though a state attempting systemic transformation of its economy must eliminate such elements of statism, decentralization during the earlier phases of transition needs to be regulated by a coordinating mechanism from above. Sudden and complete abrogation of the state sector tends to be chaotic, inefficient, and irresponsible. Upon independence, Ukraine did not possess a rationally articulated privatization policy.

Privatization in the former Communist world is even more complicated than privatization in the industrialized world, which has the advantages of resolute political will, experienced administrative personnel, plentiful financial resources and investors, and efficient institutional and structural supports. Privatization specialists in Canada, Great Britain, and France can readily attest to the difficulties Ukraine will face in implementing a privatization policy, and to the economic and sociopolitical dangers of implementing a poorly organized policy.

This chapter examines Ukraine's privatization program and draws lessons from Ukraine's experience. It consists of six sections: (1) administrative organizations; (2) objects subject to privatization; (3) privatization methods; (4) privatization certificates and intermediaries; (5) privatization programs and progress; (6) an appraisal of Ukraine's privatization policy and programs.

ADMINISTRATIVE ORGANIZATIONS

The success of Ukraine's privatization programs depends on the efficacy of its governmental institutions. The institutional players and their functions in the privatization process are described below.

The primary privatization organization is the newly created State Property Fund of Ukraine (hereafter referred to as the Fund). The nation's president nominates the Fund's chief administrator, whose appointment must be confirmed by the Supreme Rada. The Fund is accountable to the Supreme Rada, which approves, rejects, or modifies Fund-recommended privatization programs. Along with formulating the state's privatization programs, the Fund's other more significant tasks include the following:

- supervising or mandating organizational restructuring of state enterprises;
- acting on behalf of the state as the legal owner of its shares in state enterprises;
- identifying and conducting sales of public properties where state initiative is warranted;
- acting as the designated lessor of state properties to worker collectives or to leasing organizations formed by citizens;
- coordinating and/or overseeing regional and local privatization authorities;
- approving licenses to financial intermediaries;
- appointing enterprise-level privatization commissions;
- approving privatization plans submitted by the privatization commissions. (Law of Ukraine on Privatization of Assets of State-Owned Enterprises, 1992: part 1, art. 7)

The Fund establishes branch offices and exercises jurisdiction only over state-owned properties subject to privatization. Within the framework of the privatization laws, the privatization of public properties consigned to regional or local governments is within the purview of locally established privatization authorities. The Fund serves them in an advisory capacity as the national agency for the privatization process.

The enterprise commission is a grassroots organization. When a privatization proposal is initiated by a workers' collective, by a prospective outside buyer, or by authorities having jurisdiction over an the enterprise, an enterprise-level commission must be formed within a month of the proposal's initial submission. All parties having a direct interest in the enterprise proposed for privatization must be duly represented on the commission's membership composition. Experts from outside of the enterprise and representatives from the financial institution servicing the enterprise may also be part of the commission. The Fund or the local privatization authority must first approve the recommended membership list before the commission may proceed with drafting a privatization plan. Once the drafting of the privatization plan has been completed, the commission dissolves itself.

The National Bank of Ukraine and the network of the nation's savings banks are entrusted with the responsibility of issuing, distributing, and maintaining deposit accounts for privatization certificates. The National Bank of Ukraine, upon direction from the government, issues and distributes privatization vouchers to eligible recipients. After a nominal fee is paid by the recipient, the vouchers are converted to certificates, which are then kept as privatization accounts with one of the branch savings banks. The banks, therefore, are an integral component of the privatization organization.

The presence of a fundamentally sound privatization plan, however, does not guarantee success. Administrative adequacy, financial stability, and effective coordination are also critical to transformation. Ukraine needs effective institutions for successful privatization of its state sector, and its success will depend largely upon its developing these institutions.

UNITS OR ENTERPRISES SUBJECT TO PRIVATIZATION

State enterprises may be grouped under three categories: those that remain state owned, those that can be privatized only upon approval by the Council of Ministers, and those that can be readily privatized..

Among those that remain state owned and are not subject to privatization are Ukraine's space agency, communication centers, cultural institutions, and organizations that are of importance in the provision of public services. Industries that can be privatized only upon the approval of the Council of Ministers include energy and fuel complexes, local transportation systems, nuclear machine-building concerns, bakeries and macaroni manufacturers, and television and radio broadcasting stations.[1]

The third group of enterprises, those that can be readily privatized, includes all state-owned properties outside of the two categories mentioned above. The enterprises in this category can be divided into six groupings:

Group A consists of units whose value as of August 1, 1993 did not exceed 700 million *kbv*. They are small retail, service, and producing units that can be readily disposed of. Monopolistic enterprises are excluded from this group, regardless of size. In sparsely populated areas of the USSR, such units were not uncommon.

Group B consists of nonmonopolistic firms valued at between 700 and 45,000 million *kbv* as of August 1, 1993, provided the per employee worth of the firm's assets is less than 1.5 times the nominal value of a privatization certificate.

Group C comprises units also valued at between 700 and 45,000 million *kbv*, but the per employee asset worth of these units exceeds 1.5 times that of a privatization certificate. As in groups A and B above, monopolistic enterprises are excluded from this grouping.

Enterprises in group D include the following classifications: monopolistic concerns, regardless of their asset worth; enterprises whose asset values exceed 45,000 million *kbv* as of August 1, 1993; firms subject to privatization due to international agreements signed between the Ukrainian government and foreign or international entities that will be privatized with foreign capital participation, regardless of their asset values; and military-industrial complexes singled out by the government for privatization.

Group E consists of unfinished, halted, or abandoned projects, plus assets of enterprises due for liquidation.

Finally, Group F consists of state shares in enterprises of mixed capital ownership (State Program for the Privatization of State Property for 1994, 1994: part 1, ch. 2, sect. 2.1).

PRIVATIZATION METHODS

The privatization process begins when the state authority (hereafter referred to as the authority) publishes a list of enterprises being privatized. The initiative for privatization may be taken by the authority itself, by outside buyers, or by an association of employees. The authority approves a privatization commission or committee on the enterprise level and reviews the committee's privatization plan for the enterprise. The committee has two months for preparation of the plan and must then obtain the authority's approval for the plan. The authority then publishes information about the enterprise being privatized and accepts applications from prospective buyers for thirty days. The authority then publishes cogent information on the units or enterprises being privatized thereafter, and determines the method of privatization.

There are five basic methods for privatizing enterprises: worker buyout, auction, competitive tender, share offering, and buyout under a leasing agreement. Each is briefly examined below.

Worker Buyout

Worker buyout, referred to as "redemption" in official documents, is the purchase of a unit or an enterprise by an association of workers employed therein. Worker buyout may materialize from two directions: (1) a worker-buyers' association petitions the authority for a buyout settlement; or, (2) an *ex-post*-formed buyer's association, which allows workers to file a petition after an outside interest has expressed interest, prevents an enterprise from being sold to outsiders. Under part 1 of the Fund's April 2, 1993 "Regulation on Procedures for Privatization of State-

Owned Enterprises' Property," enterprises within groups A, B, and E may be privatized through this worker buyout method. They are referred to as "small state-owned enterprises" or "objects of small-scale privatization" (State Property Fund, Approval of Regulation on Procedures, 1993: part 1, sect. 1, art. 1; part 2, sect. 1, art. 1). The preface to the Law of Ukraine on Small Privatization of 1992 defines a small-scale unit or enterprise as one whose entire property complex is purchased by one buyer in a single transaction. In addition to small retail and service units, this includes "processing and local industries, building materials industries, light industry and food retail, construction, [and] special types of transportation . . . " (Law of Ukraine on Privatization of Small State Enterprises, 1992: sect. 1, art. 1). The worker buyout method thus applies to all the enterprises in the above-mentioned industries, provided that all properties of a given unit or enterprise are purchased by one entity in one transaction, and that they conform to the specifics as outlined under groups A, B, and E. The authority uses two different sets of procedures, depending on whether the unit or enterprise being bought out belongs to group A, B, or E.

Group A Units. If only one application is received within the thirty-day period, and if the worker-buyer association is the sole applicant, then the authority follows the appropriate privatization procedure until the unit is sold. If, on the other hand, two or more applications are received, then the authority first decides how privatization of the unit will proceed. Among the options are the worker buyout, auction, competitive tender, or share offering methods. If the authority favors a worker buyout format, then it notifies the enterprise management, as well as other applicants, of its decision. From then on, the procedure for privatization by worker buyout applies.

Terms of sale must be completed within a two-month period, beginning with the date on which a list of enterprises being privatized is published. Within three days of the publication of that list, before the authority decides on the form under which the enterprise will be privatized, the enterprise management recommends to the authority a panel of committee members who will evaluate the enterprise's book value. Upon the authority's approval of its membership composition, the committee takes an inventory of the enterprise's assets, estimates their combined value, and certifies the estimate's accuracy. The buyers' association drafts a buy/sell contract as soon as the authority accepts the committee's estimate. Among the contract articles are terms of payment and employment. Although not explicitly stated in the Fund's directives, minimizing layoffs is an important consideration when approving the buyer association's proposed contract. Signing of the buy/sell contract terminates the state's property rights in the newly privatized small-scale enterprise.

Groups B and E Units. The perceived book value of units in groups B and E is considerably higher than that of units in group A, and the per-employee asset worth of an enterprise in groups B and E is less than 1.5 times the nominal value of a privatization certificate. After the publication of the privatization list, and upon confirming the privatization of a B or E group enterprise via worker buyout, the authority approves the committee and itemizes specific considerations that the committee must address in the proposed buyout plan. The committee formulates the buyout plan in accordance with the Fund's October 11, 1992 directives, submitting it to the authority within a two-month period. The authority reviews and makes a determination on the proposed plan. If the plan is accepted, a buy/sell agreement is signed, concluded, and registered. The buyer's association makes payments on the purchased unit in accordance with the payment schedule specified in the approved plan/contract. Fund Regulations grant a thirty-day grace period, "provided the payment covers no less than 50 percent of the total price" (State Property Fund, Approval of Regulation on Procedures, 1993: part 2, sect. 4, art. 4). It is not clear, however, whether the 50 percent refers to each of the installment payments or to the total amount due on a given date. Whatever the case may be, the formal process of privatizing a B or E group unit is complete once the buy/sell agreement is signed and provisions therein are followed.

Auction

Objects or enterprises may be placed on the auction list either at the request of prospective buyers or at the authority's own initiative, however, not at the entreaty of worker-collective groups. That worker-led groups cannot request an auction suggests that public officials are aware of the management-worker team's two main sentiments: uncertainty over employment or working conditions after a takeover by external private capital, and unpreparedness for facing enterprise ownership by outsiders. In either instance, the management-worker team does not initiate the enterprise's privatization process unless the method is an employee buyout. Public documents, therefore, surreptitiously eschew the management-worker team as a possible source of privatization initiative, except in the worker buyout method.

The units offered for auction include enterprises, plants, unfinished projects, and parts or units of given enterprises. At the discretion of the authority, an auction can be organized and conducted either by its own representative or by an authorized legal representative. The authority publishes relevant information on the units being privatized at least thirty days prior to the scheduled auction date, designating which ones are for hard currency sale only. All persons may inspect the units offered for auction sale. Any person interested in participating in an auction sale submits an application and pays a nominal registration fee and a deposit equivalent to 10 percent of the unit's initial asking price. Three days before the scheduled auction date, the authority ceases accepting applications; if fewer than three applications have been received, the authority removes the unit from the sale list. If, after three minutes of auctioning, no participant has made a bid equal to or greater than the initial asking price, then the auctioneer may reduce the initial asking price by as much as 30 percent.

The moment a unit is sold to the highest bidder, control over the property automatically shifts to its new owner. Within a week after the auction, the buyer and the privatization authority draft a contract, which includes payment conditions and mutual obligations. Once the final installment payment is made, the authority's representative officially signs the property transfer over to the new owner, concluding the final phase of the auction sale transaction.

Competitive Tender

In the competitive tender method, the state sells property to either the highest bidder or the bidder who can use the property with greatest efficiency. Prospective buyers may petition the authority to place a state enterprise or a publicly owned unit on the privatization list, or the authority may, on its own initiative, place such a unit or enterprise on the list. Once the authority decides an enterprise will be privatized via competitive tender, a tender committee issues information on the enterprise. The committee consists of five to nine members, including representatives of the authority and the enterprise, and hired specialists. Representation of the enterprise's management or worker collective is again conspicuously absent. Within a two-month period from its formation, the committee, which is headed by a chairperson appointed by the privatization authority, itemizes the conditions of the competitive tender.

Conditions for sale vary from one state enterprise to another; among the conditions are initial price, employment status, limits on resale, environmental concerns, and, where applicable, specialized product lines. Prospective buyers may inspect the enterprise, pay application fees, and submit a buyer's plan to the committee. In the plan, buyers propose a purchase price and explain how they will meet the conditions specified by the committee. Seven days before the scheduled tender, the authority ceases accepting applications. The committee then studies the applications, removes an enterprise or object from the list if fewer than three offers are received, and selects the finalists before making its ultimate selection. The final selection must be approved by two-thirds of the committee members.

The committee announces its decision and communicates the winner's purchase offer to all participants; the other participants may submit additional offers within five days of the announcement. The committee then renders its final decision and submits its decision to the privatization authority for approval; with the signing of a contract between the winner and the authority, the privatization process by way of competitive tender is completed.

Share Offering

Share offering, the fourth method of privatization, is used for the sale of enterprises that have already been reorganized into open joint stock companies replete with shares for public subscription. If the authority determines that share offering is the method for privatizing an open joint stock company, then a committee on share offering is formed within ten days of a privatization plan. The committee includes intermediaries and representatives of both the enterprise and the privatization authority. Members of the committee are appointed by the enterprise's top official and are subject to approval by the privatization authority.

The authority publishes information on the enterprise while the committee accepts purchase applications. Share offerings are first made to the current and former employees of the enterprise being privatized. As provided by the law:

The employees of an enterprise subject to privatization shall have:

- priority rights to acquire shares at nominal value up to the value of and in exchange for the privatization certificate issued to each employee;
- priority rights to purchase shares at nominal value using their own funds in an amount up to one half the value of the privatization certificate issued to each employee.

The benefits provided to employees in this Article shall also apply to former employees. (Law of Ukraine on Privatization of Assets of State-Owned Enterprises, 1992: part 4, art. 25, para. 1, 3)

The regulation on procedures for privatization does discuss methods of arriving at competitive prices of shares under different open-market scenarios, and the Law on Privatization of Assets of State-Owned Enterprises does specify procedures for calculating an initial offering price in the case of selling an entire enterprise complex.[2] However, neither the law nor the regulation specifies what the nominal value of a share in a given enterprise of a given nature is or should be. Nevertheless, in accordance with the law, current and former employees of an enterprise being privatized may purchase 150 percent of the value of their privatization certificate. The employees have a three-month period for submitting applications, specifying amounts of payment, and purchasing shares of the enterprise. Shares not sold under those conditions are offered to the public on a competitive basis; the public, however, can buy shares only with privatization certificates. Private citizens and financial intermediaries may all apply for subscription, specifying offering prices and the number of shares desired. The committee analyzes the number and quality of offers against the number of shares available for sale. The committee then determines a competitive price per share. If an offer price equals or exceeds the committee-determined sale price, all shares subscribed to are accepted, though it is unclear what takes place when the offer price is less than the sale price. The regulation on procedures for privatization states that: "applications, where the offered price for one share is less than the sale price, shall be satisfied with the agreement of the applicant in the proportion equivalent to the number the shares applied for" (State Property Fund, Approval of Regulation on Procedures, 1993: part 5, sect. 3, art. 9). It appears that, for some unspecified formula, the low offers may still be satisfied, depending on the number of shares applied for and the price offered.

In addition to sales under the privileged conditions and open selling of individual shares via privatization certificates, the committee may also sell individual shares or blocks of shares for cash. It is unclear whether such shares or blocks of shares are leftovers from the above two categories or are designated so by the committee after the privileged sale has been completed. The procedure for selling shares for cash is the same as the procedure for selling in exchange for certificates, but the regulations governing the sale of share blocks parallel those of the competitive tender method.

Buyout under Leasing Agreement

The law on privatization permits the buyout of a leased state enterprise by its leaseholders, provided the option is contained in the lease agreement. When the lessee exercises its option, the procedure "is conducted in accordance with the Law of Ukraine on the Leasing of Property of State-Owned Enterprises and Organizations" (Law of Ukraine on Privatization of Assets of State-Owned Enterprises, 1992: art. 17, para. 1). However, the Law of Ukraine on the Leasing of Property of State-Owned Enterprises and Organizations does not stipulate procedures for converting a leasing arrangement to a buyout arrangement. A reasonable assumption is that procedures for the buyout method previously examined are applied in such circumstances.

PRIVATIZATION CERTIFICATES AND INTERMEDIARIES

The Law on Privatization, acknowledging that state enterprises have value only because of the citizen workforce, mandates that no less than 40 percent of the value of state properties be equitably distributed, through privatization vouchers, to the citizens of Ukraine. These vouchers may be converted into privatization certificates for a nominal fee, and are deposited in branch savings banks throughout the country. The government, taking inflation into account, periodically adjusts the face value of each certificate to reflect real values.

Owners of privatization certificates may use them when purchasing shares of an enterprise or unit being privatized. They may also pool the combined purchasing power of the certificates, redeeming them through a buyer's association formed by workers of a given enterprise. As envisioned in the law on privatization, the certificates may also be placed in trust associations, investment funds, or holding companies. Since the vast majority of certificate owners have neither the knowledge nor the experience for engaging in investment activities, the inchoate financial intermediaries can assist them in various ventures.

Workers do not receive more privatization vouchers than others; however, they do receive benefits such as priority claims and privileged purchasing, and they may receive extra benefits under given circumstances. If an association of workers purchases more than half of an enterprise, then the law on privatization grants it the privilege of receiving "free of charge from the appropriate state privatization agency the social and cultural facilities created with the use of financial resources of the social development fund of said enterprise" (Law of Ukraine on Privatization of Assets of State-Owned Enterprises, 1992: part 4, art. 24, para. 2). This privilege applies no matter what type of transaction is used. For many of the medium- or large-sized enterprises in Ukraine, as in most of the former centralized economies in Eastern Europe, such facilities include vacation complexes, recreational facilities, health care units, auditoriums, and cultural centers. This privilege may encourage workers' financial participation in the privatization process, helping to develop a worker-capitalist middle class and to compensate the working class for past exploitations.

PRIVATIZATION PROGRAMS AND PROGRESS

Ukraine's public pronouncements on its privatization policy have been marked by incongruity, translucency, and contradiction. The agenda for privatization has been shadowed by other concerns, such as partisan politics, inflation and economic stagnation.

The government's privatization program of 1992, which coincided with the Law on Privatization of State Enterprises, did not win the parliament's approval. Prime Minister Kuchma, despite having the extraordinary power to introduce reform measures by decree, could not advance a privatization policy. Ukraine also lacked both the bureaucratic staffing and financial institutions requisite to such a program. The bureaucracy and leadership were poorly acquainted with the privatization process. The financial intermediaries were consumed by inflation. As a consequence of this institutional unpreparedness, the program proved ineffective. By the end of fiscal 1992, property rights of only sixty-eight small state enterprises had been transferred to the private sector, mostly by auction sponsored by the International Finance Corp (IFC) or by worker-management buyout. By May 1, 1993, near the end of the Kuchma administration, the state still owned 98 percent of all productive assets. A brief analysis will suffice to demonstrate the slow pace of Ukraine's ownership transformation process.

The repetitiveness of official Ukrainian pronouncements is one clue that the process is moving at a snail's pace. For example, the first priority listed in the State Programme for the Privatization of State Property for 1993 was "completion, in essence, of groups A, D objects privatization." Likewise, the 1994 program lists as priorities "conducting mass scale privatization of objects in groups A, E; expanding privatization on objects in groups B, C, D." Obviously, group A was not completed, since it appeared again as a priority in 1994. Another priority of the 1993 program was securing the "participation of Ukrainian citizens in privatization by way of using privatization deposit accounts." The same phrase reappeared in the 1994 program. Little use was made of these privatization deposit accounts in the interim (vol. 2, no. 6:5).

The 1993 privatization program announced: "[The] State Property Fund of Ukraine, Antimonopoly Committee of Ukraine, [and] Ministry of Economics of Ukraine will carry out a sectoral analysis of markets for essential products and services in Ukraine" (State Program for Privatization for 1993, 1993: ch. 1, art. 11). However, the 1994 program again states: "Intersectoral commissions shall be created for the conduct of the sectoral analysis. . . . The results of the sectoral analyses conducted by the intersectoral commissions shall serve as basis for creation of concepts of privatization of the enterprises in the different sectors [branches] of the economy" (State Program for the Privatization of State Property for 1994, 1994: ch. 3, arts. 1, 2).

This 1994 repetition of a 1993 statement contains a disturbing element of governmental casualness toward a pivotal reform policy. The 1994 document does not even direct the implementation of an essential aspect of the 1993 privatization program: analyzing markets and sectors, an obvious prerequisite to rational action.

If the proposed actions of the administration appeared perfunctory, then the goals set in government pronouncements were also overly optimistic; the privatization slates set forth in programs would be unattainable even if the nation possessed the requisite governmental and financial institutions. The 1993 program targeted a total of 7,480 Group B units for privatization (Program, 1993: ch. 1, art. 2); yet, as of late July 1994, "the privatization program for 1993 has been only 1 percent fulfilled" (Privatization in Ukraine, 1993, vol. 2, nos. 6, 5).

The 1994 program is further littered with baffling numbers and disorganized directives. Some of these statements bear mentioning, either because they created unattainable goals or illustrated an irrational or poorly conceived facet of the nation's privatization policy.

The 1994 program directed the Fund to publish a list of at least 2,000 group A (small) units for privatization each month, and 40 group E (unfinished or abandoned) projects (Program for Privatization, 1994: ch. 5, sect. 1, art. 3). The ministries, meanwhile, were given the responsibility for corporatizing and transferring to the Fund no fewer than 1,500 enterprises by April 1, 1994. The program also called for the complete privatization of all state-owned agricultural entities by the end of 1994. The Fund, however, saddled by administrative inadequacy, could not attain figures anywhere close to these stated objectives:

Between January and December 1993, the Central Staff of the State Property Fund of Ukraine has privatized 275 objects at the cost of more than 190 billion *kbv*. But it would be more accurate to use the term "has prepared to privatize," since 202 objects of this number were transformed into leased enterprises or into leased enterprises with options to buy-out, and the remaining 73 objects were created into joint stock companies. . . . During 1993, regional departments of the Fund have privatized 722 objects in different oblasts, including 443 small-scale privatization objects.(Privatization in Ukraine, 1994: vol. 3, no. 1, 2)

Though there is doubt about the accuracy of these numbers,[3] the conclusion is evident: the Fund is not capable of privatizing industries at the rates directed by the programs. It did not accomplish in an entire year what the program had expected it to do in one month. This disparity is reminiscent of the fiat mentality of the Soviet era. Leaders who believe that economic prosperity can be achieved by decree and by plan still dominate the Ukrainian political process.

Even the rationale of the program seems suspect. The 1994 program at one point states that the highest priority for privatization should go to the units that can have the greatest impact on the development of the consumer market, including "loss making enterprises in all branches of the economy, . . . [and] enterprises with capital assets depreciated in excess of 70 percent" (Program for Privatization, 1994: ch. 2, art. 2). It is unclear why or how loss-incurring enterprises should be transferred to the private sector. They should either temporarily remain in the public domain or be eliminated altogether. No rational investor would purchase shares of such an enterprise.

At times, the 1994 privatization program even contradicts other government statements and laws. It states, for example, that the privatization authority shall "offer for sale to the citizens, for privatization certificates, not less than 70 percent of the total value of the assets subject to privatization" (Program for Privatization, 1994: ch. 6, sect. 2). The law on privatizing state assets, however, mandates that the total value of certificates should be not less than 40 percent of the value of the assets subject to privatization. Privatization certificates valued at 40 percent of total value of state property cannot be exchanged for 70 percent of state property, yet this is what the program mandates. Similarly, the 1994 program directs the district privatization authorities to recommend the means for privatizing given enterprises, as well as the allocation of shares to diverse interest groups. The law on privatizing state assets, however, accords these same responsibilities to worker collectives in the enterprises. It is the workers' collectives that "establish the methods of privatization, propose whom they wish to invite to participate in the process, and recommend how many shares to which part of the enterprise be allocated to what groups outside of the enterprise" (Bielienkiy interview, 1994). It appears that even the privatization authority itself is unclear about the parameters of its functions and responsibilities.

The progress of privatization legislation calls into question the resolve of the Ukrainian legislature. The 1995 privatization program had not been passed as of May 1995. A draft was approved by the Council of Ministers yet not accepted by the Supreme Rada. Thus, Ukraine still does not have an official privatization program for the year. The draft program for 1995 is a near reproduction of the 1994 program, enumerating the same priorities, objects, and methods of privatization. The sole distinct feature of the 1995 draft is that it proposes a slight expansion in the scope of the role of privatization certificates' in worker-management and citizen participation:

The program envisions broad participation of the population in the privatization process via privatization certificates, which are valued at *kbv* 1,050,000, about USD seven, as of November 1, 1994.... In 1995 the government of Ukraine anticipates privatization of 31,650 enterprises of various size(s) and status, and receipt of *kbv* 41,523.6 billion [about USD 277 million] income.... To provide for the broad participation of Ukrainian citizens in privatization, 100 percent of the group B enterprises, over 70 percent of shares of the group C enterprises, about 70 percent of shares of the group D enterprises are to be sold, preserving all advantages for their employees and administration. (International Market Insights, 1995: 1, 5)

The average value of an enterprise intended for privatization in 1995 is US$8,752 ($277 million divided by 31,650 enterprises.) The proposed sale of all group B units would be feasible if the average value of a group B object were exceptionally modest, while that of certificates distributed to each citizen/worker were remarkably high. However, the value of a certificate approximated only US$7 as of November 1, 1994. Though workers can purchase an average of US$10.50 (150% of US$7) with a single certificate, the price of even a small group B enterprise is beyond the range of most citizens.

Finally, for the successful privatization of the agricultural sector, Ukraine must effectively administer its antimonopoly policy. The collective farms and highly centralized state purchasing system has left a legacy of widespread monopoly in the agricultural sector; privatizing and deregulating industries with non-competitive market structures is unwise. Antimonopoly policy has only been declared, not implemented (Bielienkiy interview, 1994). Ukraine also lacks the financial resources for sufficiently staffing a ministry of justice or a judicial system. Implementing the needed reforms in the agriculture-related industry is technically complex and prohibitively expensive. Privatization in this sector should proceed only when the prerequisite infrastructural support system is reasonably adequate.

Ukrainian legislators have proven that they lack the expertise, information, and discipline for crafting coherent, logical, and reasonable annual privatization programs. The future of privatization in Ukraine is therefore uncertain. The remainder of this chapter appraises Ukraine's overall privatization performance and explains where improvements can be made, drawing from lessons observed in other newly liberalizing economies.

AN APPRAISAL OF UKRAINE'S PRIVATIZATION POLICY AND PROGRAMS

Success in privatizing Ukraine's state holdings depends on Ukraine's legal framework, political will, economic rationality, and institutional infrastructure. Ukraine lacks all these and is still in need of the groundwork for their development. Examples of weaknesses in each of the above four categories are offered below.

Legal Framework

Ukraine's privatization is marked by incongruity and inconsistencies in its legal framework; five instances help illustrate this statement.

The first example involves the leasing law, which grants worker collectives the privilege of entering into leasing arrangements with the Fund at the most favorable conditions conceivable. As a result of Ukraine's sustained inflationary spiral, the law practically allows worker collectives rent-free use of public property for the duration of the agreements, resulting in immeasurable losses in revenue. The leasing law is an appeasement for leaders of the worker-collectivess, who fear that privatization will result in layoffs and costcutting. Near zero-cost leasing discourages privatization, breeds inefficiency, and deprives the government of much-needed revenue, but persists because it appeals to a politically volatile group.

A second example concerns antitrust policy. Assuming that policy success can be guaranteed by the passage of legislative acts is presumptuous. This is clear in Ukraine's attempts at antitrust reform. Ukraine's nascent antimonopoly policy is poorly crafted, while its antitrust agency is underbudgeted and understaffed. Ukraine is incapable of effectuating a substantive demonopolization policy. Though state control over prices is not conducive to economic vitality in the long run, an economy full of privately held monopolies is equally undesirable. This is especially true in the agricultural sector, where the inherited central purchasing and distribution system can create a private-sector-based monopolistic and monopsonistic market structure. Accelerating privatization processes in the absence of effective antitrust policy is incongruent with a rational approach to promoting market competitiveness.

A third flaw rests in Ukraine's agricultural policy. Farmers, unlike their industrial counterparts, do not enjoy priority rights in purchasing and leasing government-owned capital. Thus, only the select nonfarm players can purchase shares of agriculture-based industrial enterprises. Ukraine's agricultural sector, as mentioned in earlier chapters, embodies great potential for the country's future growth; in most economies, it represents the most competitive sector. Yet, Ukraine's privatization policy may have compromised the future competitiveness of a most important facet of the Ukrainian economy.

The fourth inadequacy reflects the ideological largesse of the former Soviet Union. Unlike the privatization policies in Poland, Czechoslovakia, Hungary, and the Baltic states, Ukraine's privatization policy does not allow for the restitution of private property appropriated by the Communist regime. Incorporating such a provision into the privatization policy would expedite the transfer of state properties to the private sector. It would also reflect a governmental resolve toward private property ownership.

Finally, Ukraine's privatization laws are prone to abuse by the monied class, as well as by those with political connections. Since the official value of state enterprises is determined, in part, by outstanding credits and liabilities and since debts between enterprises are not uncommon in the liberated economies, the well-connected can intentionally undervalue firms for sale by juggling debt from firm to firm. Through an exchange of favors, buyers can take advantage, with the state and the public being the net losers.

In brief, there is ample ground for improvement in Ukraine's legislative, executive, and administrative directives for privatizing state properties.

Political

The ideology of the former Soviet Union has not vanished from Ukrainian government. Decision makers at all levels are still uncomfortable with both economic and political decentralization. The "top-down" style of the erstwhile command system is incompatible with the cooperative and decentralized approach required by privatization policy. That every new level of government administration creates a new level of political contention, partisan or otherwise, cannot be neglected. As the means and ends of power become more widely dispersed throughout the government, administrators become more concerned with preserving and acquiring power for themselves or for their agencies. As a consequence, entrenched bureaucrats now use subversive delaying tactics. Consider, for example, the "subversion of corportization plans of subordinated enterprises by different ministries and agencies. As a result, by January 1, 1994, the State Property Fund did not receive shares of [even] one corporatized enterprise" (Privatization in Ukraine, 1994: vol. 3, no. 3, 7, 8). One analysis succinctly sums up the legal and political developments in Ukraine's privatization attempts: The privatization program approved for 1992 failed. A similar program for 1993 [was] not approved. We may conclude that we have lost two years. . . . In 1994, it is envisioned that 20,000 unfinished construction projects and 8,000 medium and large enterprises will be privatized. . . . But these are plans. Reality is quite the contrary. . . . Up to now, we have no legislative basis for it [mass privatization]" (Bondar, 1994: 17–18).

The lack of political will is not limited to the regional or local levels. The Supreme Rada voted, by a ratio 3 to 1, for the suspension of the sale of state-owned units in late July, 1994, ostensibly for the improvement of the privatization institutions and mechanisms. The real reason for the moratorium, however, was largely political. Many deputies in the Supreme Rada are also directors of large state enterprises. Losing property and management control to an unknown private interest is an unattractive venture for many members of the legislature. As a consequence, procrastination in reform in general, and in privatization in particular, continues to be nearly a way of life with Ukraine's political decision makers.

Economic Rationality

The primary justifications for denationalizing state properties are improved efficiency, increased competitiveness, and enhanced consumer surplus. The means to these ends, corporatization and leasing, are not ends in themselves. They possess little intrinsic worth.

The dominant form of privatization in Ukraine has been the leasing of proprety by worker collectives. This is the format that the workers and management feel the most comfortable with in the midst of growing economic uncertainty. Few enterprises, however, will enjoy success through leasing because they still lack organizational efficiency and financial resources. The efficiency of leasing is also lower than full-fledged privatization because offering competitive wages and employment levels ranks low among lessee priorities. Leasing out the old Soviet capital stock may also undermine the most important of national initiatives: restructuring and reorienting the highly specialized inherited plants. Many firms now survive by allowing deterioration of existing capital. The state's construction association estimates that "by 1995, the total amount of capital depreciation not renovated . . . will reach 1,807, 367.5 bln. *krb.*, or (US) $71.7 bln. according to the official exchange rate of the National Bank of Ukraine" (Mayetniy, 1994: 4). As the old capital stock falls into disrepair and disuse, and without the introduction of more efficient capital replacements and new technologies, the firms' net worth declines, existing productivity dwindles, and the economy continues its downward spiral.

In short, extensive leasing of state properties erodes rather than contributes to social and economic well-being. In this instance, in light of Ukraine's recent experience with the Soviet system, the nation's defective privatization policy has failed to accomplish even the most modest of objectives.

Institutional Infrastructure

Even if legal, political, and economic conditions were favorable, privatization on a mass scale would either stall or fail without the support of an adequate and appropriate institutional framework. Ukraine lacks the administrative capability, organizational experience, institutional efficiency, and financial resources that would constructively and productively move the privatization process forward. Legislative and executive fiat from above places lower level administrations constantly on the defensive, impassively reacting to wistful and optimistic directives rather than methodically and effectively executing a rationalized policy. Ukraine is in need of improving its administrative/bureaucratic system, as well as reforming its financial intermediaries. Privatizing tens of thousands of enterprises and organizations without the assistance of developed financial intermediaries can be compared to speeding down a freeway with a nearly empty gas tank. Ukraine's inherited institutions and arrangements are not capable of expediting the nation's ambitious privatization program: ". . . we need a complete revision of approaches to privatization in Ukraine. . . . It is obvious that the institutional, organizational and financial support of the transfer of property rights has completely failed" (Privatization in Ukraine, 1994: vol. 3, no. 3, 8).

Thus, administrative inadequacy, unfamiliarity with decentralized governance, a poorly endowed financial system, and fundamentally unsound legislation have combined to render Ukraine's privatization policy largely unsuccessful to date. Worse, pursuing privatization policy without these institutions has destroyed more wealth than it has created. An important lesson herein is that hasty and cosmetic reform efforts without first adequately assessing the economy's relative strengths and weaknesses could be highly counterproductive in the short as well as in the long run.

NOTES

1. The Supreme Rada's "State Programme for the Privatization of State Property for 1993" listed "television and radio broadcasting stations" as "not subject to privatization," yet also declared "television and radio broadcasting centers" to be subject to conditional privatization. This inconsistency sheds some light on the parliament's lackadaisical posture toward reform. There are also numerous, seemingly trivial, units such as bakeries and macaroni plants, that are not subject to unconditional privatization. These are usually consumer goods industries in which the government wishes some control over the quantities and prices of outputs. The consumers' disturbing loss in purchasing power compels the state's temporary retention of ownership rights to enterprises providing basic consumer goods and services. Although prices of basic goods and services have risen, the price increases remain state regulated. Complete price decontrol would precipitate even more rapid price increases. Such enterprises, therefore, may be privatized only if the council's approval is given. It is likely that they will be subject to privatization once economic stabilization materializes.

2. According to the Law of Ukraine on Privatization of Assets of State-Owned Enterprises of April 12, 1992, "the initial offering price of a privatization object or the amount of the initial capital [statutory fund] of a commercial enterprise [an economic association] founded on the basis of a state-owned enterprise shall be determined by calculating the adjusted value of the fixed assets, allowing for depreciation, the actual value of its current assets including accounts receivable and liabilities on loans outstanding obtained in accordance with recommended methods for approval by the Cabinet of Ministers of Ukraine" (Law of Ukraine on Privatization of Assets of State-Owned Enterprises, 1992: part 3, art. 20, para. 1). The 10 percent deposit paid on a unit by a participant is returned within ten days after the auction if the prospective buyer did not make the purchase.

3. In a September 1993 article, Lada Pavlikovskaya, Ukraine's Deputy Minister of Economy, affirmed that "1,040 units of state-owned and municipal property [with a total value of more than 70 billion roubles—*karbovantsi*] have been privatized by September 1, 1993" (Pavlikovskaya, 1993: 2). The citation in the text, however, was based on official numbers

published by the Fund itself at the beginning of 1994. The statistical discrepancy reveals the frequent and inexact usages of statistics in public pronouncements. More important is the concern that perhaps the government lacks information as well as knowledge about what indeed has been transpiring in the Ukrainian economy.

8

Foreign Investment

Despite Ukraine's languid economic performance since independence, the nation displays much untapped potential. It is richly endowed with mineral deposits and fertile soil, and it has a skilled and educated labor force. However, the disintegration of the USSR, the breakdown of the centralized purchasing and distribution system, and the collapse of markets in CIS nations have rendered an immense portion of Ukraine's productive assets idle. The outmoded capital structure makes production costly and inefficient, and depreciates rapidly. Asset fixity reduces the salvage values of productive resources for no longer marketable goods to near zero. Meanwhile, the Ukrainian economy has become inhospitable to investors. High inflation rates create perverse domestic savings disincentives, promoting dissaving and limiting the possibilities for domestic investment. Instead of substantive gains in foreign capital inflow, there has been a steady outflow of underground domestic capital into foreign markets.

Most firms encounter difficulty in replacing the capital they deplete; they cannot contemplate either capital restructuring or plant expansion. As a result, many firms go bankrupt, the nation's capital base erodes, and productive capacity keeps decreasing. Economic development pivots around the efficient allocation of human, financial, and natural resources. These elements are even more crucial to the Ukrainian economy, since it is still in the process of effectuating a systemic and structural transformation.

With a disintegrating domestic capital stock, and with conditions unfavorable to domestic investment, an influx of foreign capital is vital to economic resurgence. Foreign investment and foreign assistance will be needed in repairing, replacing, and restructuring existing capital, and in introducing new technology, managerial techniques, and overall human resource development.

Ukraine, however, must compete for the limited sum of foreign investment capital available from abroad. Though the total size of the foreign investment pie is expanding, as Japan and Western Europe have finally shaken off their recessions, investors will not be inclined to tilt in favor of Ukraine. Other newly liberalized economies, particularly Poland, Hungary, and the Baltics, have shown greater investment potentials than has Ukraine. Moreover, the recent investment debacle in Mexico has reminded investors everywhere of the risks of investing in less stable economies. Ukrainian foreign investment legislation, therefore, must create a social, political, and economic environment that is uniquely attractive to prospective foreign capital. This chapter analyzes Ukraine's foreign investment potential, policy, and performance. It consists of four parts: policy, priorities, performance, and appraisal and recommendations.

FOREIGN INVESTMENT POLICY

Inducing foreign capital inflow was not a high priority for Ukraine during the Soviet era. The nation's Law on Business Enterprise provided that foreign investors could "enjoy the same rights and bear the same responsibilities as citizens of [the] Ukrainian SSR" (Law on Business Enterprise, 1991: art. 16). The Ukrainian government of 1991 granted no privileges and provided no special incentive to foreign capital beyond what its own citizens were accorded. Since Ukraine's economy was still an integral part of the USSR, and since many of its expenditure and investment requirements were met by the national budget, attracting outside capital was not an important priority. The notion of creating an environment attractive to foreign capital evolved only gradually, though the evolution became more pronounced after Ukraine regained its independence.

Principal legal and administrative provisions regarding foreign investment are contained in the Law on Foreign Investment of March 11, 1992, in the Law of Ukraine on Privatization of Assets of State-Owned Enterprises of April 12, 1992, in the Decree of Cabinet of Ministers on Procedures for Foreign Investments of May 20, 1993, in successive economic programs, and in numerous executive decrees.

Governmental action has been marked by the same disturbing patterns that have been displayed in other areas of reform. Executive actions have been characteristically noncommittal and lackadaisical. Their pronouncements reflect their relaxed posture. Legislation on foreign investment has been drafted without concern for other economic problems. Programs have been marked by unrealistic, almost naive optimism. In all cases, the government has mistakenly assumed that government policy, once legislated, will be successful, no matter how implemented by bureaucracy, mitigated by economic problems, or received by the public. This section discusses first the policies of the executive branch—decrees and administrative programs—and then the actions taken by the legislative branch.

Government Programs

In its February 1992 plan for urgent economic reforms, the government envisioned a two-pronged approach encouraging foreign capital inflow: direct new foreign investments, either in jointly or wholly foreign-owned enterprises, coupled with foreign participation in Ukraine's privatization process. The program attempted to attract foreign capital by guaranteeing foreign ownership rights, freedom of economic activities, and "substantial financial privileges . . . , more so than in the republics of the former USSR" (Cabinet of Ministers, 1992a: ch. 3, sect. 3). The only financial incentive, however, lay in limited customs privileges.

The incentive package was expanded and more explicitly elaborated in the government's subsequent reform program, the Programme of Economic Reform and Policy, which appeared in the latter part of the same year. It sought accelerating Ukraine's integration into the world economy through increased interaction with foreign economic interests. In addition to the incentive provisions cited in the February Plan, this program pledged simplified procedures for foreign capital entry, guaranteed rights to local bank accounts, and granted free access to stock exchanges, reduced the profit tax, expanded the depreciation allowance, and reduced rent on land and natural resources (Cabinet of Ministers, 1992b: 10).

The government's May 20, 1993 Decree on Procedures for Foreign Investments provided a much stronger incentive for foreign investment prospects: the decree granted a five-year tax holiday to foreign investments. Investment projects consisting of either more than 20 percent or more than $100,000 worth of foreign capital qualify for these benefits. The decree attempted to discourage repatriation of profits, thus encouraging reinvestment, by placing a 15 percent tax on repatriated profits (Decree of the Cabinet Ministers, 1993b: article 31). This restriction seems shortsighted; with many strong options for investment in the immediate area, and with a highly competitive worldwide investment market, aggravating conditions would seem to prohibit entry.

The benefits were even further expanded. The December 1993 State Programme for Encouraging Foreign Investments extends the tax holiday beyond the previously granted five-year period for large foreign investments, with a ten-year period as the limit to those exceeding $50 million in initial capitalization.[1] In addition, the resolution grants "a three-year exemption from a wide range of local and municipal taxes, as well as from the value-added tax," if such foreign investments should be in the spheres of agricultural and electrical appliance production, and in food processing (Zubaniuk, 1994: 25).

Furthermore, a newly created Agency for International Cooperation and Investment of Ukraine issued a directive on March 31, 1994 entitled Temporary Procedure On the Grant[ing] of Additional Privileges for Foreign Investors. This directive granted new foreign investors the liberty of applying for privileges beyond those stipulated in the law and in programs on foreign investment. The additional benefits may include "low interest loans and investment insurance," if foreign investment activities are in "light industry, machine-building, medical industry, metallurgy, [and] the energy sector" (Mycyk, 1994: 1).

These decrees, taken by themselves, create an enticing milieu for investment. Whether Ukraine actually attracts foreign investment, however, depends on more than the economic incentives it can offer.

Leonid Kuchma has presented two reform programs containing references to foreign investment: one from 1993, during his tenure as prime minister, and one in his 1994 address to the Supreme Rada as the nation's new president. His 1993 Plan of Action dwells only briefly on the subject of foreign investment. It acknowledges the potential role of foreign capital in contributing to Ukraine's technologies and science-related projects (Cabinet of Ministers, 1993: 66). It also pledges a list of state-owned enterprises for convertible currency privatization. The list appears in the government's resolution No. 635 of August 12, 1993, offering fifty-three state enterprises for convertible currency privatization.

President Kuchma's directive on foreign investment is contained in his address to the Supreme Rada on October 11, 1994. Kuchma views improving foreign investment incentives as only one facet of a more comprehensive strategy for enhancing investment. He stresses, for example, stimulating domestic savings. Instead of redirecting productive activities toward Western markets, as is a common and tempting tendency among the newly liberalized economies, Kuchma emphasizes the traditional importance of close commercial relations with economies of Eastern European countries. He also cites the need of foreign investment in "processing sectors of industry, agriculture, transport, communication, and other entities that [would] help increase the quality of economic potential" in Ukraine (Kuchma, 1994: 36). In addition to his emphasis on new technology via foreign investment, Kuchma also advocates importing advanced organizational and management techniques through foreign capital. The most significant element encouraging foreign investment comes in his statement demanding that Ukraine introduce "comprehensive measures aimed at the radical improvement of the investment climate in Ukraine" (Kuchma, 1994: 37).

Legislative Provisions

Ukraine's March 11, 1992 Law on Foreign Investment updated and expanded the September 18, 1991 Law on Investment Activity and the September 10, 1991 Law on Protection of Foreign Investments. The Law on Foreign Investment stipulates that foreign investment consists of the real or equivalent inflows of convertible currencies in liquid or material forms, including intellectual properties. Foreign capital may assume any form of investment activity. No foreign investors may be excluded from engaging in the investment ventures of their choice unless the activity is explicitly prohibited by law.

Foreign capital may purchase shares in existing enterprises, enter into joint ventures with domestic entrepreneurs provided that at least 20 percent of the initial authorized capital is of foreign origin, acquire productive assets that will become wholly foreign owned, and lease land properties for the purpose of exploiting Ukraine's natural resources. The law protects foreign investments against legislative changes less favorable to the investors by guaranteeing the continuation of all privileges effective at the time of the investments' registration (Law on Foreign Investment, 1992: art. 9). If bureaucratic error or negligence results in losses to the foreign investor, the investor may seek full compensation from the erring party.

Since the disposal of profit constitutes a major concern to foreign investors, the law explicitly states that "Upon payment of taxes and other mandatory duties, foreign investors are guaranteed the right to the unimpeded and prompt remittance abroad—repatriation—of their revenues, profits, and other funds in foreign convertible currency obtained legally in connection with their investments"[2] (ibid: art. 13).

More important for many prospective investors is the provision that grants foreign entrepreneurs rights for using profits derived from the investment "to purchase goods on the domestic market of Ukraine for their export abroad without [a] license" (ibid: art. 14). Since export licenses to domestic entrepreneurs have remained in short supply for domestic investors, the law creates a major advantage for foreigners. The only activities that require special permits are trading in commercial paper and in insurance and banking operations. The Ministry of Finance oversees the licensing of commercial and insurance activity. The National Bank of Ukraine regulates foreign banking operations.

Combining the government's legislative and administrative provisions governing foreign investment, the updated economic incentives are comparable to those of the newly liberalized economies of Eastern Europe. Ukraine, however, must still convince investors that the nation's political and economic scenarios are stable and conducive to safe investment. Until greater stability emerges, a "radical improvement of the investment climate in Ukraine" is not likely.

PRIORITIES

Foreign capital inflow should ideally complement and augment domestic investment activities. Investment efforts should thus focus on the maximization of value-added spheres, on export-oriented industries, on consumer goods industries whose domestic production is stymied by supply inelasticities, and on affordable high technology industries. Ukraine needs to encourage and attract foreign capital inflow into these spheres. Ukraine's decision makers meanwhile must also acknowledge that relying exclusively on foreign capital for securing the desired investment objectives, without reforming domestic investment priorities, invariably imposes high opportunity costs on the economy.

Table 8.1 presents foreign investment priorities as identified by the Ukrainian government in May 1993. A brief analysis of the table will be followed by a discussion of current investment shares in various categories of the economy, a survey of the government's more recent articulation on the subject, and an evaluation of Ukraine's official foreign investment priorities.

Some of these priorities seem well placed, reflecting the areas where the Ukrainian economy displays the most promise. A few, on the other hand, appear misdirected.

Table 8.1

Official Foreign Investment Priorities, May 1993

Classification	Millions of US$	Specification
Fuel Industry	314.0*	Coal, oil, gas refinement and transport
Machine building	234.0	Compressors for refrigerators, urban transit for L'Viv
Metallurgy	506.7	Iron, tin, magnesium
Chemical/petro	627.2	Polyalkene plastics, vinyl, synthetic. rubber
Wood processing	130.6	Three new plants
Cellulose	42.3	Straw, cardboard, bleached pulp
Food processing	99.5	Baby food, vegetable oil
Agriculture	210.0	Hybrid strains, sowing and harvesting machinery
Medical	416.8	Expanded productive capacity for insulin and antibiotics
Transport/Communication	486.5	Renovating Kiev airport
Construction	128.8	PVC pipes, shipping and packaging
Light industry	430.6	Spinning and weaving facilities

* plus DM 174.3 million

Source: Decree of Cabinet of Ministers, 1993a

There are also some ambiguous priorities, making some growth possible, yet at high opportunity costs.

The $210 million sought for agricultural research and for farm machinery upgrading is economically sound in view of Ukraine's agricultural productive capacity. This should be a top priority for investment expansion, as should food packaging and processing. Improved energy processing and energy transport capacity likewise holds potential for foreign investors since a significant portion of the USSR energy processing and refining was performed on Ukrainian soil. Improved energy refining and transport capacity can establish Ukraine as a competitive processor in the region.

A questionable target for foreign investment is in the chemical and petrochemical industries, the largest category. Since demand for products made by these industries (gasoline and other fuels, plastics, etc.) has slackened in Ukraine, it is not clear whether expansion of these industries is intended for civilian or military use.

The $486 million solicited for the reconstruction of Kiev's airport is a misplaced priority. The government's intent is reminiscent of third-world "white elephants," expensive projects designed with the intention of making key cities look more attractive to outsiders, while adding nothing to the nation's productive capacity. There are far more productive alternatives to the expansion of an airport for a city whose business volume does not justify such expensive renovations. Constructing three new wood processing plants also seems a misplaced priority. The government should instead focus first on privatizing and revamping existing plants, adding progressive managerial and organizational techniques.

Foreign capital has been, is, and will in the foreseeable future be one of the scarcest of resources in Ukraine. Efficient distribution among competing opportunities requires painstaking analysis. An official listing of foreign investment priorities should reflect economic opportunities for prospective foreign investors, as well as for resulting gains to the domestic economy. The priority list should ideally embody realistic expectations articulating how the desired foreign investment activities can directly stimulate or indirectly strengthen Ukraine's export sector, can help create backward or forward linkages, or can contribute to the development of competitive markets. Efficiency consideration over capital investment, especially over that of convertible currency investment, needs significant fine tuning on the part of Ukraine's decision makers.

PERFORMANCE

Ukrainian total investment has plummeted since independence. After gains of 3.7 and 1.9 percent in 1989 and 1990, respectively, total investment fell by 8.2 percent in 1991 before an even more precipitous decline began. Investment fell by 50 percent in 1992, and by 22 percent in 1993 (Secretariat of the Economic Commission for Europe, Geneva, 1993: 28). In the first six months of 1994, Ukraine suffered an additional 25 percent decline in investment in heavy industry. Production for the first six months of 1994 was 36 percent less than for the first six months of 1993 (Kuchma, 1994: 4). In the thirty-month period from January 1992 to July 1994, investment thus fell by a cumulative 71 percent.

As a result, the steepest losses in production occurred in the most capital-intensive industries between 1990 and 1993: natural gas (a loss of 32 percent), coal (28 percent), steel (39 percent), synthetic fiber (55 percent), rolled metal sheets (38 percent), and paper (51 percent). These declines are attributed to both the supply and demand sides. Declining investment has hampered production, while many of Ukraine's export markets have significantly weakened. Since most of the industrial enterprises are still state-owned, enterprise management looks to the government for solutions. The familiar practice of enterprise subsidies during the Soviet decades remains in Ukraine. A sizable share of state budget thus still covertly subsidizes the loss-incurring enterprises. Part of the subsidies are allocated for capital replacement in economically nonviable enterprises. Table 8.2 outlines the nation's investment by sector for the first quarter of 1994.

Table 8.2

Ukraine's Investment Distribution, lst Quarter, 1994

	billion *kbv*	%
Properties of State Enterprises	**13893.1**	**76.9**
Collective property	3344.8	18.5
Foreign	15.6	<0.1
Joint venture	51.0	0.3
Housing construction	764.7	4.2
TOTAL	18069.2	100.0

Source: National Bank of Ukraine Monetary Policy Administration, 1994: 46

This table shows how pale foreign investment in Ukraine has been. State and collective property, taken together, accounted for more then 95 percent of all investment in Ukraine for that period. Foreign and jointly-owned ventures, on the other hand, accounted for less than .05 percent of the investment total.

The small share held by foreign investors, however, understates the growth of this sector, which has been somewhat encouraging since 1991. According to one estimate, there were approximately 500 registered joint ventures in Ukraine as of

January 1, 1991, with the majority in nonindustrial production (Frydman, 1993: 111). However, according to a study conducted by the Vienna Institute for Comparative Economic Studies, there were only 214 joint ventures in Ukraine by the end of 1991 (Boss and Havlik, 1994: 31). A United Nations Economic Commission for Europe estimated that 2,000 joint enterprises existed by the end of 1992, and that by June 1993, the number had risen to 2,400 (Secretariat of the Economic Commission for Europe, Geneva, 1994: 87). Ukraine's own National Institute for Strategic Studies reported a 78 percent increase in foreign investment during the period of January to September 1993 (National Institute for Strategic Studies, 1994: 122). Finally, the Ministry of Foreign Economic Relations reported that 3,500 foreign investment ventures were registered "after the Law on Foreign Investment had been adopted" (Ukrainian National Information Service, 1994: 35). The law was enacted in 1992.

Precisely determining the volume of foreign capital inflow into Ukraine is difficult. One estimate places the cumulative foreign capital in Ukraine at $500 million as of mid-1993 (Boss and Havlik, 1994: 61). The Ministry of Foreign Economic Relations estimated the total at only $350 million by the end of 1993 (Unian, 1994: 35). Ukraine's deputy foreign minister, meanwhile, estimated the sum to be $1.5 billion as of mid-1994 (Mararenko interview, 1994). Whatever the correct amount, the total is small. In addition, the investment dollars are highly concentrated among a few major international players. Pepsi-Cola and Johnson & Johnson rank among the largest investors in Ukraine, while 40 percent of the foreign ventures in Ukraine have an initial capitalization of less than $1,000 (Ukrainian National Information Service, 1994: 35).

It is painfully clear that Ukraine has failed to induce foreign capital influx to any meaningful degree. For example, the Baltic states of Estonia, Latvia, and Lithuania, whose combined population is approximately one-fourth that of Ukraine's, have each attracted more foreign capital inflow and more foreign and joint ventures than Ukraine through 1995 (Secretariat of the Economic Commission for Europe, Geneva, 1994: 87).

APPRAISAL AND RECOMMENDATIONS

The investment difficulties Ukraine presently experiences can be attributed to several factors: the capital stock the nation inherited from the FSU, the high inflation rate, and political instability.

The capital structure of the Ukraine was adopted by a bureaucratically crafted plan, not by profit-maximizing firms interested in minimizing long-run average costs. Plants that once produced goods under the supervision of Soviet-directed managers have, on the average, become nearly worthless to private-sector entrepreneurs.

Inflation, which has ravaged the economy for four years, prevents Ukrainians from meaningful savings. Since domestic investment must be drawn from either domestic savings or foreign borrowing, and since the Ukrainian currency is unattractive as an asset, investment possibilities are curtailed. Inflation has eroded citizens' purchasing power, to the extent that most Ukrainians must expend their entire monthly earnings on basic household items. Little remains for savings.

Correcting the third problem, surrounding political instability, might prove most difficult. The creation of a politically stable and socially unified environment is time consuming. Given Ukraine's lack of experience in democratic government and its inherited ethnic diversity, the nation appears as a risky investment to prospective foreign capital. Since virtually every other former SSR has undergone some civil unrest, many foreign investors fear the same for Ukraine. Creating a politically stable environment is imperative for attracting foreign investment. In the words of the deputy foreign minister, given political stability, "money talks": "Our main problem is to convince our parliament that we do need changes in our legislation with the aim of creating a favorable investment climate. There is no problem with money [shortage] in the world. Take China, for instance. Its economy is booming. Even Taiwan is investing heavily in China. Money talks. Money smells very good" (Mararenko interview, 1994).

On a more practical level, a survey of foreign ventures in Kiev specifies the following as primary obstacles encountered by businesses from abroad:

- constantly changing laws and regulations, mentioned by 73.1 percent of the respondents;
- an underdeveloped banking system, 59.6 percent;
- unclear and unfavorable legislation, 46.2 percent;
- complicated currency conversion procedures and poor communication systems, 44.2 percent each;
- deficiency in information availability and shortage of choice business locations, 42.3 percent each; and,
- difficulties in securing essential factor supplies, 38.5 percent.(Manninen and Snelbacker, 1993: 20)

Other factors detracting from foreign investment are corruption, difficulties with local partners, and language barriers.

There are signs of promise, however. Nearly 51 percent of the respondents cite expected high returns on investment as their primary consideration for entering into the Ukrainian market; 32.1 percent are drawn by competitive factor costs, and 24.5 percent are attracted to cheap labor (ibid: 23). With the favorable and competitive conditions provided for by the December 1993 State Programme for Encouraging Foreign Investments, the "unfavorable legislation" that so many business leaders bemoaned should no longer be a major factor deterring prospective foreign investment.

Foreign investors seek competitive profit in politically stable, socially tranquil, legally secure, and administratively uncomplicated settings. Added economic incentives may serve as neutralizing forces where political and social factors are less favorable. The favorable conditions need strategic and active publicity, emphasizing the permanency of the nation's foreign investment law and regulation thereafter.

Administrative improvements can be made on three principal fronts: first, adequate training and staffing of personnel in key offices of the Foreign Investment Agency; second, simplification of application, registration, and reporting procedures; and third, closer administrative relationships between the Foreign Investment Agency and the State Property Fund. On the institutional level, six primary areas require priority attention. First, a concerted effort at demonopolizing existing factor and product markets must be made. Second, the National Bank of Ukraine must be granted functional autonomy as the nation's sole monetary authority. Third, the *karbovantsi* must be replaced with a permanent and stable domestic currency, pegged against either a strong convertible currency or the weighted averages of a basket of hard currencies. Fourth, steps must be taken to encourage the establishment of foreign branch banks to expedite domestic financial flows and foreign investors' business transactions. Fifth, the nation must undertake an accelerated program of developing capital markets, creating a climate more conducive to exchange activities. Finally, the development of a state-of-the-art infrastructural support system by granting the most favorable investment concessions to multinational corporations in relevant spheres is also an essential step. These recommendations are more reform than Ukraine is capable of undertaking simultaneously. Furthermore, none of these reforms will be without short-run costs. Ukraine cannot finance these reforms by floating bonds. No potential bond buyer would take such a risk since Ukraine's public debt is already virtually unserviceable. It is likely, therefore, that creating a healthy investment climate, including investment from abroad, is a viable option Ukraine possesses for expediting the reform process.

In conclusion, Ukraine needs to analyze its foreign investment performance, update and upgrade its foreign investment legislation and policy, reorganize its administrative apparatus, and introduce other institutional and infrastructural elements that encourage foreign investment. Substantive foreign investment is still a possibility for Ukraine. Despite its inferior performance to date, Ukraine's external economy remains one of superior potential.

NOTES

1. Foreign investments capitalized between $10,000 to $50,000 enjoy a one-year tax holiday. A five-year tax exempt status is granted to foreign legal entities investing more than $500,000 in cash or $50,000 in kind (Zubaniuk, 1994: 25). On an ascending scale, an extended tax-exempt privilege is accorded those who invest from $0.5 to $50 million, with the privileged period ranging from five to ten years.

2. As discussed earlier, the tax on repatriated profits has been waived by the December 1993 State Programme for Encouraging Foreign Investment.

9

Foreign Trade

Many of the most pressing problems Ukraine presently faces were not difficulties until the nation gained its independence. Attracting foreign investment was not a priority until ties with Moscow were severed. Price stabilization policy was severely hampered because Ukraine had no currency but the ruble, whose supply it could not control. The balance of foreign trade has likewise created difficulties that did not exist during the Soviet era. Whereas Ukraine once received strategic raw materials from other SSRs at subsidized prices, Ukraine must now pay world-market prices to purchase those materials from foreign sources. For the first time, Ukraine is in need of a foreign trade policy.

An effective foreign trade policy should encourage the import of goods most essential to structural transformation, fostering foreign trade as an engine of both restructuring and development. This chapter examines Ukraine's foreign trade problems, policy, and performance. It consists of four parts: (1) pre-independence performance and policy; (2) trade policy since independence; (3) post-independence performance; (4) evaluation and recommendations.

PRE-INDEPENDENCE PERFORMANCE AND POLICY

The centralized system's distribution regime controlled the flow of goods and services beyond the boundaries of the Ukrainian Republic; the Central Planning Commission (CPC) determined and coordinated the volume, as well as the direction, of Ukraine's interrepublic exchanges. The CPC also synchronized the volume and direction of Ukraine's exports to and imports from non-USSR trading partners, most of which were former members of the COMECON organization. Table 9.1 illustrates the relative strengths and weaknesses of Ukraine's foreign trade sector, and offers insights into the appropriate course of action for Ukraine. In the table, commodity values are priced at both foreign and domestic rates to reveal the practice of cross-subsidization under the centralized system.

Several important economic trends can be observed in Table 9.1 with little or no analysis. The table shows that Ukraine ran a trade deficit in 1990; imports of oil and gas from Russia and from the central Asian SSRs more than account for the entire deficit. The table shows that more than three-fourths of that year's commerce was carried out with other former SSRs.

Table 9.1
Ukraine's External Trade, 1990 (billions of rubles)

	World market prices		Domestic prices	
	Export	Import	Export	Import
TOTAL	43.8	51.8	45.6	54.1
foreign	7.8	9.3	7.3	15.1
interrepublic	36.0	42.4	38.3	39.0
Machine Building	20.3	19.4	17.9	18.7
foreign	3.0	4.3	2.4	5.0
interrepublic	17.3	15.2	15.5	13.7
Ferrous Metals	9.0	3.1	7.6	2.7
foreign	1.7	0.3	1.6	0.2
interrepublic	7.3	2.8	6.0	2.4
Oil and Gas	1.4	10.9	0.6	3.9
foreign	0.6	0.1	0.3	0.1
interrepublic	0.8	10.8	0.3	3.8
Food Industry	3.0	2.2	6.7	4.0
foreign	0.2	1.5	0.5	2.2
interrepublic	2.8	0.7	6.1	1.8

Source: World Bank, 1992: 402–403

The heavy interrepublic import and export of machine-building materials reflects the chain of production in the former Soviet system. Most of the production in Ukraine added value to, yet did not finalize, goods whose production was begun in other regions of the country.

The data also help reveal a less obvious trend: plan-mandated cross-subsidization. Imports from non-Soviet sources were intentionally overvalued, while exports to non-Soviet outlets were intentionally undervalued. This discouraged Ukraine from seeking external markets for its products, forced the Ukrainian trade sector into subsidizing the USSR central budget, and contributed to the overvaluation of the ruble. The practice also reflected the Soviet quest for self-sufficiency. While other industrial nations were encouraging foreign trade, the Soviet government and other Eastern European governments tried undermining the expansion of foreign commerce.

Since the Soviet planning system merely invented the prices for interrepublic trade, allocative inefficiency was widespread. In addition, commerce between two Communist nations was made difficult by the fact that each preferred that their own arbitrary price system be used. In practice, unless trade represented an open subsidy from one Communist country to another, two Communist economies engaged in bilateral trade invariably resorted to prices determined by free market nations for the goods they traded. Marshall Goldman, an American economist who has studied the Soviet Union and post-Soviet reforms, once asked the minister of the Soviet economy how, if all the world's nations were Communist, any international trade could take place. The minister responded with a laugh, "We'll have to leave one [country] capitalist, then."

Since the interrepublic prices of oil and gas understated the world market price by almost two-thirds, Ukrainian industry received an essential factor at low cost. Today, the nation can no longer purchase fuel at the subsidized price. They must pay the full international market price for oil. Since all nonbarter transactions between CIS nations now take place with convertible currencies, Ukraine must now import essential production and consumption factors at much higher prices, but it sells less of its exports for lack of markets. As a result, production has declined as firms' marginal cost curves revert upward and leftward.

The only glimmer of hope comes from the agricultural sector. It is the only export segment that has remained stable, even when expressed in terms of convertible currencies, and it is the only sector that apparently possesses realizable potential for growth in the near future. Since demand for food products in the CIS community remains highly elastic, any supplier of low-cost goods still can easily export to the CIS. This advantage can bolster the benefits stemming from foreign investment and economic restructuring discussed in previous chapters.

In 1992, after the Soviet Union and its subsidizing mechanism had dissolved, Ukraine's trade deficit swelled to $2.9 billion, owing mostly to the soaring prices of imported oil and natural gas. The turnover of meat, cotton, crude oil, coal, iron ore,

ferrous metal manufactures, steel tubing, and many other products declined sub-
stantially between 1991 and 1992. The only notable exception was natural gas,
whose import volume remained relatively stable (International Monetary Fund, 1993:
111–112).

Exposure to world market prices has reduced the import ability of all former
Communist states. By introducing a rational, effective trade policy, Ukraine can reap
significant benefits.

TRADE POLICY SINCE INDEPENDENCE

Trade immediately after independence continued primarily along the lines of pre-
independence practices. There have been few legal trade barriers. Other than the
articles explicitly prohibited by law, all economic subjects may import goods or
services after paying relatively low import duties. The imposition of tariffs began in
early 1993, and tariffs range from zero to 10 percent on most imports. The rates are
slightly higher on luxury goods and on goods whose domestic producers require
some degree of protection from undue foreign competition. Tariffs have been
reduced on imports from the few countries that have signed free trade agreements
with Ukraine, or have been eliminated altogether if the imports are from the poorest
economies in the world, as specified by the General System of Preferences
(International Monetary Fund, 1993: 52–53).

Bilateral agreements between the Ukrainian government and its CIS partners have
determined most external trade, primarily with respect to exports. Ukraine's
Ministry of Foreign Economic Activity, paralleling Soviet practices, assigned
composite quotas to branch ministries, which in turn allotted apportionments to state-
designated firms for fulfilling the authorized export quotas.

Many of the state-assigned export quotas were fulfilled by enterprises exercising
monopolistic powers. The state-authorized export quotas attach additional power to
the enterprises, authorizing them as export monopolies as well. Along with ready
entry into state-brokered foreign markets, the authorized exporters enjoyed
"centralized provision of critical inputs, better access to bank credits, . . . [and] in
1993 exports under quota [were] also exempt from export tax" (ibid: 51). Such
noncompetitive benefits were unavailable to other firms, which had to cope with the
sudden dissipation of product markets upon the dissolution of the USSR.

The exporters, as authorized by the state, negotiated export prices directly with
recipient enterprises in CIS countries. The retained foreign currency earnings from
the transactions enabled the designated exporters to import the much-needed capital
goods and other essential factors from either the CIS or Western markets as they
deemed appropriate. This added amenity was denied the nonexporting producers.
Since trade benefits were awarded by government sanction, Ukraine could not readily
be considered a free-trade nation.

Under the banner of market reform, former president Kravchuk issued a decree on March 19, 1992 entitled Regarding Steps to Stimulate Foreign Economic Activity. The decree featured three focal points:

- To establish that all subjects of foreign economic activity in Ukraine have the right to realize foreign economic operation in the export of goods . . . and the import of goods;
- [directing the Cabinet of Ministers] to present for parliamentary review a shortened—not more than 200 trade items—list of export products, which will be subject to a regime of export licensing and quotas;
- Subjects of economic activity on the territory of Ukraine have the right without specific permission to settle accounts in any freely convertible currency [until a permanent national currency is introduced]. (Decree of the President of Ukraine, 1992)

It was not clear whether "all subjects of foreign economic activity in Ukraine" refered to all Ukrainian citizens or only to those designated by the state for foreign trade activities. The May 1993 Decree of the Cabinet of Ministers of Ukraine on Liberalization of Foreign Economic Activities stipulates that the "basis for granting of (export) license is (the) receiving of quota or guarantee of export tax payment by crossing a customs border of Ukraine, if goods are exported above quota" (Decree of the Cabinet of Ministers, 1993b: para. 6).

Thus, it was not until May 1993 that enterprises outside of the quota system were granted export licenses, on the provision that they purchase export quotas at the Ministry of Foreign Economic Relations–sanctioned quota auctions. Despite these slightly liberalized export provisions, state regulations and constraints on foreign trade still remained as of mid-1993. Other administrative decrees of early 1993, under the guise of liberalizing trade, "actually expanded the number of goods subject to quotas, . . . and added a new category of 'strategic exports.' Quotas were extended, covering 390 products, as opposed to 180 the year before" (International Monetary Fund, 1993: 51, 52).

A March 1992 presidential decree granted firms the freedom to "settle accounts in any freely convertible currency" until a permanent Ukrainian currency is introduced (Decree of the President of Ukraine, 1992). The February 19, 1993 government decree, however, directed that 50 percent of foreign earnings from all exporters must be converted into local currency and traded on the local currency market (Ministry of Economy, 1993c: 20). "Trading on the local currency market" means interbank auction of convertible currencies, with the number of banks, as well as which banks, participating in the auction being determined by the state. As a result, distortions emerged in commodity markets, and, worse, exporters only reluctantly remitted their foreign earnings back home.

It was in late 1993 that huge amounts of foreign earnings began to accumulate abroad. It became unprofitable to return the hard currency earnings paid to Ukraine. This is related to currency exchange policy. Before, enterprises tried to produce quality products which could be exported for convertible currencies. With that, the firms could import the needed factors from the West. Firms also used to purchase hard currencies at free-market exchange rates to import needed factor supplies. Now, the hard currency earnings are taken away, and in return the firms are given a certain amount of *karbovantsi*. (Dorofeyev interview, 1994)

In summary, the state's intent on short-term gains in exchange for control over foreign earnings, especially under a contrived foreign exchange regime, has resulted in extensive long-term loss. The unrealistic interbank foreign exchange auction rate, combined with the mandatory 50 percent surrender of foreign earnings at this contrived exchange rate, adversely affected foreign trade and encouraged capital flight. A closer examination of ramifications from these two factors follows.

Although the official, auction, and black market rates were synchronized in August 1993, vast divergences among the three emerged shortly thereafter, discouraging the retention of convertible currencies in domestic markets. This compromised the orderly conduct of external transactions.

As may be observed in Table 9.2, the official, auction and street exchange rates nearly paralleled each other between April and August 1993; the official exchange and the UICE auction rates were officially and artificially aligned during the months of April through August 1993. In addition, at least in the short run, the obligatory exchange of 50 percent of foreign earnings by domestic exporters spuriously increased the supply of convertible currencies, temporarily buoying the *karbovantsi*'s exchange value.

In August 1993, the auction rate was separated from the official exchange rate. The auction rate then plummeted to roughly one-third the value of the official exchange rate. Since only state-designated enterprises have ready access to the official exchange rate, independent traders must compete for convertible currencies on the domestic market at either the interbank auction rate or at rates approaching those of the black market. Consequently, trade monopoly endures, excluding the majority of firms from fair competition for external markets and for cheaper convertible currencies at the official exchange rate.

Equally detrimental to the economy is the state-designated exporters' practice of holding convertible currencies abroad. After the law requiring that 50 percent of foreign earnings be converted into local currency came into effect, underreporting and falsifying of profits became widespread. Many exporters, afraid of holding the wildly unstable *karbovantsi,* kept their unreported foreign earnings abroad. Instead of productive capital accumulation, capital leaked into foreign financial markets. In the words of a high government official: "There are between 6 to 8 billion dollars in the country. But there are between 15 to 18 billion abroad in foreign banks. Nobody keeps hard currency here in local banks" (Mararenko interview, 1994).

Table 9.2

Official, Auction, and Street Exchange Rates of the *kbv* to the U.S. Dollar

(January 1993–December 1994)			
Date	**NBU Official Rate**	**Auction Rate***	**Street**
1/01/93	638	749	2
2/01/93	931	1002	2.7
3/01/93	1036	1502	2000
4/01/93	2180	2180	2200
5/01/93	3000	3000	3000
6/01/93	2999	2999	3100
7/01/93	3980	3980	3350
8/01/93	5760	5760	n/a
9/01/93	5970	16900	8400
10/01/93	5970	16950	15850
11/01/93	5970	31000	25000
12/01/93	7090	31150	25000
1/01/94	12610	25000	37000
2/01/94	12610	25000	39500
3/01/94	12610	30200	38500
4/01/94	12610	31120	43000
5/01/94	12610	36800	45000
6/01/94	15100	39950	54000
7/01/94	17500	39970	4600
8/01/94	19500	39970	46000
9/01/94	20500	40400	52500
10/01/94	28000	47200	72000
11/01/94	79800	79800	95000
12/01/94	110200	110200	133000

* The auction rate is the UICI (Ukrainian Interbank Currency Exchange) rate.

Source: Ministry of Economy, 1994c: 27

An unrealistic official exchange rate, combined with the public's lack of trust in local financial institutions, promotes the leakage of one of the nation's scarcest resources. Decreed measures proudly proclaiming trade liberalization have, in fact, restrained competition. Economics is the study of cause and effect, not the study of hopes and intentions.

These perversions were finally eliminated in the cabinet of ministers' decree No. 734 of November 1, 1994. Under pressure from the International Monetary Fund (IMF), the Ministers eliminated nearly all trade quotas, in effect voiding the restrictive and inconsistent provisions of twenty-three other decrees or legislative acts (Frishberg, 1994: 8). Since foreign trade constitutes a vital aspect of Ukraine's economic lifeline, decree No. 734 may have finally removed the bulk of obstacles to the emergence of a potentially vibrant and competitive foreign trade sector in Ukraine.

POST-INDEPENDENCE PERFORMANCE

President Kuchma's directive for reemphasizing and restoring Ukraine's traditional trading relationship with other republics of the FSU is a move toward recapturing some of the lost ground in the trade sector. The president had potential markets in CIS countries in mind when he repeatedly criticized the previous administrations' impulsive attempts at distancing Ukraine from the republics of the FSU. The fact that trade with non-CIS nations declined in the short run should not be surprising. This can be traced to Ukraine's minimal contact with the rest of the world's markets for the previous seven decades. A sizeable share of the steep decreases in interrepublic trade, however, came as the result of decision makers' distancing Ukraine's economy from the other republics of the FSU. This policy detracted from Ukraine's efforts at a systemic transformation. Kuchma, in his October 11, 1994 address to the Supreme Rada, thus insisted that "decisive measures be taken, aimed at reestablishing artificially-broken economic ties (with CIS countries), eliminating economically unsound tariff and payment obstacles affecting export and import operations. At the same time, measures will be carried out aimed at the radical reconstruction of existing systems for cooperation with these countries on the basis of mutual benefit and economic expediency" (Kuchma, 1994: 36).

The emphasis on reestablishing close cooperation among the republics of the FSU is Kuchma's attempt at stabilizing Ukraine's disrupted external economic relationships. His rationale is sound: since the move toward world market pricing for exports and settling accounts in convertible currencies became fashionable among newly liberalized economies, interrepublic trade among CIS economies has contracted. In realigning domestic prices with those of the world market levels and exact payments in hard currencies, Ukraine and other newly liberalized economies have aimed at selling in Western markets, erroneously assuming that their products are competitive.

Ukrainian products, however, are not of the caliber that the West demands. Other than raw materials and products from the agricultural sector, the majority of Ukraine's exports previously destined for interrepublic exchanges were only parts or semi-finished products. The demand for these products on the world market is tepid at best. More than one-seventh of the firms in Ukraine are no longer viable now that subsidies have been withdrawn. These firms cannot even make an accounting profit, much less cover their opportunity costs. Especially in the industrial sector, the quality of the products Ukraine intends for export is low. As a result, any efforts at cracking Western markets are likely to be futile. An analysis of the nation's post-independence trade performance can help reveal some of the distinct characteristics of Ukraine's trade sector.

Trade in 1992

Despite severe contractions in its external sector since independence, Ukraine is still heavily dependent on CIS economies for trade, as is evident in the figures presented in Table 9.3.

Table 9.3
Ukraine's Trade Performance for 1992 (in billion *kbv*)

	Exports	**Imports**	**Turnover**	**Balance**
Manufactured	1072	987	2059	85
interrepublic	773	922	1695	-149
rest of world	299	65	364	234
Consumer	135	123	258	12
interrepublic	117	94	211	23
rest of world	18	29	47	-11
TOTAL	1207	1110	2317	97
interrepublic	890	1016	1906	-126
rest of world	317	94	411	223

Source: Ministry of Economy, 1993a: 16

The first full year of trade statistics for Ukraine are not as bleak as a visceral glance might suggest. The trade sector can become an engine for growth in Ukraine, if the correct policies are pursued.

Eighty-two percent of Ukraine's commercial activity for 1992 was conducted with other former SSRs, including 93 percent of Ukraine's imports and 72 percent of its exports. Though imports from these nations declined by 34 percent from the previous year and exports fell by 27 percent, Ukraine continued to be heavily dependent on other CIS and Baltic states for both inputs and markets.

That Ukraine incurred such a large trade defecit with these nations is both reason for concern and reason for optimism. The primary cause of Ukraine's interrepublic trade deficit stems from oil and natural gas imports, especially from Russia and Turkmenistan. If this segment of the commercial sector is excluded, Ukraine's exports in 1992 exceeded its imports. This suggests markets exist for Ukrainian products, especially in the former Communist world, and that an import substitution policy is feasible. Ukraine is in a better position than any other former SSR except Russia for achieving self-sufficiency.

A well-crafted energy policy, therefore, can significantly reduce Ukraine's costly financial outflows owing to oil and natural gas imports. Such a policy would necessarily phase out subsidies for energy consumption. The state can offer tax incentives for improved energy efficiency in industry, agriculture, and mining, and tax privileges for energy efficient new investments. It can also use tax policy for discouraging inefficient energy consumers, and offer privileges to foreign investors interested in establishing energy-refining processes in Ukraine. Policy along this line could help weed out nonviable industries whose energy consumption imposes opportunity costs, could enhance investment, and help the nation develop the trade surplus it needs for the acquisition of hard currency.

Despite significant decreases in both imports and exports in 1992, Ukraine's 1992 trade performance underscores its potential in exploiting foreign trade as a potent mechanism for growth. According to official estimates, Ukraine's 1992 trade turn-over equaled 47.4 percent of GDP, a significantly higher percent than in either the United States or Japan. Sustained expansion in the foreign trade sector can contribute to a speedier systemic and structural transformation.

Trade in 1993[1]

A direct statistical comparison between 1992 and 1993 trade performance in Ukraine is difficult due to the hyperinflation sustained in 1993. Table 9.4, however, can render a varied perspective on Ukraine's 1993 foreign trade relationships and performance.

By 1993, the foreign trade outlook for Ukraine stood in contrast to the promising figures for 1992. Instead of a trade surplus, Ukraine sustained a 549 billion *kbv* deficit in 1993. Although the trade deficit in 1993 represented a meager 0.7 percent of the trade turnover for the year, it was a notable departure from the 4.2 percent surplus in 1992. Ukraine registered trade surplus against all trading partners other than Russia, Turkmenistan, and Lithuania. Its trade deficits for the year with Russia, Turkmenistan, and Lithuania were 7.1, 5.7, and 0.5 billion *kbv*, respectively.

Ukraine's interrepublic trade deficit in 1992 was 127 billion *kbv*, or 6.7 percent of interrepublic turnover for the year. It reached 13.3 trillion *kbv* in 1993, or 23.1

percent of interrepublic turnover.[2]   Much of this can be attributed to the rapid
increase in the price of oil and other imported products. The year 1993 also marked
a departure from Ukraine's traditional trading patterns. While in 1992, 74 percent
of the nation's exports headed to other former SSRs, interrepublic activity accounted
for only 60 percent of exports in 1993. Likewise, the proportion of imports coming
from non-Soviet sources rose from 8.0 percent in 1992 to 10.7 percent in 1993.
Although ill prepared, Ukraine attempted to redirect the focus of its trade toward
Western markets. Ukraine's 1993 trade surplus against "the rest of the world" was
14.5 percent that of the year's total turnover, up from 9.7 percent over 1992. This
suggests Ukraine's continued disposition toward expanded trade with "the rest of the
world."

Table 9.4

Ukraine's Foreign Trade in 1993 (in billion *kbv*)

Areas	Foreign Trade Turnover	Exports	Imports	Balance
Total Invest. Goods	77119.5	38285.4	38834.1	-548.7
Total Consum. Goods	68644.8	31073.7	37571.1	-8497.4
Azerbaijan	1176.9	904.7	1263.0	5949.7
Belarus	3115.5	1708.0	1407.5	300.5
Armenia	70.9	45.0	25.9	19.1
Georgia	132.5	69.5	63.1	6.4
Kazakhstan	957.6	557.9	399.7	158.2
Kirgizstan	83.8	42.3	41.5	0.8
Latvia	317.0	163.7	153.3	10.4
Lithuania	1120.7	304.0	816.7	-512.7
Moldova	529.6	369.0	160.6	208.4
Russia	41726.8	17312.4	24414.4	-7102.0
Tajikistan	48.6	27.9	20.7	7.2
Turkmenistan	7490.6	950.9	6539.7	-5588.8
Uzbekistan	714.5	453.9	260.6	193.3
Estonia	163.3	55.8	107.5	-51.7
Rest of world	19471.11	15320.41	4150.7	11169.7

Source: Ministry of Statistics of Ukraine, 1994e: 89–91

Ukraine's combined trade deficit against Russia and Turkmenistan in 1993 was 12.7 trillion *kbv*. Its negative balance of payments in natural gas for the year was 18.0 trillion *kbv*. For diesel fuel imports, it was 2.1 trillion *kbv*, oil 2.0 trillion *kbv*, gasoline 0.95 trillion *kbv*, and coal 0.24 trillion *kbv* (Ministry of Statistics, 1994e: 89). Ukraine's combined negative balance in energy imports alone, therefore, was already 23.3 trillion *kbv* for the year, nearly doubling its combined trade deficits against Russia and Turkmenistan. In other words, abstracting deficits from energy imports, Ukraine's exports to Russia and Turkmenistan in 1993 exceeded its import needs from the same two energy-rich economies.

Although Ukraine registered a positive trade balance against the other republics of the FSU for 1993 (973 billion *kbv*), the surplus constitutes only 1.26 percent of the year's total trade turnover. Export promotion in these CIS countries needs a more determined approach.

Trade 1994 (January-June)[3]

By mid-1994, clearer patterns began emerging, as the severest of economic distortions had begun subsiding, and as institutional reforms began to take shape. Though it had become painfully clear that Ukraine would not likely make major inroads into Western markets, several promising trends had developed among other economies in the Eastern hemisphere.

The interrepublic scenario remained largely unchanged. Ukraine incurred large trade deficits with Russia and Turkmenistan, solely because of energy purchases. The balance of interrepublic trade for the first half of 1994 broke down as follows:

Table 9.5
Interrepublic Trade, January–June 1994 (in billions of $US)

	Export	Import
Belarus/	.14	.14
Moldova	.13	.05
Russia	1.12	1.73
Turkmenistan	.03	.17
Lithuania	.09	.10
Other FSSRs	.16	.16
TOTAL	1.67	2.35

Source: Ministry of Statistics, 1994c

If energy imports are excluded, Ukraine ran a small surplus with the former Soviet republics. This demonstrates continued export potential. Though heavy industry still accounted for three times as much of the export total as did agricultural products, Ukraine continued to develop markets for meat and dairy products throughout the FSU.

In the rest of Europe, meanwhile, Ukraine ran a small surplus, based on trade with select nations. (See Table 9.6.) Contrary to popular belief, more than 60 percent of commercial dealings in Europe were performed with established Western democracies.

Table 9.6

Trade with Europe, January-June 1994 (in millions of $US)

	Export	Import	Turnover	Balance
Eastern Europe	266.8	229.9	496.7	36.9
Western Europe	440.3	407.0	847.3	33.3
total Europe	707.1	636.9	1344.0	70.2

Source: Ministry of Statistics, 1994c

This is not necessarily cause for optimism, however. The non-Communist nations with which Ukraine ran the largest surpluses—Greece, Ireland, and Italy—were not the wealthiest nations of Europe. Ukraine has not generated much trade with France, the United Kingdom, Germany, or the Benelux nations, the "inner circle" of the European Union (EU). Germany accounts for more of Ukraine's import total than any nation except Russia; Ukraine has incurred a $120 million trade deficit with the "economic engine of Europe."

Ukrainian industrial products, such as rolled steel, automobiles, and synthetic compounds, have proven themselves to be inferior goods in Europe. Ukraine's agricultural output, however, can appeal to nations of all income levels.

This is especially true of Asia, in which populations are continuing to grow. That even the poorer nations of Asia, such as China and Vietnam, have begun experiencing rapid economic growth suggests a booming market for Ukrainian agricultural products.

In sum, Ukraine's foreign trade since independence has outperformed its foreign investment sector. Ukraine's heavy reliance on oil and natural gas imports from Russia and Turkmenistan has been one of the two prime factors for its negative trade balance in recent years. The other is the fact that Russia and Turkmenistan have implemented policies aligning oil and natural gas export prices with world-market levels. Other than significant trade deficits with Russia, Turkmenistan, Germany, and Sweden, Ukraine's overall trade with the "rest of the world" paints a promising picture for future foreign earnings. However, much improvement is needed in Ukraine's foreign trade policy and practices before Ukriane can reap the full benefit of external trade. The remainder of this chapter evaluates Ukraine's foreign trade position, its policy and procedures. The chapter concludes with recommendations for possible consideration.

EVALUATION AND RECOMMENDATION

Ukraine's economy is neither Communist nor market. It is a transitional economy undergoing severe disruptions and dislocations, complicated by distorted visions and unwilling politicians. Amidst deep gloom in most economic spheres, and despite its negative balance of payments in recent years, Ukraine's foreign trade sector still projects a ray of hope. Ukraine can offer much to markets abroad, provided it promptly focuses on the more competitive sectors of the economy while system-atically reducing resource flows to the nonviable sectors.

Currently 115 nations worldwide have trade relationships with Ukraine. Republics of the FSU remain Ukraine's major trading partners, with Russia leading the way. In 1993, Ukraine's exports consisted mainly of semifinished products and raw materials, followed by heavy industry (32.6 percent) and agricultural products (11.3 percent). Exports in the service sector remain elusive. The world market for industrial raw materials and nonstrategic metals is highly competitive and nearly saturated. Unless Ukraine uses well-coordinated and assertive export strategies, there is little oppor-tunity for expansion in this sector.

Ukraine's heavy industry, as a whole, remains mired in inefficient productive practices from the past. Other than CIS economies, where limited markets still exist for rolled metal, lorries, cast iron, cars, aluminum, buses, and ferrous alloys, Ukraine's export potential from its heavy industry is limited at best. In particular, Ukraine should expect steady decreases in demand from Russia for these products, as that nation continues pursuing self-sufficiency.

Ukraine's heavy dependence on energy imports casts a long shadow over its balance of payments scenario. Nearly 60 percent of Ukraine's current imports and less than 0.5 percent of its exports are in energy-related fields. Natural gas alone accounted for 46.5 percent of Ukraine's 1993 total imports, followed by diesel fuel (5.6 percent), oil (5.3 percent), and gasoline (2.5 percent). Ukraine's energy imports originate nearly exclusively from Turkmenistan and Russia and account for approxi-mately three-fourths of Ukraine's 1993 total gross imports. Ukraine's largest deficits have consistently been with Russia and Turkmenistan; there has been a moderate surplus from rest of the world. It is nonetheless highly significant that if fuel imports are excluded, Ukraine holds a larger trade surplus with Russia than with any other nation.

Ukraine's largest non-CIS trading partner is China, with a total turnover of $837 million in 1994. Most of Ukraine's exports to China in 1994 were chemicals and metals. The current balance of payment with China is overwhelmingly in Ukraine's favor, with exports constituting 90 percent of turnover. More importantly, China has begun to purchase machinery from Ukraine, including hardware produced by its military-industrial complex. It was toward that end that Ukraine's defense minister, Valerii Shmarov, visited China in early April 1995, as a participant in a meeting of the Chinese-Ukrainian Commission on Trade and Economic Cooperation (OMRI, April 4 & 10, 1995). A potentially vast market exists in China for Ukraine's select science and technology exports.

Ukraine's potential for exporting to developed market economies depends on two main variables: how promptly Ukraine's manufacturing sector can begin producing cost-effective quality finished—in contrast to semi-finished—products, and how effectively Ukraine can negotiate the lowering of nontariff barriers in respective developed economies. Approaching both these imposing tasks in the near future requires Ukraine's short-term strategy to focus on export activities wherever a comparative advantage exists. Japan's post–World War II trade policy can serve as a point of reference for Ukraine's economy. Finally, in view of Ukraine's current state of economic conditions, export growth in less developed economies must be given more serious consideration. A humble yet realistic approach to foreign trade promises more rewarding dividends than theorizing and planning lofty but largely unattainable objectives.

Objective circumstances dictate the necessity of reevaluating Ukraine's foreign trade bearing. Terms of trade have been turning against Ukraine's trade sector, especially in view of world market pricing on imported oil and natural gas in recent years. Practical difficulties are encountered on nearly all levels of attempts at penetrating the developed economies' markets. In tapping into Ukraine's potential in its foreign trade sector, two principal domains merit undivided attention.

First, Ukraine's parliament and administration need to conclusively enact and implement a consistent and progressive foreign trade policy. As it stands, "there is a notable lack of state programs for foreign trade development" (National Institute for Strategic Studies, 1994: 41). Influenced by the traditional mentality of exercising control, Ukraine's government continues mending legislative flaws and administrative inconsistencies by incessantly issuing new laws, decrees, edicts, and regulations governing foreign trade. These corollary laws often confuse rather than clarify, and irritate rather than appease domestic and foreign economic subjects alike.

For example, in response to the question "How do you assess current legislation regulating the import/export activity (in Ukraine)?" two representatives from a foreign trading firm in Kiev answered as follows:

Frankly speaking, it is difficult to keep track of your laws. We understand that young Ukraine seeks after and improves something continuously and adopts three decrees a day (over foreign trade). We will wait until you find it at last and just then will (we) sit and study everything thoroughly. We expect that laws hold on for a longer time.

And,

I have not met such export laws anywhere in the world. . . . The state of legislation is such that if one obeys to the letter, nothing can be achieved at all. That is why many run away from here. (quoted in Chini, 1994: 34)

Ukraine is in need of a definitive piece of foreign trade legislation and a conclusively articulated import/export policy. These reforms must possess clarity, consistency, credibility, feasibility, simplicity, and practicality. The element of practicality should include competitive tariffs for imported capital goods and export incentives for products for which foreign markets exist. Ukrainian trade policy can liberalize exports by eliminating the existing export quota system, as well as the mandatory conversion of 50 percent of foreign earnings into national currency. The creation of economic opportunities and incentives for domestic subjects is in itself a safeguard and stimulus for hard currency reinvestment in the domestic economy.

The second sphere warranting coordinated efforts lies in a critical reevaluation of Ukraine's import needs and export potential. Wherever international agreements permit, higher tariff barriers would discourage the import of nonessential consumer goods. Conversely, the government may grant additional incentives for the import-ation of goods and services, thus creating and strengthening forward and backward linkages in productive activities.

On the export side, Ukraine is capable of aircraft manufacture and shipbuilding, as well as the manufacture of select military engineering and metallurgical products. This potential, however, exists only for a limited duration. As CIS economies stabilize and as the Chinese economy continues its rapid growth, future external demand for products in these industries will dwindle. Ukraine's traditionally industry-based economy is neither economically viable nor functionally efficient. Given objective circumstances, Ukraine's restructuring efforts must depend proportionately more on its most promising sector instead of attempting haphazard preservation of its existing structure on a dysfunctional life-support system.

Ukraine's most overlooked potential, at least in the short run, resides in its primary sector. Ukraine is eminently endowed with productive potential in the agricultural sector, and it is surrounded by republics of the FSU whose natural environment is less benevolent to agricultural production. Therefore, exploiting Ukraine's produc-tive and export potential in the primary sector is sensible, as well as economically sound. As Ukraine's National Institute for Strategic Studies suggests: "Improvement of agricultural technology, and re-equipment of the processing and grocery [sic] sectors with up-to-date technology will result in rapid rewards and should be a priority in terms of export growth potential" (National Institute for Strategic Studies, 1994: 38)

Concerted efforts in agricultural production, storaging, processing, packaging, and exporting can significantly improve Ukraine's current account scenario and strengthen other sectors' endeavors at structural transformation. It was along this line of reasoning that president Kuchma demanded the formulation of

an export oriented strategy for economic development on the basis of the comprehensive formation and effective implementation of Ukraine's export potential in the primary sector of the economy. . . . It is precisely this strategy which is intended to become a material basis for the integration of our country into the world economic arena, to serve as one of the veritable "locomotives" that will pull the Ukrainian economy out of its deep crisis, and to safeguard the institutional transformation of the economy. (Kuchma, 1994: 35)

Comparative advantages in Ukraine's agricultural sector exist in ample proportions. Current and future external markets also exist. Therefore, aside from selectively emphasizing export potentials in given industrial branches, proportionately heavy emphasis could be placed on Ukraine's agricultural sector. Policy direction in this respect should include market information, farm credits, reduced tariffs on imports of essential inputs, tax credits to agriculturally related industries, supplementary incentives to foreign investments therein, and active market research abroad for product distribution.

In conclusion, Ukraine's foreign trade policy needs overall reevaluation, further liberalization, and governmental coordination. Ukraine must conclusively and permanently redefine its long-term foreign trade policy. A liberalized trade policy must also seek the reestablishment of trade relationships with both traditional and new partners. A rationally crafted foreign trade policy can serve as a veritable engine for Ukraine's economic restructuring and growth.

NOTES

1. The principal supplementary reference for this part of the analysis is: *Statistical Bulletin*, January-February 1994, the Ministry of Statistics of Ukraine.

2. Detailed data for this section's analysis are derived from the Ministry of Statistics's *Statistical Bulletin*, 1994e.

3. Detailed data for this section's analysis are derived from the Ministry of Statistics's publications, 1994e and 1994f.

10

Public Finance

Ukraine's public policy has on the average been characterized by an inconsistent, ambiguous, and uncoordinated series of desultory laws and decrees. Nowhere have these characteristics been more evident, or more counterproductive, than in the field of fiscal policy. Fiscal policy, when rationally applied, can encourage stability and promote growth and structural transformation. As applied in Ukraine, however, public finance policy has intensified existing crises and dislocations. Since economic stability is a prerequisite for transformation, fiscal reform should be a top priority.

This chapter presents an examination of the budgeting and allocating processes, government revenues and expenditures, and recommendations for a more rational approach to fiscal policy for Ukraine.

BUDGETARY PROCESSES AND PRACTICES

In the United States, the federal, state, regional, and local governments prepare their own budgets, levy taxes, and apportion disbursements. Consolidated budgets, as practiced in Ukraine, encompass aggregated revenues and expenditures of all levels of government. Comparable to revenue sharing in the United States, regional and local governments receive shares of taxable revenues and disbursement responsibilities based on their respective characteristics.

In Ukraine, the main sources of government revenue include personal and corporate income taxes, payroll deductions for social security contributions, value added (VAT) and excise taxes, and import and export duties. The personal income tax is progressive in nature. Marginal tax rates range from zero for the lowest levels of income to 50 percent for income earned beyond thirty times the minimum wage. Enterprises pay taxes on profits, payroll, value added, property, and export/import duties. An 18 percent tax is imposed on enterprise profit, 28 percent on value added, and 52 percent on the payroll; 31.8 percent of the total payroll goes to the Pension Fund, 5.2 percent to the Social Security Fund, 3 percent to the Employment Fund, and 12 percent to the Chernobyl fund[1] (International Monetary Fund, 1993: 125–126). Excise tax is levied on select commodities, with rates ranging from 10 to 85 percent. VAT and enterprise profit taxes formed the largest segments of total revenue during fiscal 1992. By 1993, the government shifted the emphasis of its corporate tax policy, reducing the burden of VAT and increasing indirect taxes like excise and import/export duties.

Tax exemptions and reductions are granted to various economic subjects or productive activities. Income tax exemption, for instance, is granted to agricultural producers and coal miners, while VAT is waived for exports to convertible currency markets. Social security and pension benefits are exempt from personal income taxes. Hard currency foreign investments are granted a host of tax exemptions, with added tax privileges for those engaged in food production, agricultural processing, and select electrical appliances manufacturing (Zubaniuk, 1994: 25).

Ukraine's state budget consists of budgetary and extrabudgetary disbursements. Budgetary apportionment covers expenditures on the national economy, administrative expenses, social safety net expenditures, health, education, science, and the Chernobyl Fund. Expenditure on the "national economy" has largely become a euphemism for subsidizing agriculture, energy consumption, manufacturing, and public transport. Extrabudgetary allocation, on the other hand, consists of employment, pension, and social insurance funds.

Expenditures on social programs account for more than two-thirds of the budgetary account, with general subsidies alone absorbing nearly one-third of the total budgetary disbursement. General subsidies are channeled to consumers, households, enterprises, and health and education programs. Consumer subsidies, for instance, are extended by way of controlling prices over food, medicine, housing, and public utilities. More than twenty categories of allowances or cash benefits apply to household subsidies, including grants to low-income families and adjustable allowances to families with children of diverse age groups.

In addition to budgetary and extrabudgetary expenditures, there exists a third category of quasi-government disbursement. Informally referred to as nonbudgetary allocation, it refers to amounts designated extemporaneously by the parliament for lending to specific sectors or for designated purposes. Since nonbudgetary appropriation has no source of revenue, the parliament, via the Ministry of Finance, directs the National Bank in extending government-guaranteed long or short-term credits to the designated recipients at nominal interest rates. The practice is part of the Soviet legacy. Agricultural and industrial producers alike benefited from the practice during the Soviet era.

In 1991, nonbudgetary expenditure equaled roughly 4 percent of the nation's GDP. By 1992, this figure had climbed to 16 percent (International Monetary Fund, 1993:

28).   Much of the loose credit has served consumption rather than productive purposes, including credits to select enterprises with debt payments due. This policy of easy credit and subsidy has fueled Ukraine's incendiary inflation.

BUDGET 1992

Frequent administrative changes, bureaucratic inertia, and ideological divisions between the branches of government have brought frequent tardiness in budget submissions. The 1992 budget, for example, was not approved until June 1992. Governments thus operate on temporary authorization from parliament.

The Ukrainian government under former prime minister Fokin envisioned tight controls over budgetary expenditures for 1992. Planned fiscal reforms included the introduction of VAT, more direct taxation, a legislatively mandated limit on the state budget deficit (not to exceed 1 percent of GNP for the year), a legislative prohibition on deficit financing through borrowing from the National Bank of Ukraine, reductions in consumer and enterprise subsidies, including the cessation of assistance to financially insolvent enterprises, along with the abolition of all extrabudgetary funds outside of the Pension, Social Security, Employment, and Chernobyl Funds (Cabinet of Ministers of Ukraine, 1993: 2.5.1).

In *The Programme of Economic Reforms and Policy in Ukraine*, a 1992 document adopted by the Council of Ministers for presentation to the IMF, Fokin's ambitious agenda was reemphasized. Proposed measures for improving fiscal discipline included the following:

- Grants and subsidies to non-profitable enterprises are being canceled, expenditures on defense are being cut;
- Reducing budget expenditures (by limiting) the sums of subsidies for prices for goods and services;
- Legal limitation of ensured deficit of the state budget is going to be introduced. (Cabinet of Ministers of Ukraine, 1992b: ch. 2)

Government plans, including adopted budgets, however, often differ from outcomes. According to the IMF, Ukraine's projected budget deficit was set at 2 percent of its GDP, with revenue equal to 43 percent of the GDP and expenditure equal to 45 percent. Total expenditure for the year did not vary much from the IMF projection; however, total revenue did not approach the 43 percent expectation—the government collected only 29 percent of GDP for 1992. The budget deficit for the year thus equaled 16 percent of GDP. Factoring in nonbudgetary disbursements, total government disbursement in excess of total revenue for 1992 approximated a record 32 percent of GDP (International Monetary Fund, 1993: 25–26). Ukraine's deficit is put in perspective when compared with the much-publicized United States budget deficit, which equaled about 2 percent of GDP for the year 1992.

According to Ukraine's Ministry of Statistics, the receipt for 1992's consolidated budget was 1,227 billion *kbv,* while actual expenditures totaled 1,920 *kbv.* The total deficit, including budgetary and extrabudgetary accounts, was thus 693 billion *kbv,* or 56.5 percent of the year's total revenue. Since 1992's GDP was 5.127 trillion *kbv,* the budget deficit for the year amounted to 13.5 percent of GDP. However, nonbudgetary disbursement comprised of subsidies and assorted funneling of funds reached 660.5 million *kbv,* appending the equivalent of an additional 12.9 percent of GDP to the government's 1992 outlays. The year's aggregate deficit, therefore, reached 26.4 percent of 1992's GDP, approximately 6.5 percent lower than the IMF's figure (Ministry of Statistics of Ukraine, 1994a: 4, 14).

Whether the Ministry of Statistics' or the IMF's figures are used, it becomes clear that the deficit Ukraine incurred during its first year of independence was less than rational. Ukraine's fiscal policy of 1992 actively fueled the inflationary spiral without simultaneously advancing the economy's productive capacity.

The deficit of 1992 did not emerge from a vacuum, nor was it a consequence of previously unforeseen trends. The overestimation of revenues and underestimation of expenditures can be attributed to poor bureaucratic staffing, poor legislation, and traditional political values. The inherent political flaws that caused this fiscal debacle bear further mention.

The overestimation of revenue was largely a consequence of inadequate tax-collection procedures. High tax rates encourage "underground" economic trans-actions, effected in cash, while high inflation rates encourage barter arrangements that do not involve the turnover of cash. These types of transactions went unreported. Worse, the law demanding that 50 fifty percent of repatriated foreign earnings be converted to *karbovantsi* gave many firms engaged in foreign transactions the incentive to underreport profits.

The underestimation of expenditure can be attributed to traditional political practices. Though at the beginning of the year, decision makers did not intend to run a massive deficit, they found expanding consumption subsidies, bailing out failing industries, and continuing other outmoded practices politically expedient. However, these priorities impeded economic performance and the process of economic transformation as the year wore on. Likewise, unemployment was not tolerated during the Soviet era. Though Khruschev questioned the purpose of engaging citizens in highly unproductive activities, the Soviet administrators took pride in the virtual nonexistence of unemployment in the nation. This value had passed into Ukrainian political culture. As a result, the government shored up failing firms, even those that were, and are, clearly nonviable, wasting scarce social resources.

Political unwillingness, administrative inadequacy, and cultural values thus have contributed to an overwhelming and crippling deficit.

BUDGETS: JANUARY 1993–SEPTEMBER 1994

In a nation with few trained market-oriented economists, estimates of macro variables are often imprecise and quite frequently vary widely from agency to agency. Though this problem exists even in the United States, where the Office of Management and Budget and the Congressional Budget Office routinely quibble over the budget deficit, these discrepancies pale beside the magnitude of some of the deviations seen in Ukraine and in other less developed economies. For the sake of consistency, only statistics adopted by the Ministry of Statistics and the Ministry of Finance are used in this section. Since these statistics are produced by administrators largely isolated from partisan political pressures, political agendas are less likely to be reflected in these figures than in other groups' estimates.

The state's budget for 1993 was adopted on April 9, 1993, anticipating a deficit of 6.2 percent of the year's GDP. Hyperinflation, however, promptly rendered the approved revenue and expenditure figures obsolete. The Ministry of Finance adjusted the budgetary forecast in July 1993, revising the year's deficit upward to 12.3 percent of GDP. Such upward revisions became necessary during subsequent time periods, raising doubts about whether decision makers would exercise fiscal restraints in the foreseeable future. Analysis for the period is based upon data presented in Tables 10.1 through 10.3.

Table 10.1 presents quarterly revenues and expenditures for 1993 in nominal terms, whereas Table 10.2's data are in March 1993 constant values. The analysis is divided into two respective fiscal years, 1993 and 1994.

BUDGETARY PERFORMANCE, 1993

The government entered 1993 with optimism. The Ministry of Finance anticipated greatly increased revenue. As excise and export taxes and VAT were increased, tax collecting procedures were purportedly improved, and expenditure, particularly for consumer subsidies, was reined in.

As may be observed in Table 10.1, the first quarter's total expenditure for 1993 exceeded total revenue for the same period by only 56.7 billion *kbv*, a mere 1.2 percent of the quarter's GDP. Combined revenues from VAT, corporate profit, personal income, and excise taxes accounted for 1,333.9 billion *kbv*, or 82 percent of the quarter's total government receipts.

The government, however, failed to keep its expenditures under control. The first quarter's combined expenditures for "national economy," "social/cultural," and "other" purposes amounted to 1,169.7 billion *kbv*, almost 70 percent of the quarter's total government outlays. Classifications such as "national economy" and "social/cultural" disbursements often conceal transfer payments and subsidies for agriculture, mining, and so forth. Nonetheless, the shortfall of only 1.2 percent of GDP equivalent for the first quarter appeared to represent a success on the part of the government.

This apparent success, however, was artificial and short-lived. The near balance was accomplished mainly at the expense of delayed subsidy disbursements and spending freezes on all nonessential expenditures. The promising fiscal performance continued into April 1993, with growth in revenues for the month notably exceeding expenditures, which resulted in a cumulative budgetary surplus of 568 billion *kbv* for the first four months of 1993 (Popiel, 1993: 37).

Table 10.1

Quarterly 1993 Budgets at Current Values (in billion *kbv*)

Budget Item	Q1-93	Q2-93	Q3-93	Q4-93
Corp. Income Tax	424.7	1512.7	2460.7	9922.5
Pers. Income Tax	109.1	200.0	499.3	2055.2
VAT	698.8	1652.6	3963.7	10655.0
Excise Tax	101.3	205.3	466.6	1719.0
Foreign Activity	19.8	219.4	395.4	1389.8
Chernobyl Fund	98.6	152.2	449.4	1791.4
Pension Fund	n/a	n/a	n/a	n/a
Other Revenue	172.0	512.5	2583.3	5358.1
TOTAL REVENUE	1624.3	4454.7	10818.4	32981.0
Social Security	258.9	974.7	1566.8	15841.0
Social/Cultural	511.3	1121.8	2655.1	9582.3
Pension Fund	n/a	n/a	n/a	n/a
Chernobyl Fund	124.5	264.8	502.0	906.2
Nat'l Economy	400.9	1469.1	3117.5	7636.7
Defense	127.9	233.6	634.1	1765.2
For Econ. Activity	0.0	424.4	426.9	1592.5
Other Expenditures[A]	257.5	1518.5	3963.6	-177.9[B]
TOTAL OUTLAY	1681.0	5996.9	12866.0	37146.0
BALANCE	-56.7	-1542.2	-2047.6	-4255.0
GDP	4950.0	10721.0	39633.0	98645.0
Deficit/GDP (%)	1.1	15.0	5.2	4.3

Source: Ministry of Economy, 1994c: 23-24

[A]The "Other Expenditures" category is arrived by subtracting the itemized columns from the total. The "Total Revenue" listed in the original document was not quite equal to the sum of all itemized entries.

[B]The negative "Other Expenditure" amount for Q4-93 is most likely the result of inaccurate rounding, estimations, and discrepancies between different models in the cited reference. The amount was less than 0.5 of one percent of that period's total outlay.

By May of 1993, these apparent successes had vanished. The deficit for the second quarter alone amounted to 1,542.2 billion *kbv*, more than 15 percent of GDP. The most significant increase in government expenditure arose from additional grants to agriculture and industry, necessitating a net transfer of 1.38 trillion *kbv* from the National Bank of Ukraine to the year's budgetary account.

The government secured an additional 2.35 trillion *kbv* of credit from the National Bank of Ukraine in July, thus borrowing almost 4 trillion *kbv* from the monetary authority in only two months' time. With this borrowing, the government financed even more irresponsible spending for the remainder of the year. The year's cumulative deficit at current values was 7,901.5 billion *kbv*.

Total revenue and expenditure in real values for 1993 were 7,683.4 and 9,211.6 billion *kbv*, respectively, resulting in a deficit of 1,528.2 billion *kbv*. The year's real value deficit was 6.7 percent of GDP, an apparent fiscal improvement over 1992's performance. The improvement was nevertheless more apparent than substantive. Despite a budgetary deficit of 6.7 percent GDP-equivalent, the Ukrainian economy sank deeper into depression instead of slowly emerging from the 1992 crises. Expenditures in excess of revenues neither contributed to the economy's systemic conversion nor advanced the cause of structural transformation. State disbursements only helped brake the fall, without concurrently rendering the economic subjects more competitive or viable in the longer run. On the basis of real-value revenue/expenditure data in Table 10.2, several noteworthy phenomena—distinct from those given earlier under nominal-value presentation of the statistical evidence—can readily be identified as follows:

- Fourth quarter 1993's real value tax revenues from corporate profit, personal income, VAT and excise—the foundation of revenue sources for the government—all experienced decreases instead of gains from their respective first quarter receipts.
- Revenue surge in real values during the second quarter of 1993 was due to a "one time large inflow of revenue(s) from corporate income taxes resulting from the collection of back taxes" (Ministry of Economy, 1994a: 23). As may be observed in Table 10.2, the largest revenue increases during the second quarter of 1993 originated from the corporate income, VAT, and "foreign activity" taxes.
- Outside of receipts from the category of "other revenue," the government's real income plunged abruptly during the third quarter of 1993, with revenues from the corporate income category alone dropping by more than 46 percent in a three-month period.
- Fourth quarter 1993's revenues in real values further decreased in all income categories, registering a 33.0 percent aggregate loss when compared with the previous quarter, and a 46.9 and 15.2 percent decrease, respectively, when contrasted with the second and first quarters.
- The most drastic proportional decrease over the quarters occurred in the VAT category. Real value receipts from VAT during the first quarter of 1993 accounted for 41.6 percent of revenue total during the three-month period. It dwindled to only 26.5 percent during the fourth quarter.

Table 10.2

Quarterly 1993 Budgets at Constant Values (in billion *kbv*)

Deflator index[A] Budget item	100.0 Q1-93	171.7 Q2-93	518.4 Q3-93	2387.3 Q4-93
Corp. income tax	424.7	881.0	474.6	415.6
Pers. income tax	109.1	116.5	96.3	86.1
VAT	698.8	962.5	764.6	446.3
Excise Tax	101.3	119.6	90.0	72.0
Foreign activity	19.8	127.8	76.3	58.2
Chernobyl Fund	98.6	88.6	86.7	75.0
Pension Fund	n/a	n/a	n/a	n/a
Other revenue	172.0	298.5	498.3	224.4
TOTAL REVENUE	1624.3	2594.4	2086.8	1377.8
Social Security	258.9	567.7	302.2	663.6
Social/cultural	258.9	567.7	302.2	663.6
Pension Fund	N/A	N/A	N/A	N/A
Chernobyl Fund	124.5	154.2	96.8	38.0
Nat'l economy	400.9	855.6	601.3	319.9
Defense	127.9	130.2	122.3	73.9
Foreign econ. activity	0.0	247.2	82.3	66.7
Other expenditures[B]	257.5	884.4	764.5	-7.5[C]
TOTAL OUTLAY	1681.0	3492.6	2481.7	1556.0
BALANCE	-56.7	-898.2	-395.0	-178.2
GDP	4950.0	5981.9	7644.9	4132.1
Deficit/GDP (%)	1.1	15.0	5.2	4.3
Gvt. exp/GDP (%)	34.0	58.4	32.5	37.7

Source: Ministry of Economy, 1994*c*: 23–24

[A]The deflator index is derived from retail price indexes for the corresponding periods.

[B]The "Other Expenditures" category is arrived at by subtracting the itemized columns from the total. The "Total Revenue" listed in the original document was not quite equal to the sum of all itemized entries.

[C]The negative "Other Expenditures" amount for Q4-93 is most likely the result of inaccurate rounding, estimations, and discrepancies between different models in the cited reference. The amount was less than 0.5 percent of that period's total outlay.

- Significant real-value income losses over the quarters reflected general economic crises in Ukraine during fiscal year 1993. The occurrence severely compromised the government's ability to steer the economy out of the quandary via the otherwise potent tool of fiscal measures.
- While unpredictability on the revenue side may, in part, be attributed to factors exogenous to government controls, the nearly systematic oscillations in expenditure evidences the government's whimsical indifference to fiscal discipline and restraint.
- The second quarter's total revenue in real values increased by 59.7 percent over the year's first three months. The corresponding expenditure increase in the "national economy" category was 113.4 percent. Government disbursement under the "national economy" category was a euphemism for covert state subsidies, which led to a short-lived "from famine to feast" scenario for the beneficiaries.
- The third quarter's total revenue decreased by 19.6 percent. Expenditure decreases for "national economy" concurrently fell by 29.7 percent, causing a "from feast to famine" diet for subsidy recipients.
- More pronounced was the extreme growth in the government's disbursement to "other expenditures" during the second quarter, a net increase of 233.5 percent over the year's first quarter. Unlike the third quarter's 29.7 percent decrease in benefits received by beneficiaries under the "national economy" category, receipients under the category of "other expenditures" experienced only a modest 13.5 percent decrease in government disbursement. Despite this slight decline, beneficiaries under the "other expenditures" category were still 196.9 percent better off during the year's third quarter than during the first.
- The combined government expenditure for the "national economy" and the "other" categories was 39.2 percent of total expenditures in the first quarter. It climbed to 49.8 percent during the second quarter, regressed to 39.1 percent during the third, and ended at a mere 20.1 percent during the fourth. Such casual decisions on the part of the government chisel away instead of fostering the imperative of rational planning and decision making by economic entities at large.
- While expenditures in real values for the fourth quarter declined significantly in all other spheres, social security disbursements more than doubled from the preceeding quarter. The social security to total outlay ratio during the first quarter was 15.4 percent. It grew slightly, to 16.3 percent, during the second quarter, only to fall conspicuously to 12.2 percent in the third. As is almost consistent now with the government's other unpredictable decisions, it spiraled to more than 42.6 percent during the year's final quarter. This quasi-roller-coaster ride for social security recipients points to the decision makers' overall problem-solving routine: remedial appeasement, not judicious circumspection.
- Wild fluctuations in real GDP for the second half of 1993 reflect the most turbulent wage and price spirals, especially for the months of September and December.
- The quarterly deficit/GDP ratios for 1993 were 1.1, 15.0, 5.2, and 4.3 percent, respectively. And the corresponding government expenditure/GDP ratios were 34.0, 58.4, 32.5, and 37.7 percent, respectively. Since the year's second quarter experienced the most drastic increases in revenues as well as expenditures, the 15.0 percent deficit/GDP ratio illustrated the government's unwillingness to exercise restraints in its objective to orderly withdraw enterprise and consumption subsidies. It also suggests the government's casualness in dealings with either budgetary surpluses or deficits.

- Finally, abrupt fluctuations in the government's real-value revenues and expenditures from one quarter to another underscore the government's vulnerability in attempts to maintain fiscal stability and effectiveness. Impulsive and tumultuous expenditure practices compromise a nascent economy's attempts at a systemic and structural transformation. It actively promotes macro disturbances and erodes public confidence in the merits of a market system.

In sum, the government's 1993 fiscal practices did not help curtail the force of hyperinflation, nor did it constructively promote an orderly transition to a market-oriented system. Fiscal policy, a potentially potent instrument for stabilization and growth, has instead become a tool of destabilization and waste in Ukraine.

FISCAL YEAR 1994

Despite the failures of the previous two years, the government anticipated fiscal success in 1994. The proposed budget forecasted a balanced budget, with both expenditures and revenues equal to 418 trillion *kbv*. The process began inauspiciously. Since presidential elections were held in mid-1994, the budget was not approved until the third quarter, forcing government operations to depend on legislative and administrative authorization for another lengthy period.

The differences between projected and actual performance again proved dramatic. Table 10.3 presents both planned and actual fiscal performance for the first three quarters of 1994.

The draft of the 1994 planned budget balanced to six significant figures, a perfectly balanced budget. That both expenditure and revenue added up to precisely 418.029 trillion *kbv* in the document perhaps reflects the naive optimism of the parliament, or the enduring fiat mentality: the eternal hope that the budget will balance if only the legislature says so assertively. Obviously, no government can project its revenues and expenditures to six figures a year in advance.

By the end of the first quarter of 1994, the government was already operating in the red, with expenditure exceeding revenue by 14.1 percent. Instead of the projected revenue increases from corporate profit, personal income, VAT, and excise taxes, there was an aggregated decrease of 66.5 billion *kbv* between the fourth quarter of 1993 and the first quarter of 1994. Relatively tight disbursement during the first quarter of 1994 succeeded in holding the deficit/GDP ratio to 5.5 percent, enabling Ukraine to maintain some semblance of fiscal discipline.

Many of Ukraine's most disturbing fiscal patterns continued through 1994. Expenditure grew faster than revenue in the periods when revenue increased. Overall, real expenditure grew slightly faster than real revenue for the year. Even though the most dismal period of performance had passed by late 1994, the deficit/GDP ratio soared to 16.1 percent, the highest level since the debacle of 1992, and government expenditure accounted for more than two-thirds of the nation's GDP.

Table 10.3
Planned and Factual Quarterly Budgets in Nominal and Real Values, First Three Quarters, 1994 (in billion _kbv_)

Budget Items	Planned		Nominal			Real		
	Rev.	Exp.	Q1-94	Q2-94	Q3-94	Q1-94	Q2-94	Q3-94
Corp. Inc. Tax	58470		13511.7	28733.9	42879.0	399.0	733.0	973.1
Pers. Inc. Tax	16700		4233.9	6543.5	9809.5	125.0	166.9	222.6
VAT	88486		12959.7	25336.3	37005.8	382.7	646.3	839.8
Excise Tax	25387		1586.1	2885.2	5064.7	46.8	73.6	114.9
Foreign Activity	22686		2426.9	2285.8	4524.4	71.7	58.3	102.7
Chernobyl Fund	15827		3115.5	4238.9	6462.4	92.0	108.1	146.7
Pension Fund	61260		11576.3	17154.3	23952.3	341.8	437.6	543.6
Other Revenue	116603		6760.3	10271.2	14945.9	199.6	262.0	399.2
TOTAL REV	418029		56170.4	97449.1	144644.0	1658.5	2485.8	3282.6
Soc.Security		51984	7880.8	11878.8	16586.0	232.7	303.0	376.4
		11342	15880.7	24174.5	31333.2	468.9	616.7	711.1
Social/Cultural		65960	11979.2	16319.3	20127.7	353.7	416.3	456.8
Chernobyl Fund		16363	2078.6	4408.7	5926.4	61.4	112.5	134.5
Nat'l Economy		100798	11146.8	33135.1	70919.3	329.1	845.2	1609.4
Defense		17744	2456.4	4957.7	4862.9	72.5	126.5	110.4
For. Econ. Activity		24945	2297.5	5055.3	5733.0	67.8	129.0	130.1
Other Expenditures		128893	10393.2	13152.6	34448.5	306.9	335.5	781.8
		418029	64113.2	113082.0	189937.0	1893.0	2884.5	4310.4
BALANCE		0	-7942.8	-15632.9	-45293.0	-234.5	-398.8	-1027.9
GDP		—	144651.0	210217.0	280910.0	4271.0	5362.3	6375.0
Deficit/GDP (%)			5.5	7.4	16.1	5.5	7.4	16.1
5.5Deflator Index [B]						3386.8	3920.3	4406.4

Source: Ministry of Finance, 1994b: 13–14; 1994c: 23

[A] The "Other Expenditures" category is arrived at by subtracting the itemized columns from the total. The "Total Revenue" listed in the original document was not quite equal to the sum of all itemized entries.

[B] The deflator index is derived from retail price indexes for the corresponding periods.

The most distressing trend is the growth in supports to the "National Economy." Disbursements to the "National Economy" during the first quarter of 1994 totaled 329.1 billion *kbv*, accounting for 17.4 percent of total expenditure. Factoring for inflation, expenditure on these supports more than doubled during the second quarter of 1994, and nearly redoubled during the third quarter. Disbursements under the "National Economy" category are predominantly disguised subsidies to agriculture, industry, and mining, especially to the coal industry. Being consumptive rather than constructive in nature, such subsidies help create false expectations and breed lasting inefficiency.

"Social safety net" programs, though rapidly expanding, at least have autonomous sources of funding. Sporadic wage and price indexations constitute the primary source of revenue growth in the Social Security, Pension, and Chernobyl Funds. Despite dramatic increases in all three programs' receipts and disbursements, they have been roughly deficit neutral since their inception.

The revenue side also shows many disconcerting trends. In 1994, the government attempted to place more emphasis on indirect business taxes and less on corporate taxes and VAT. Corporate income/profit tax constituted 28.2 percent of total government receipts in 1993. The 1994 budget plan attempted to reduce this figure to 14 percent; however, the burden placed on profit earners remained virtually unchanged for the first three quarters of 1994. Similarly, the 1994 plan expected VAT to comprise 21.2 percent of total revenue, down from 38.5 percent for 1993. VAT's share of total revenue declined, yet only to 25.2 percent.

Poor economic performance and irresponsible levels of government expenditure for the latter part of 1994 pushed the government spending/GDP ratio to 67.61 percent by September 1994. According to one estimate, the expenditure total was to rise to 75 percent of GDP by the end of the year, and "the budget deficit for the whole of 1994 was projected at 19.5 percent of GDP" (Aslund, 1994: 4). Even developed and stable market economies cannot sustain such high deficit-to-output ratios without devastating consequences. In a volatile economy like Ukraine, fiscal indiscretion of such magnitude can neutralize the few positive market elements that have emerged since reform efforts began.

Economic performance was not worse for the sole reason that the government used borrowed money for propping up the soft economy. The consequence of this borrowing has been a sustained reduction in the private sector's savings and, therefore, a reduction in the private sector's investing ability. An autonomous monetary authority would never allow this; invariably when politicians get control of the money supply, credit policy becomes too easy, and the entire nation suffers in the long run. The National Bank of Ukraine's subordinate status prevents it from ending the haphazard circulation of credit for the purpose of political appeasement.

UNCERTAIN FISCAL PERFORMANCE FOR 1995

After three years of economic independence and lax fiscal discipline, the year 1995 could witness some improvement in the government's management of public finance. Three main factors suggest that improvement is probable. First, the election of Leonid Kuchma and his commitment to solid reforms give hope for more responsible leadership. His directives and public pronouncements have substantiated his resolve. Second, the resignation of Vitaliy Masol as Ukraine's prime minister in March 1995 removes one large political hurdle for Kuchma.[2] Masol, a former leader of the leftist faction in the parliament, was characterized as an obstacle to "many of Kuchma's measures to reforming the country's Soviet-style economy" (OMRI, March 2, 1995). Third, Ukraine's need for international assistance and credits compels the government to comply with demands for fiscal restraint.

A single incident shows how all three of these factors interacted. The 1995 draft budget, prepared by former Prime Minister Masol's administration in January 1995, sought to trim social welfare programs, as well as to curtail subsidies to agriculture and industry. The budget proposal projected 4.32 quadrillion *kbv* in revenue, a 465 percent rise in wholesale prices, a wage increase of 340 percent, the elimination of several tax privileges, and a 2,000 percent increase in property tax (OMRI, February 3, 1995).

Shortly after the Supreme Rada received the proposal, a vote of no confidence was taken. Although Masol survived the vote, "deputies from both the Left and the Right complained about the austerity measures and cuts in both social spending and subsidies to ailing industries and farms" (OMRI, March 16, 1995). Masol resigned as prime minister on March 1, 1995. While the budget proposal languished in the hands of parliamentary commissions in February and March of 1995, the IMF postponed its decision over a proposed $1.8 billion standby credit to Ukraine. Convinced that the much needed IMF credit was premised on an austere 1995 budget, Speaker Moroz read Kuchma's statement to the parliament, calling for its passage. After months of opposition to the budget proposal, the parliament finally acquiesced to the IMF's demand; it adopted the proposal on April 6, promising the deficit would not exceed $2.2 billion for 1995, or 7.3% of projected GDP. Whether decision makers will adhere to the proposal remains uncertain.

A CONCLUDING NOTE

It is imperative that decision makers comprehend the situation at hand, clearly define attainable objectives, and responsibly pursue those goals with the policy instruments at their disposal. These imperatives are singularly urgent in Ukraine, which has inherited a system overwhelmed with structural rigidity, allocative inefficiency, and operational wastefulness. Ukraine's independent economy, which was thoroughly integrated into the Soviet system only a few years ago, has also encountered abrupt disengagement from the FSU's extensive exchange systems. This setting challenges the effectiveness of fiscal policy.

The Ukrainian government has thus far failed at capitalizing on the potential effectiveness of fiscal policy, not fully grasping the economy's innate flaws. With no clearly defined objectives, the government has been careless in the formulation and execution of fiscal policy.

A rational fiscal strategy applies prudent tax and expenditure policies, thus achieving desired objectives. Taxation results in a withdrawal of purchasing power from businesses and households, reducing the private sector's spending capability. Government spending, on the other hand, represents an injection into the economy. The respective levels and configurations of taxation and government spending impact the degree of aggregate demand. That is, the government's tax policies and spending practices can affect the levels of employment, output, prices, and external exchange. Public finance can thus effectively foster stabilization, mitigate disturbances, and promote growth. A well-formulated and methodically implemented fiscal policy is, therefore, capable of steering the economy toward the envisioned objectives.

In view of the prolonged inflationary recession currently plaguing Ukraine's economy, the government must decide between how much inflation and how much unemployment it can tolerate. The British economist A. W. Phillips demonstrated the inverse relationship between unemployment and inflation in the early part of the twentieth century. The Ukrainian government has not made any value judgment on this matter. Though employment is a highly valued commodity, stable prices are a necessity in a nation that desperately needs to foster financial intermediation and investment.

Until Ukraine can balance its budget, it cannot keep inflation in check. The persistent gap between total revenues and expenditures over time needs narrowing first, then closing in a deliberate and constructive manner.

Throughout its independence, Ukraine has consistently run budget deficits. The economy has enjoyed neither price stability nor full employment because of poorly operated fiscal policy. Clearly, there is an alternative; that is, both unemployment and inflation can be reduced if the correct policies are enacted. A recommendation is presented to conclude this chapter.

Even in mid-1995, Ukraine claims an unemployment rate of less than .05 percent. Maintaining such a contrived full employment scenario is not an option. Even in industrial nations operating at "full employment," roughly 5 percent of the population will be classified as unemployed. This is a natural market phenomenon. Markets do not clear instantly, though they do clear. Interfering with this equilibrium only creates inefficiency in yet another sector of the economy. The government must acknowledge that less competitive factors and nonviable producing units face inevitable and eventual elimination from the marketplace. The longer the state attempts to suppress and hide the inevitable rise in open unemployment through wasteful subsidies to nonviable firms, the higher the opportunity costs the nation will incur, and the more budget deficits will cripple the nation's reform efforts.

Since price levels must be brought under control, curtailing wasteful spending and eliminating subsidies from nonessential consumption in the private sector is a logical approach to balancing the state's budget.

Deliberate and planned withdrawal of enterprise-consumption subsidies in conjunction with increased tax burdens on less competitive producing units and factors can help hasten the planned eradication of inefficiency. Both these policies would help alleviate the deficit, enabling a slow rise in Ukrainian savings and investments, rather than mere consumption. Privatization of state enterprises can further diminish the deficit and encourage efficient resource use.

Finally, direct injection or indirect subsidies via credits and tax relief for potentially competitive segments of the society can encourage growth. Given sufficient incentive, underground economic activity and barter transactions will decrease, enabling fuller expansion of credit through the multiplier principle. This will allow for more activity, more revenue, more growth, and more rapid stabilization and recovery of the Ukrainian economy.

NOTES

1. The pension, social security and employment funds make up the extrabudgetary fund. The Chernobyl fund, on the other hand, is a part of the regular budgetary account.

2. Vitaliy Masol was also the prime minister of the Ukrainian Socialist Soviet Republic until 1990. Forced out of the office by student demonstrations in 1990, he returned later as one of Ukraine's numerous new prime ministers. He resigned as Ukraine's prime minister, for the second time, on March 1, 1994.

11

Financial Sector Development

Development in a market economy prompts corresponding development in its financial sector, which, in turn, promotes the economy's real growth. A well-developed financial system responds and adjusts to market signals, channeling financial resources toward productive and efficient uses. Real and financial flows interact, sustain, and nurture one another, propelling the economy forward in an orderly progression of mutual support and benefit. Developing a well-coordinated financial system is thus critical to economic development.

This chapter consists of four sections: (1) Ukraine's financial system and its functional problems; (2) monetary policy and performance; (3) reform needs and priorities; (4) a concluding note.

UKRAINE'S FINANCIAL SYSTEM AND ITS FUNCTIONAL PROBLEMS

Ukraine's financial system functioned passively alongside plan-directed real flows during the Soviet era. Money served primarily as accounting units, since the central planning bureaucracy determined how money was spent. Balance between real and financial flows was achieved through administrative controls, not market coordination. Monetary policy did not exist in reality, since neither financial intermediaries nor producers played a role in resource allocation. Systemic reform in Ukraine thus requires a fundamental reorientation in the function of money and the role of the financial system.

Ukraine's current financial system has seen minimal changes since the Soviet era. Ownership of banking institutions is concentrated in the state sector, with minimal private-sector activity. The financial system still consists mainly of the six state banks inherited from the Soviet decades. The six banks are: the National Bank of

Ukraine, the Import-Export Bank, the State Savings Bank, the Social Investment Bank, the Agricultural-Industrial Bank (hereafter referred to as the Bank of Agriculture), and the Industry-Construction Bank (hereafter referred to as the Bank of Industry). These banks are vulnerable, however, to the whims of the legislature; they do not enjoy de facto functional autonomy.

Though commercial banks, trust funds, investment funds, insurance companies, and credit unions have proliferated in the few years since independence, these institutions account for less than 2 percent of the financial sector's total assets. Most of the private banks in Ukraine are owned and organized by enterprises or enterprise organizations, and exist primarily for the purpose of catering to their parent enterprise. These institutions generally do not extend credit to other private-sector borrowers. They do not consider this to be part of their function.

The National Bank of Ukraine (NBU) was a branch bank of the USSR's Gosbank. In the Soviet era, NBU issued no currency, performed no regulatory function, and had no role in mapping the republic's financial policies. Ukraine's five other state banks were likewise branch banks of the USSR's national banking system. They followed directives from their respective head offices in Moscow.

The absence of a competitive financial network in an economy attempting to effectuate a structural transformation is cause for concern. Of greater concern is the state's interminable directives to state banks for credit emissions, which severely compromise sound banking operations. A select few of the problems involving Ukraine's banking sector are briefly highlighted below. They exemplify the imperative of a new course for action in the immediate future.

The four state banks most affected by traditional practices are the State Savings Bank, the Bank of Agriculture, the Bank of Industry, and the National Bank of Ukraine.

The State Savings Bank

The State Savings Bank accepts household savings, holds a limited number of foreign currency accounts, and finances a small portion of real estate operations. Continuing the traditional relationship between the State Savings Bank and the NBU, the bulk of the Savings Bank's assets are credited to the nation's central bank. This practice prevents the Savings Bank from channeling resources to the most constructive possible investment opportunities.

Four years after Ukraine declared its independence from the USSR, more than one-fourth of Ukraine's Savings Bank assets still remain frozen in Moscow, with no satisfactory solution in sight. The amount represents the Ukrainian Savings Bank's liability to Ukrainian depositors. It also hampers the bank's productive use of financial assets rightfully belonging to its depositors.

In response to high inflation, the state has, on numerous occasions, directed the indexation of household deposits with the Savings Bank. It remains unclear whether all or only some of the additional claims will eventually be assumed by the state. This creates further uncertainty for the Bank, rendering it even less capable of mapping out long-term investment strategies.

This problem is exacerbated by the uncertain future the bank faces. It is not yet clear whether the bank will be privatized. Until privatization occurs, the financial resources of this institution will not play a constructive role in restructuring Ukraine's economy.

The Bank of Industry and the Bank of Agriculture

The Bank of Industry and the Bank of Agriculture maintain current accounts of state enterprises, of state farms, and of farm collectives, and are principal lenders of credits to the industrial and agricultural sectors. Under the centralized system, fulfilling plan directives superseded concerns over profits or losses. The banks were responsible for extending credit to their clientele group, regardless of the financial position of the enterprise or the probability of success. Inexperienced in evaluating credit applications and unseasoned in overseeing client performance, banking officials can do no better than continue their traditional function as bookkeepers. The sector's inherited systemic arrangements, its relationship with the state, and the politicians' penchant for issuing directives have helped deepen instead of alleviate Ukraine's economic crises.

The downward spiral in Ukraine's economy began on the macro as well as the micro levels. On the macro level, inept and inconsistent reform programs abruptly dismantled an incumbent system without creating a viable replacement. On the enterprise level, the average management is drawn by profit motivation. However, it lacks the knowledge, experience, resources, markets, and political will for effectuating the desired enterprise restructuring. Confronted with widespread macro dislocation brought on by unexpected economic independence and by chaotic reform measures, enterprise management as a whole expends more energy on crisis management than on restructuring.

Given the state's preference for full employment, enterprise management keeps plant doors open if at all possible. Maintaining full employment, even at exorbitant opportunity cost, still ranks among the most cherished of values. However, as price liberalization raises the costs of supplies used in production, producers must now either lay off workers or seek the assistance of the state. Traditional practices incline management toward the latter.

The state, the Bank of Industry, and the Bank of Agriculture, then, play a role in maintaining nonviable enterprises. The parliament has habitually abandoned its rhetorical commitment to maintain fiscal discipline by extending credit to these enterprises. The parliament or the administration orders the Ministry of Finance to secure additional credits from the NBU for supplementary budgetary disbursements. The borrowed credit is then coursed through the Bank of Industry and the Bank of

Agriculture to the dependent sector. In addition to these unplanned budgetary expenditures, the state also resorts to nonbudgetary disbursements in the form of government-guaranteed credits to enterprises through the Bank of Industry and the Bank of Agriculture.

The practice of subsidizing these suspect industries and agricultural enterprises is clearly not conducive to economic health. Invariably, the credit secured by the enterprise drives the firm deeper into arrears, while the budget deficit expands. Enterprises nonetheless reduce work days, eliminate unpaid leave and other benefits, cut shifts, and resort to decapitalization for survival.

The macro consequences of decapitalization are profound. Production decreases, while the tax base erodes, and the production process becomes even more inefficient. One apparent explanation for the increase in real tax revenues in recent years is the state's incessant injections of borrowed money.

For the Bank of Industry and the Bank of Agriculture, credit emission is not counterbalanced by timely debt servicing. Rampant inflation, negative lending rates, and default on payments continuously corrode the banks' asset values. Yet, without authorization from the state or directives from the NBU, the two banks are kept from restructuring their lending portfolios to protect their own viability. Meanwhile, state-mandated lending to marginal enterprises severely curtails the banks' extension of credit to competitive and viable entities in the economy. Instead of fostering or forcing efficiency and growth at the enterprise level, the two banks operate as the state's proxies in perpetuating inefficiency and insolvency. Many enterprises thus survive with no pressing incentive for managerial reorganization or physical and financial restructuring. Consequently, the banks cannot contribute to enterprise reform, and are inhibited in reforming their own structure toward minimizing risk and maximizing returns.

The National Bank of Ukraine

The NBU issues currency, manages financial flows, regulates the exchange rate, supervises financial institutions, and receives de jure autonomy of operation. The government nominates members to the board of governors with the consent of the Supreme Rada. Ukraine does not possess a two-tier banking system, as other developed economies do. For all practical purposes, Ukraine's system consists only of the state banks and the NBU since minimal private financial activity exists. Financial flow thus remains more directed than managed, and directed more by parliament than by the NBU. Parliament is not prepared for relinquishing control of the money supply. According to Victor Suslov, chairman of the Supreme Rada's Finance and Banking Committee, the time is not yet ripe:

Our banking system is still being created. The system is not yet right. I want to emphasize the fact that our central bank is absolutely independent with respect to all operational issues. It is subordinate to the parliament only in the sense that it reports to us. There are different proposals [in the parliament] regarding the National Bank of Ukraine. There are proposals that it be subordinate to the government. There are proposals to redefine the relationship between the parliament and the National Bank of Ukraine. And there are also proposals that the Bank be completely independent from the government. But the deputies do not support the idea that the Bank be completely independent. It is not true that such complete independence is possible. Under the conditions of our economy which is in a transitional phase, it is neither advisable nor acceptable. (Suslov interview, 1994)

Thus far, the National Bank of Ukraine has not pursued an independent monetary policy. The state has directly and indirectly tempered the central bank's management of financial flows.

The parliament now may direct the NBU in matters relating to money supply, including standby credits to the government. For instance, when the average inflation rate for the fourth quarter of 1994 reached 100 percent per month, the NBU could not apply the brakes on growth rates in money supply because the government demanded additional credits from the NBU to cover a swiftly growing deficit. Furthermore, the parliament has also repeatedly directed additional credit emissions to subsidy recipients. The NBU must extend credits to commercial or state banks because the parliament has so directed.

The parliament's action thus enables negotiations between banks and the NBU for privileged lending rates, mandating subsidized and unsecured credits to enterprises at large. Therefore, though the NBU may be de jure autonomous, its emission of credit and monetary reins are de facto controlled by the whims of parliament.

The state's overall policy has had the perverse consequence of driving nearly half of all business transactions into the shadow economy. Both state enterprises and private entrepreneurs resort to nonmarket transactions thereby avoiding growing tax liability caused by the government's growing revenue needs. A significant portion of the underground economy's earnings is exchanged into hard currencies and leaked into financial markets abroad. At least, when money is "laundered" in the industrial developed world, the funds remain at home.

The irrational monetary policy has produced many adverse effects in the economy. It fuels inflation, depreciates the real liability of enterprises, diminishes lending institutions' liquidity, reduces the banking sector's accumulation of real-value resources for circulation, promulgates consumptive spending, neutralizes incentives for enterprise restructuring, and encourages borrowers to demand continual subsidies in the future. Political decisions have, thus far, severely handicapped the NBU's effectiveness in regulating financial flows. Until the parliament and the government permit factual operational independence to the NBU, stabilization will not return and structural transformation will continue to stall.

In brief, the inherited single-tier financial system in Ukraine is as much in need of reform and restructuring as is the rest of the economy. Because enterprise reform requires the proper functioning of a market-based financial system, restructuring of the financial system itself depends on the success of enterprise reform. The future of

Ukraine's economy rests with the political decision makers' granting market forces a greater role in resource allocation. Politicians still decide to what extent the market may coordinate real flows with the financial flows. Unless and until the decision makers relinquish their traditional preference for state regulation of economic activities, especially in the banking sector, the NBU will remain incapable of actualizing the full potential of a rational monetary policy.

The ensuing section examines Ukraine's monetary operations and consequences in recent years. This analysis will make clear that substantive reform in the financial sector can no longer be delayed.

MONETARY POLICY AND PERFORMANCE

The National Bank of Ukraine nominally formulates and executes the nation's monetary policy. In practice, it is the Ukrainian parliament and government, which do not have a policy regarding monetary flows, that dictate whether the NBU's targets will be realized. Monetary restraint is seldom a politically popular decision anywhere in the world. In Ukraine, in particular, political whims and tradition have prevailed over economic rationality. Among major consequences have been rapid monetary growth, high inflation, wage losses, accelerated income velocity, increased underground activity, currency destabilization, and overall deepening of economic crises. The combination of abrupt price liberalization, fiscal laxity, and the lack of monetary discipline have struck a severe and costly blow to the economy.

Bank credits from the six state banks to the "national economy" by January 1, 1992, only five months into independence, totaled the equivalent of 97.2 billion *kbv*. A year later, credits to the government grew to the equivalent of 2,510 billion *kbv*, a twenty-six fold increase. Money supply likewise increased by 178 percent during the second quarter of 1992, by 106 percent during the third, and by 95 percent during the fourth (Ministry of Economy, 1993a: 11, 17). Predictably, waves of galloping inflation followed shortly thereafter.

Inflation outpaced both wage and pension increases, culminating in pressure for more frequent and substantial adjustments reflecting real values. These demands were countered by international organizations such as the IMF, which cautioned fiscal and monetary restraint. Nevertheless, habits from the Soviet era persisted; the government continued to subsidize enterprises. By one means of accounting or another, subsidies to consumers and to enterprises found their way into the Ukrainian budget.

By mid-1993, credit emissions from the central bank to the government had skyrocketed. The NBU's claim against the central government in June 1993 was 2,796.2 billion *kbv*. It rose to 16,945.92 billion *kbv* in July, 26,139.1 billion *kbv* by September, and 41,241.9 billion *kbv* two months later (Ministry of Economy, 1993d: 8). Monthly inflation rates climbed into the high double-digit figures, necessitating further wage and pension indexations, and therefore additional borrowings from the NBU. The vicious cycle thus continued in perpetuum.

The velocity of money supply (MVv), or income velocity, measures the rate or the number of times that money stock turns over annually for spending purposes. It is obtained by dividing NNP into money stock at a given time period.[1] The expression MV=PQ is the money stock (M), multiplied by the average rate of turnover or velocity (V) equals total expenditure, or GDP. GDP must, by definition, equal the quantity of all goods produced (Q) by their respective prices (P). This expression is true by identity of all economies at all times.

In a healthy economy, velocity, particularly of the more inclusive definitions of money, is roughly constant. Thus, money stock is directly proportional to nominal GDP. The question is whether change in GDP will be expressed more in prices or in real output.

Ukraine, however, is not a healthy economy. As was discussed earlier, the money stock has expanded rapidly, while real GDP has fallen quickly. The increase in the money supply, the rapid growth in velocity, and the sudden and pronounced decline in real output must, *by definition*, all be balanced by higher prices. Table 11.1 shows how both the money stock and velocity have grown since 1993.

Table 11.1

Quarterly GDP, Money Supply and Velocity of Monetary Aggregates January 1993–October 1994 (in billion *kbv*)

Period	M1	M2	Qtr. GDP	Vel. M1	Vel. M2
Jan 1993	2310	2758	1708	2.96	2.48
Apr 1993	4664	6181	5251	4.50	3.40
Jul 1993	9527	12714	14320	6.01	4.51
Oct 1993	28757	42822	41801	5.81	3.90
Jan 1994	21246	40972	92147	17.35	9.00
Apr 1994	34517	58366	144651	16.76	9.91
Jul 1994	54587	94135	210217	15.40	8.93
Oct 1994	97082	157000	280910	11.57	7.16

Source: Ministry of Economy, 1994c: 25; 1993d: 18

Figure 11.1

Velocity of Monetary Aggregates, 1993–1994 (Velocity: GDP/Money Stock)

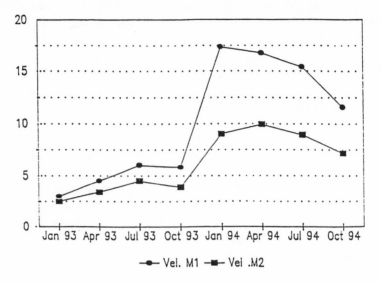

Source: Ministry of Economy, 1994c: 25; 1993d: 18. Secretariat of the Economic Commission for Europe, Geneva,1993: 41

Even before 1993, the money stock was roughly doubling every quarter; for the final three quarters of 1992, the growth rates in M1 were already 178, 106, and 95 percent, respectively (Ministry of Economy, 1993a: 10). Between October 1992 and January 1993, the rate of growth had decreased to 30 percent, before beginning another rapid expansive phase throughout 1993. The phenomenal growth in the money supply can be attributed to government directives to the NBU and special-purpose banks for credit emissions.

As noted in Table 11.1, M1 more than doubled between January and April of 1993, while M2 significantly more than doubled for the same time period. The velocity of M1 increased by 34.2 percent, and the velocity of M2 by 27.1 percent during the same time period. On January 1, 1993, nearly all prices were deregulated. Seeking their own levels, prices in March 1993 had roughly trebled from three months before. Meanwhile, real production continued to decline. With a larger money stock, a higher velocity of money, and less production, the dramatic rise in prices was a given, as the identity MV=PQ dictates. That nominal GDP actually rose while real GDP fell indicates how counterproductive these price increases were.

For the first few months of 1993, the government actually showed surprising restraint in indexing prices, keeping real incomes and thus aggregate demand very low, hoping to stem the tide of sustained inflation. Such "shock therapy," whatever its merits or demerits in a newly liberalized economy, is ill-suited for the tradition-bound Ukraine. The government eventually indexed wages heavily to the extent that real incomes did not decline as much as they might have otherwise.

By December, the stock of M1 stood at 9.19 times its level in the previous December, while the velocity of M1 increased by 5.96 times. This means that nominal GDP increased by about 53-fold for the year; however, since the price level rose more than 100-fold, real GDP fell by half.

The most drastic increases in monetary velocity materialized during the period between October 1993 and January 1994. The nominal money stock actually declined during this period, while the instability of velocity caused nominal rises in GDP anyway. Once velocity becomes unstable, as the U.S. Federal Reserve learned in the early 1980s, charting a monetary policy becomes exceptionally difficult.

"This period happened to coincide with political crisis, and [with] the resignation of [then] Prime Minister Kuchma and his government" (Ministry of Economy, 1993d: 4). This period was the second half of 1993, when hyperinflation continued, production decreases persisted, and political crisis deepened. "On 17 December [1993], Parliament tacitly approved the Cabinet of Minister's plan for controlling hyperinflation. The program is the eighth attempt in two years at bringing Ukraine's collapsing economy under control" (Brzezinski and Zienchuk, 1993: 1). Despite the nation's deepening crises, the parliament still would not base decision-making processes on economic rationality.

As presented in Table and Figure 11.1, despite the government's eighth attempt at stabilization, velocity of broadly defined money increased immediately after January 1994. Though the rate of turnover in money slowed throughout the year, nominal GDP continued to rise.

Ever since Ukraine regained its independence in late 1991, the NBU has had no clear control over monetary issues. Irresponsible political decisions in the financial sphere have deprived the NBU of its primary function, implementing a rational monetary policy, which is crucial for curtailing the rising force of destabilization. Blueprints for reform have remained on the drawing board, while the government has pieced together irrational shards of monetary and fiscal policy. As a consequence, the Ukrainian economy has been unduly debilitated.

Real Wages

In the long run, real wages reflect productivity, the most important measure of economic performance. Since productivity is measured in output per man-hour, wages, or compensation per man-hour, are the most accurate gauges of productivity. Since Ukraine gained its independence, real wages have eroded.

The decline in real GDP incurred since the breakup of the FSU can be attributed to losses of purchasing power in other markets, the dissolution of the "chain" of production held together by central planning bureaucrats, and supply inelasticities, among other factors. As prices rose, productive inputs became more expensive, increasing the marginal costs of production at all levels.

Figure 11.2
Real Wages in Ukraine, 1992–1994

(Real Wage Index: Dec. 1991=1.00)

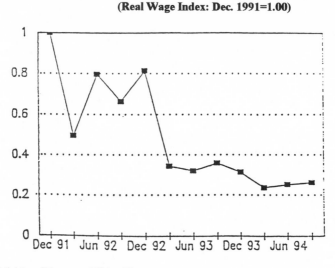

Source: Ministry of Economy, 1994c: 19

Real wages moved sporadically from March through December 1992. Mounting political pressures obliged the government to authorize wage increases for state-sector employees and to adjust inflation-ravaged pension funds and savings accounts. Real wages would thus rise for a brief period. However, the ensuing increase in aggregate demand quickly drove prices higher. With aggregate supply conditions being price inelastic, monetary and fiscal measures designed to stimulate demand could only result in higher prices.

The state continued its practice of subsidizing consumers and nonviable industries, ever expanding credit and fueling inflation. In time, real wages steadily declined throughout 1992.

By March 1993, real wages had fallen to 34 percent of their December 1991 level. The pattern of sudden wage adjustments and ensuing inflationary gusts continued throughout 1993 and 1994. The most significant observable trend is the inverse relationship between the velocity of money and real wages. The periods in which monetary aggregates were turning over the most rapidly (such as early 1994) were also the periods in which real incomes were falling the most rapidly.

Obviously, the impact of inflation is unambiguously negative. Sustained inflation and erosion of purchasing power encourages decapitalization, creates structural rigidities, reduces supply elasticities, jeopardizes the financial system, destabilizes the currency, fosters trade deficits, and increases the number of elderly and retired in need of state assistance. Nevertheless, unless both the politicians and the average economic subjects, especially subsidy-hungry enterprises, perceive the unavoidable necessity of monetary discipline and reform, Ukraine's free-falling economy will continue its downward spiral.

REFORM NEEDS AND PRIORITIES

Economic reform in Ukraine can succeed only if accompanied by parallel reform in the structure and functioning of the financial sector. An inherited single-tier banking system notwithstanding, strides must be taken toward creating an environment conducive to the development of a two-tier system, with a growing commercial banking sector increasingly active in allocating financial resources. The state, the NBU, the private sector, and the banks' clientele enterprises must each play a role in this restructuring. Reform needs and priorities in each of the four are examined below.

The State

The state's most basic requirement is creating a political environment that facilitates transferring economic activities to the private sector. Undue governmental paternalism merely prolongs the economy's structural rigidities and functional inefficiencies.

The state must first redefine its relationship with the banking sector. The purpose of a bank does not include extending credit to the government for the purpose of covering its debts, or to any economic entity the legislature deems expedient. Financial institutions must assume financial risk so that productive firms, which otherwise would not accept a venture, can operate and enhance the society's standard of living. Banks are not charitable organizations, nor are they the government's clearinghouses.

The state must grant full operational autonomy to the NBU and the other state banks. Though the actions of the monetary authority can have profound effects on society, political intervention in economic decision making is largely unjustified. The state should continue communications with, and make suggestions to, the monetary authority. However, it must refrain from issuing directives or exerting political pressures that would force the central bank into conforming to a select political agenda. Distance from the political milieu, as other countries have learned, helps the central bank retain objectivity in financial policy making.

The state must also authorize genuine independence to the management of special-purpose banks. This need will be assessed later in the chapter. These banks, in turn, must decentralize their own authority, giving branch banks authority to decide which firms are most worthy of credit, expanding their services beyond their clientele groups, and, ultimately, to privatize. Basing the allocation of credit on credit worthiness and risk assessments is clearly more conducive to efficient flows of funds than is basing allocation on government controls.

Once these reforms have been effectuated, the opportunity costs inflicted upon the economy by inefficient industries should gradually dissipate. No bank operating independently of the government would extend credit to an industry or other venture as inefficient, insolvent, or otherwise nonviable as the firms that the government currently offers easy lines of credit to. Even if this practice does not coincide with the politicians' ideological preference for full employment, the nation must understand that rooting out inefficiency ultimately yields long-term rewards. On the other hand, prolonging the existence of weak enterprises and, along the same vein, inefficient financial institutions prevents more efficient alternative uses of resources from being realized.

Reforming the nature of credit emissions and eliminating wasteful government subsidies will also enable the government to implement more disciplined yet responsible fiscal policy. Disbursements to nonproductive enterprises fuel inflation, distort proper economic relationships, and exacerbate the budget crisis. The employees of the beneficiaries of the subsidies themselves suffer because, tradition-bound as they are, they lack the confidence to seek more productive and thus higher-paying work elsewhere. The state must instill sufficient economic disincentives into those who still engage in inefficient practices. Since the inefficiency was almost entirely inherited from the USSR, social programs and unemployment assistance must accompany such reform. Since the largest and fastest-growing segment of the budget is paid as support to farmers, miners, and other workers, the state could easily introduce such social insurance measures in its budget, provided the state exercises discipline in phasing out subsidies.

Making the government compete for funds on the open market, as the rest of the economy must, is another budget-based reason for pursuing financial privatization. Eliminating a guaranteed line of NBU credit injects a sense of resource scarcity, and therefore of responsibility, into the thought processes of decision makers. The cost of being socially responsible dims in comparison with being economically irresponsible. Viable enterprises should ultimately eliminate their own debts, without assistance from the state. The government might, however, extend some credit to more viable firms, particularly if they possess strategic value. The cost of such subsidies must be made explicit in the state budget, and not be covertly underwritten by the NBU.

There are some firms that would remain insolvent if the government did not extend them further credit. However, they might survive if the government did assist them on a temporary basis. There also are firms that are of strategic importance that will continue to bear heavy debts well into the future. The proper line of policy here should depend on the nature of the debt. If the creditor is a potentially viable enterprise, the state may liquidate the arrears through budgetary disbursements to the creditor enterprise. This would assist both firms. If, on the other hand, the state is the creditor, then tax rescheduling measures can be implemented to permit the enterprises time to regain their footing. The government could set its own conditions for debt restructuring, demanding enterprise-level reform measures. If firms become more responsible in exchange for deferred payment, the interests of both the debtor firm and the state are served. A policy of short-term intervention in this respect could be of constructive assistance. A clearly defined repayment schedule for the state's temporarily assumed arrears may serve as an added incentive for enterprise management to implemente realistic and accelerated restructuring measures. Thereafter, it will be enterprise management who responsibly chooses between survival and growth or plant closing. For the financial sector, settlement of arrears can also provide a clearer picture of current and expected financial flows for planning and regulation.

The National Bank of Ukraine

It is not the NBU's fault that Ukraine does not possess a monetary policy. Only by independence from political tampering can the NBU create a financial system that is conducive to market operations and responsive to market forces. Any discussion of the future role of the NBU, therefore, must be based on two assumptions: first, that the state grant full operational independence to the NBU, and that NBU credit no longer be conveniently used to cover the state deficit;[2] and second, that effective measures be taken toward privatizing and commercializing the branch banks of the state's special-purpose banks.

Improving the NBU's effectiveness and elevating it to the standing of a bona fide central bank requires the immediate implementation of a tight monetary policy and the upgrading of institutional arrangements.

The bank's most urgent task is the restoration of price stability. Given its current capability and experience, concerted efforts in interest and reserve determinations can promise the most effective results.

Imposing monetary discipline in Ukraine entails regulating flows of M1 and M2. Targeting the more inclusive definitions of money is not necessary. Assets held by nonbanking financial institutions, which are components of the more broad-based monetary aggregates, are negligible in size in Ukraine. There is also very little commercial or government paper that has any stable value. As a benchmark for the NBU, the Federal Reserve Board of the United States does not exercise the authority for regulating M2. Tthough it publishes estimates and forecasts of the measure, its purview extends only to depository financial intermediaries, those responsible for creating M1 medium-of-exchange money. The Fed does not control investment-based intermediaries, savings accounts, pension funds, and other creators of relatively liquid assets. Thus, control of M2 should be more than enough authority for Ukraine.

Tightening credit emissions requires the NBU to place flexible and periodically adjusted borrowing ceilings on member banks, based on the lending performances of the institutions. In addition, payments from member banks in real-value terms must be exacted, both on principal as well as on positive interest.[3] Both measures oblige member banks to conduct operations strictly on a commercial basis and spontaneously reduce flows to less viable enterprises. Though higher real interest rates may temporarily hamper investment, offering unrealistically low interest rates on loans encourages reckless debt accumulation and misallocation of funds.

Four major operational modifications can improve competition in the financial market:

First, the NBU should eliminate subsidized lending rates to directed credits. A uniform lending rate among financial institutions results in private commercial banks vying for NBU credits on a competitive basis, and encourages an appreciation of scarcity.

Second, as warranted by changing economic conditions, the imposition of a lending ceiling on member banks obliges them to extend credit to their clients on a competitive basis. The branch banks of the Banks of Industry and Agriculture, in their present form, engage in no commercial activity other than meeting the financial needs of founding enterprises. A policy limiting how much a bank can lend would prevent the whimsical extension of credit to weak and wasteful enterprises, encourage banks to make the best decisions possible with their limited funds, and help keep the flow of funds under control.

Third, involving private financial institutions in exchange auctions can help close the discrepancy between official and street-level exchange rates. Currently, a sizable amount of currency remains in the hands of profiteers, with speculators concentrating on earning rapid profits as sudden changes in the value of the currency are incurred. A market-based foreign exchange rate, on the other hand, would eliminate parasitic speculation, releasing the potentially productive financial resources into constructive investments.

Finally, the NBU needs to raise the reserve requirement, or the percentage of assets that a bank must store with the monetary authority. This limits the money supply, which would otherwise become theoretically infinite as funds are moved from bank to bank. In the United States, for example, the reserve requirement has traditionally been 12 percent, meaning that for every dollar the Fed pumps into the economy, total credit can expand by up to $8.33.[4] Changing the reserve requirement is radical medicine, so potent that the monetary authorities may set the reserve requirement and yet hardly ever touch it. Ukraine's monetary policy, however, needs nothing less than the most potent medicine available.

Institutional Improvements

Enhanced effectiveness in exercising its supervisory functions depends on the NBU's ability to develop and standardize financial reporting procedures by all member banks. Uniform accounting would promote sound banking practices, expedite the enforcement of banking regulations, and make strict enforcement of the monetary policy possible for the NBU. Uniform accounting would also insure that banks keep exact account of loans to enterprises, many of which are of dubious merit. If banks' lending practices were exposed to a disciplined monetary authority, extending highly wasteful lines of credit would be much more difficult for the commercial banks.

In conjunction with institutional reform, the financial system needs to acquire more experience and expertise through training programs. The human resource areas most in need of improvement include accounting, auditing, financial analysis, and super-vision. Improving the quality of these services will speed up matching funds to the most worthy recipients.

As the banking system begins operating on a commercial basis, the NBU should begin parallel development of new control mechanisms in anticipation of auxiliary financial intermediaries appearing on the market. In brief, an updated and upgraded central bank can help smooth the path for the development of a functional two-tier banking system. A smoothly functioning financial system helps effectuate macro-level stability, improve allocative efficiency, and promote enterprise restructuring.

Special-Purpose and Commercial Banks

Financial assets within the banking sector are disproportionately concentrated in the NBU and the state's special-purpose banks. The Bank of Industry alone held more than one-third of the sector's total assets in 1992. The distribution of assets among the banks still reflects the relative importance the Soviet Union placed on each sector; each bank performed a designated function under the centralized system. The banks were never intended as establishments to foster allocative efficiency. Rather, they served as clearinghouses for accounting units.

In the Soviet system, the financial system was not used for expediting the flow of goods. It was used for keeping track of plan-dictated production. Now, the flow of funds and the flow of real goods must become interdependent and interchangeable. The flow of credit must become a tool for enhancing, not merely measuring, the standard of living of Ukraine's citizens.

Though even some of the world's developed nations have favored state involvement in the commercial banking system, the efficiency of the private sector compels the state to withdraw most of its interest in the commercial banking sector. Ukraine, in particular, needs to reconsider the relationship between its banks and its public sector, for the consequence of the current arrangement has been enduring allocative inefficiency.

The state must withdraw both its institutional and its operational interests in the financial system. That is, ownership of banks must be transferred from the state to the private sector, while the state must refrain from leaning so heavily on the banks and from expecting credit for covering its unscheduled expenditures.

Privatizing state banks under current developments in Ukraine, however, is neither realistic nor rational. After years of state-directed credit emissions and desultory accounting and auditing procedures, no state bank has much of a grasp of its real-value assets and liabilities. Most of the recent credit the banks have extended has been used for consumptive, not productive, purposes, and will thus never be recovered. Portfolio restructuring by state banks, therefore, must precede divestiture of ownership by the state.

Portfolio restructuring itself, however, can and should involve the state. The bulk of the nonprofitable or loss-incurring loans originated from state-directed bank-enterprise relationships. Unless the state assumes responsibility for the seriously enfeebled financial position of the state banks, their coordination and promotion of efficient financial flows will be compromised.

A possible resolution of bank losses involves the creation of a special agency, as was done in the former Czechoslovakia. The agency may include experts from world organizations and representatives of developed economies. The agency could assess the risks associated with debts and establish credit ratings, determine the value of recoverable loans outstanding, and determine the net worth of each bank.

The government can cover the bank losses with long-term bonds, or write off the losses altogether. In either case, the banks will more accurately assess their values, which will allow for more objective sale prices.

The agency can also demonopolize banking operations by the state banks. Taking into account enterprise and geographic needs for banking services, and factoring in the relative financial positions of each bank's branch offices, the agency may direct the partitioning of state banks into independently incorporated banking entities. Once this process is completed, the agency may consign the newly incorporated state banks to the privatization authority.

Once the privatization authority completes its process of declaring an enterprise for sale, accepting offers, making contracts, and so forth, privatization is finalized. It must be emphasized that, though privatization is a vital step in transforming the financial system, it is a concluding step, not a starting point.

Over time, the increasingly competitive character of financial institutions will nurture the growth of commercial banking operations, foster efficient allocation of scarce financial resources, and oblige state competition for credits on the open market. The efficiency gains made from advanced competition will also clear up any doubt as to which sector is more adept at allocating funds.

Finally, reform in the slowly emerging private banking sector needs to focus on the NBU's licensing and supervisory functions. The extremely low capitalization requirement set forth by the NBU has meant that most of the private commercial banks have been extremely small in size, in some cases smaller than a fraction of a rural branch bank in developed nations. Most of these banks engage only in small, short-term activity. Correcting this problem, the NBU has on occasion ordered bank mergers, as well as license suspension, for smaller entities. Since economies of scale exist in banking, and since small firms cannot handle much risk, it is vital that the size of the average private-sector financial institution increase.

Closer supervision must also be given to the enterprise-sponsored private banks, which often extend credit inefficiently and recklessly to their clientele. The NBU can monitor these banks by creating credit ceilings, by helping them service their debts, and by eliminating the growing practice of borrowing by "dummy" corporations for the purpose of skirting the credit ceiling. Closer scrutiny can make these banks use their financial assets for the benefit of all of society, not just for the privileged members of the clientele sector.

Major Bank Clientele: State Enterprises

Enterprises must also play a role in the restructuring of the state's financial system. Much as Ukraine's economic restructuring and growth depend on the performance of the financial system, the financial institutions depend on the performance of the economy's producing sector. Reform in the financial sector, therefore, must be accompanied by corresponding efforts in industrial and agricultural restructuring, including the timely privatization of all entities subject to the process.

Enterprise reforms conducive to financial improvement include organizational modification, factor and product restructuring, financial reorganization, and physical remodeling. Reconstruction of this kind invariably produces human suffering and loss. However, indefinitely delaying the reforms only imposes higher opportunity costs. It is only through change and adaptation to the dynamics of the marketplace that long-term gains and financial health materialize. Only through improved enterprise performance can growth and development in the financial sector be reasonably expected.

A CONCLUDING NOTE

Reform in Ukraine's financial/ banking sector as in many other facets of Ukraine's economy, has been more cosmetic than substantive. The banking sector's inefficient allocation of financial resources among competing users originates from the ancillary roles the USSR assigned to money and the financial system. These anomalies persist because the state lacks discipline and restraint in its monetary and fiscal practices.

An underlying norm for reforming Ukraine's economy in general, and reforming its financial sector in particular, is long-term loss minimization on the aggregate level. Reforming the financial sector requires concurrent enterprise reform. The success of each depends on the success of the other. Banks are burdened with bad loans because of state directives. Enterprises allow growing arrears because they see no ready alternatives. The remainder of the chapter sums up the basic measures needed for reforming both these ailing sectors.

Reforming the financial sector requires the establishment of a real monetary authority capable of controlling the money supply and overseeing and supervising the efficient distribution of credit. Banks must enjoy true autonomy, without the constant threat of political intervention. The state must temporarily assume some of the bad loans the banks hold in order to rebuild the banks' equity so they can be privatized. Runaway government spending is preventable if the government must borrow at the same rates as the rest of the nation, on an open market. Accounting procedures must be standardized, preventing further abuses of credit, and all forms of financial institutions, not just depositories, must be bolstered to create true competitiveness for financial resources.

Reforming Ukrainian enterprises will require the removal of loss-incurring, wasteful, or inefficient enterprises from the economy, debt assumption and/or forgiveness by the state, as well as conditional loans encouraging structural improvements, expanded job-training programs, and accelerating privatization.

It can be readily seen that the state will perform many of the same tasks in reforming the financial sector as it did in reforming the productive sector. Enterprise-level performance depends on restructuring both the financial and product sectors. Restructuring facilitates enhanced enterprise-level performance, which in turn strengthens economy-wide stability and growth. It is the state that must ensure and promote an environment that facilitates restructuring and reform in both the financial and the real sectors.

NOTES

1. No official publication from Ukraine contains data on NNP. Velocity of monetary aggregates in table 11.1 and figure 11.1 are obtained by dividing GNP into money stock instead. Since both GDPS and MS are presented at current values, no deflator is needed in calculating the velocities of money stocks.

2. The chairman and members of the NBU's board of governors must expect and be prepared to withstand intense political pressure from the parliament's left and center for a monetary policy that is more liberal than the bank's current course of action. Such political pressure has been applied to all boards of central banks in the more progressive reforming economies of the former Eastern Bloc, most notably in Estonia and in the former Czechoslovakia.

3. The real positive rate should also apply to interest payments on time and savings deposits by competing banks. This helps instill confidence and promotes growth in savings, increasing credit availability to competitive concerns while simultaneously reducing consumptive spending.

4. Once the initial dollar is placed into a bank, the institution can loan out 88 percent of it, or $0.88. If that $0.88 is spent, it will become an asset of another bank, which can loan up to 88 percent of $0.88, or $0.7744. This amount will be spent, and the new creditor will place it in another bank, which can loan out up to 88 percent of *that*, or about $0.6815. This process continues indefinitely; but elementary calculus shows that the sum of the infinite series converges to the reciprocal of 0.12, which is eight and one-third.

12

Summary, Conclusion, Recommendation

During the Soviet era, Moscow's domination and integration of all republics of the USSR was thorough and strict. Ukraine was held under closer scrutiny than the rest of the republics because of its strategic importance to the USSR. The Union's system held all regional economies together. If separated from the others, no single republic's economy could function without substantial dislocations. The centralized system permanently maintained the status quo and prevented the possibility of relapsing into other forms of structure. Ukraine was a pivotal part of this rigidly structured and strictly controlled system. It functioned, or seemingly functioned, as long as all the other important parts remained closely held together.

The CIS's declaration of political and economic independence from the USSR precipitated more than the disintegration of the USSR's centralized command system. It prompted instant and extensive dislocations throughout republics of the FSU.

The depth and duration of economic crises, which all fifteen republics of the FSU have encountered, depend on inherent and inherited characteristics unique to each of these republics. Prospective reform programs, therefore, should be mapped, tested, fine-tuned, and promulgated in light of each republic's distinctive characteristics, including historical, cultural, social, political, and economic considerations.

Ukraine's decision makers did not map a coherent reform strategy. Ukraine did not, and still does not, have a consistent reform program. Governments have kept changing. Reform efforts have lacked clarity. Reform emphases have lacked continuity and focus. Reform measures since independence have accentuated rather than mitigated macro dislocations. The inherited distortions have persisted, amplified, and deepened rather than consolidated or mitigated. Costly yet valuable lessons can be learned from Ukraine's experiment with economic reform.

This concluding chapter comprises five parts. The first segment discusses prerequisites to systemic transformation, including noneconomic factors as they impact reform endeavors. Part two capsulizes obstacles to the reforms in Ukraine's inherited economy. The third section traces policy errors. Lessons derivable from Ukraine's reform experience constitute the fourth part. The chapter concludes with select recommendations for possible consideration by decision makers in Ukraine as well as in other newly liberalized economies.

PREREQUISITES TO SYSTEMIC REFORM, INCLUDING NON-ECONOMIC FACTORS

Crafting a rational reform program dictates the primary imperative of judiciously assessing the inherited systemic deficiencies. Tentatively settling on a reform strategy follows. An elementary guideline is the mini-max criterion: minimizing social and economic costs, maximizing positive outcomes. A tentative reform strategy does not suggest indecisiveness. Rrather, its intent is incorporating the elements of flexibility and adaptability in implementation. Reform objectives remain absolute. Approaches to their realization must therefore remain adjustable. Too frequently, reform architects do not fully comprehend the tenacity of built-in reform obstacles. Decision makers in select newly liberalized economies do not appear overly cognizant of the long-term social and economic costs consequent upon policy mistakes. Intractable reform strategies, even when objectively proven inappropriate, have continued while an already enfeebled economy heads toward avoidable, ever-deeper crises. The rigidity and inflexibility of the past must be replaced by adaptability and flexibility in policy implementation.

Political Constraints

In Ukraine, inadequacies and obstacles abound as inopportune social, political, and economic forces intertwine. Ukraine's experience with independence has been circumscribed by military and political developments in the region. Two years of independence after World War I provided Ukraine with a less than ample heritage for self-governance. Ukraine lacks the independent political, social, and economic traditions upon which reform could solidify, or around which it could modify. Recent independence descended upon Ukraine with minimal preliminaries, propelling it, with few forewarnings, from a fully integrated component of a rigidly structured whole—politically, socially and economically—to a sovereign and autonomous entity. What Ukraine has inherited from the Soviet era is a group of politically polarized decision makers and a population that remains ideologically diverse. The parliament, composed of a conservative majority and a reform-minded minority, continuously changes hands, from one group of old-timers to another. Unaccustomed to clear divisions of authority, the legislature and the executive branch of government keep a constant struggle going, each claiming ultimate authority over key decisions.

Political unity is absent from the government and from the general populace as well. Ethnic tension endures between easterners and westerners, while political wrangling persists among the different regions of Ukraine. In sum, Ukraine is a politically divided and socially dissonant entity.

Economic Consideration

Ukraine has had no experience in independent reforms. By the time Ukraine regained its independence in late 1991, Poland, the former Czechoslovakia, and Hungary had less than two years of experience with attempts at a systemic transformation. Even world organizations lacked experience in steering a formerly centralized economy to becoming market-based. Ukraine was entering into uncharted waters, with few precedents from which it could derive lessons.

Among the prerequisites for charting a rational reform policy is a full recognition of the inherent obstacles to a systemic transformation. The formulation and implementation of a rational reform program presupposes political will, wisdom, and harmony. Yet, decision makers in Ukraine have demonstrated no such political will, having disregarded the full force of inherent reform obstacles. As a result, reform programs have not been consistent or conducive to Ukraine's unique predicaments.

As a rule, economic success helps neutralize negative influences of political, cultural, and social divergences. Conversely, economic failures magnify and intensify them. Successful economic reforms can help unify Ukraine into a new political and economic entity. Failures may predispose Ukraine once again to political and economic subordination to regional powers.

Yet, in Ukraine, instead of unifying social and political forces against economy-based obstacles, political discord has created additional obstacles and hazards to economic reform. In addition to the inherited economy-based obstacles to systemic transformation, human factors in Ukraine have also contributed hindrances to the realization of the desired transformation. Political discord has heightened instead of mitigated social tensions and ethnic disharmony.

With these added constraints to reform, the question synthesizes into whether and how strongly the majority of the population and decision makers are willing to persevere in a painful, necessary phase of restructuring and reorientation. It is upon the answer to this question that the future freedom and independence of Ukraine as an independent state rests. On the premise that the nation can endure further hardships for a promising tomorrow, the ensuing sections successively outline the inherited obstacles to reform, highlight policy errors, and derive lessons therefrom.

OBSTACLES TO REFORM

Ukraine is faced with internal obstacles and external hindrances to reform. Internal obstacles emanate from structural deficiencies and functional deficiencies. External impediments originate from beyond Ukraine's jurisdiction. Each of the two internal obstacles is briefly examined below.

Structural Deficiencies

As a constituent component of a centralized system during the Soviet era, Ukraine's economy was structured toward being dependent on other republics of the USSR. The state sector dominated all aspects of economic activities. State ownership of the means of production, plan-directed investment, production, distribution and consumption, and the suppression of market exchanges negated opportunities for the emergence and development of creative initiatives by the private sector.

The economy Ukraine has inherited from the Soviet system is laden with state monopolies that produce large quantities of semifinished products for interrepublic distribution. Policy-created distortions from the past have left Ukraine with a productive capacity disproportionately concentrated in the military and heavy industries, with consumer goods industries accounting for less than 30 percent of the economy's total. Although many direct and indirect consequences flow from this simple reality, only a select few need underscoring.

First, even if external markets currently existed for parts and semifinished products from Ukraine, the policy-induced dependence on factor supplies from other republics of the FSU obliges sustaining Ukraine's import needs with adequate export-generated foreign earnings. However, Ukraine has not developed an independent trade regime that can naturally balance its current import needs with export turnovers.

Second, the economic independence of the CIS countries has plunged the previously internal demand—now the CIS countries' external demand—for Ukraine's heavy industry exports to critically low levels. Although Ukraine's effective demand for factor imports has decreased as well, the idled productive capacities have caused additional severe dislocations.

Third, disproportionate investment concentration in heavy industries during the past has left Ukraine with capital assets of minimal salvage value. Supply inelasticities in consumer goods industries meanwhile remain stationary for lack of investments therein.

Fourth, repressed inflationary pressure in the consumer goods sector has erupted into open inflation, with minimal control mechanisms in place. Real incomes dwindle. Life savings dissipate. Decapitalization accelerates in industries.

Fifth, despite abrupt upward price adjustments for consumer goods, the perennial discrepancies between inelastic demand for, and the even less elastic supply of, consumer goods remain. Impoverished by rising expenditure needs and sustained inflation, neither the state nor the private sector possesses the needed financial resources for extricating the economy from the supply inelasticity predicament. Import of consumer goods rises without a measurable pressure-release from the upward assent of prices.

Sixth, unbalanced emphasis on heavy industries has dictated the concentration of human resource development in technical specialties not useful in the production of consumer goods or the provision of consumer-oriented services. It has reduced the mobility of the skilled labor force from traditional production to where demand inelasticity prevails.

Seventh, the absence of market exchanges during the Soviet era has left Ukraine with a severe shortage of entrepreneurs and managers seasoned in efficiency-based decision making. The built-in rigidity and anomaly of imbalances cannot be readily rectified.

Eighth, in fulfilling plan directives, many monopolistic state enterprises used to operate on the basis of sustained state subsidies that covered perennial financial losses. Though no longer financially viable under an abruptly liberalized regime, the operationally autonomous enterprises still expect continued state subsidies to keep plant doors open. Asset fixity in loss-incurring enterprises poses the dilemma of choosing between a surge in unemployment or continued resource wastefulness, a difficult choice for Ukraine's socialist-dominated parliament.

Ninth, state ownership of the banking system and the state banks' monopolistic positions in conjunction with the plan-assigned relationship between clientele enterprises and special-purpose state banks severely constrains the banking sector's development of a market-based commercial banking infrastructure.

Tenth, state monopoly of asset ownership renders difficult the establishment of an orderly, efficiency-based and yet equitable privatization process. Ukraine lacks trained personnel as well as established institutional frameworks for mass privatization. Yet, without a successful privatization program, the economy's ingrown inertia and inefficiency remain institutionalized.

The above impediments pertain to the internal structure of Ukraine's inherited economy. There are also externally related built-in obstacles and deficiencies that temper Ukraine's smooth transition from a centralized to a market-based economy.

Unlike the other newly liberalized economies of the former COMECON nations, Ukraine did not have an independent existence before late 1991. It had neither an independent currency nor an autonomous foreign economic policy. Except for its relationship with the predominantly interrepublic markets, Ukraine must begin from ground zero, establishing an export and import relationship with markets outside of the CIS countries. Although Ukraine is heavily dependent on imports of factors, goods, and services from beyond its boundaries, the largest segment of Ukraine's inherited economy can find no ready markets abroad. The rigidly structured producing entities lack export-supported factor imports, but are incapable of flexibly adjusting to market signals from the world's increasingly aggressive competitiveness.

Russia's unilateral price liberalization measures after the formation of the Council of Independent States compounded the problem of foreign currency reserve shortages. The spillover effects from Russia's hyperinflation and money printing adversely impacted Ukraine's independent monetary policy, since Ukraine was still within the ruble zone. Among the adverse effects of currency instability was Ukraine's problem converting local currencies into hard currencies for essential factor imports. Finally, upon independence, Ukraine had neither the structure nor the institutions for foreign capital inflows. Inexperienced in marketing abroad and unclear of the potential contribution of foreign investments in development, Ukraine lags far behind many newly liberalized economies in competing for hard currency investments. As a result, with insignificant trickles of small ventures from the West, Ukraine is left practically isolated in its struggle toward a structural transformation. Fossilized in the grip of an uncertain mentality over reform approaches, Ukraine thus suffers from a lack of infusions for progressive ideas, experiences, and resources from developed economies.

Functional Deficiencies

Competitiveness induces efficiency. Efficiency reinforces competitiveness. Ukraine has inherited a system that lacks both. In the past, plan-determined commodity prices facilitated the attainment of an artificial balance between material and financial accounts. The system helped perpetuate misallocation of scarce resources. Overproduction of industrial products with increasingly lower marginal value productivity was accompanied by increasingly more acute shortages of basic goods and services of high marginal utility. The problem of perennial commodity shortages was conveniently circumvented through the rationing of consumer essentials. The state-determined prices not only contrived a feigned appearance of stability, they also institutionalized consumer and producer subsidies. The system deprived prices the preeminent function of reflecting relative abundance and scarcity, yielding neither signals nor incentives for efficient resource allocation and consumption. Repressed inflationary pressure accumulated, with not even a valve for monitoring the extensiveness and depth of state induced distortions. Apprehensive of relinquishing state authority over economic relationships, while unsure of appropriate remedies for deteriorating distortions, wastefulness continues while commodity imbalances remain uncorrected by domestic producers.

What Ukraine has inherited is a system of control mechanisms devoid of established market relationships. Abrupt discontinuation of centralized directives leaves no functional mechanism for coordinating the traditionally controlled economic activities. The disintegration of the Soviet distribution system has left the traditionally passive enterprise management with uncertain factor supplies and loss in product markets. Directors of enterprises lack managerial and organizational skills, on the one hand, and technical and financial resources on the other, yet must undertake enterprise restructuring and reorientation. Responding to market signals and adapting within active market relationships, long-established practices in developed economies are painfully deliberate activities for the hitherto cloistered enterprise management.

Accustomed to state-maintained price stability and state-guaranteed financial security, only a small minority of enterprise directors have capitalized on the rapidly changing price structures following price liberalization. Majority enterprises react rather than respond when given untested reform policies. Increasing prices has been more a function of meeting the anticipated revenue needs than of price-utility alignment as warranted and tested by market forces. Upward spiraling prices reflect inflationary expectations, not real costs in production or real values in consumption. No longer as secure over continued state subsidies, enterprises barter or reschedule arrears as partial compensation for the income shortfalls following interrepublic market losses. Complementing such nonmarket relationships is the enterprises' accustomed approach when meeting revenue needs: pressuring the state for sustained financial assistance.

Functional impediments also spontaneously arise from structural anomalies. Plan-directed investments in state monopolies impose extensive asset fixity on monopoly enterprises. Much of the productive capacity of the inherited capital assets can produce only goods that have narrow markets in republics of the FSU. Inconvertibility of existing productive assets into market-oriented product mix places enterprise management in a quandary that resists ready solutions. Meanwhile, monetary overhang from the Soviet decades has already dissipated into thin air with hyperinflation, leaving enterprises needing credits without adequately circulating financial resources. Physical restructuring of industrial enterprises becomes a near impossibility without external injections. Neither the state nor Ukraine's banking system is capable of supplying adequate credits without concurrently fueling the inflationary spiral.

On the external frontier, capital obsolescence and continual decapitalization further erode capital productivity, culminating in increased production costs and further reduced international competitiveness. Lack of foreign earnings, in turn, constrains an enterprise's effectiveness in physical restructuring.

Another significant external development adversely impacting Ukraine's economic performance has been the rise in Russian and Turkmenistan energy export prices to world market levels. Prior to the formation of CIS, crude oil and natural gas were two primary foreign earning assets that the USSR possessed in plentitude. Since other Soviet exports could find no ready markets abroad, except in the former COMECON organization, hard currency earnings from energy exports constituted the primary source for subsidizing imports from the West. Domestic consumption of energy, on the other hand, was heavily subsidized in lieu of state-determined prices, which were significantly below world market prices. The formation of the CIS meant each republic of the FSU became an independent political and economic entity. Ukraine's former levels of interrepublic energy supplies from Russia and Turkmenistan, as allocated by the system's centralized plan, must now be imported using convertible currencies at world market prices. Inevitable price increases for domestic energy consumption, including consumption for industrial and agricultural use, have further escalated production costs and product prices, eliminating a large number of Ukraine's raw materials and industrial products from effectively competing for export shares in the world market.

Finally, the absence of a competitive financial system impedes the efficient allocation of resources to the more progressive and innovative enterprises in need of investment capital. It passively, yet definitively, curtails the growth of the more promising segment in the economy, especially in the foreign trade sector, which could otherwise provide impetus and incentives to the economy. The transformation from a rigidly controlled and highly centralized system to a flexible and adjustable one is more difficult without a decentralized and competitive financial system.

POLICY ERRORS

Structural transformation requires relative economic stability. However, Ukraine was already experiencing recessionary inflation by 1991. Since macro dislocations can be expected upon independence, intensified destabilization forces are predictable. Therefore, stabilization measures, such as securing political consensus, averting unnecessary additional dislocations, and formulating a reform program uniquely suited to Ukraine's inherited characteristics, should logically precede a liberalization policy.

Not fully comprehending the devastating effects of economic destabilization, Ukraine instead has adopted the strongest of recommendations from a world financial organization. It subscribes to a destabilizing, inflationary policy.

The background forces at work require a brief review to comprehend the ramifications of this approach. All important facets of economic life in Ukraine were severely controlled and regulated. This was a way of life. Rendering sound economic decisions was not an aptitude that enterprise management had in abundance. Economic liberalization, as Eastern European economies have tended to perceive, means letting go of what once was. Among the abrupt measures are the following: enterprise autonomy displacing state controls, price liberalization replacing centralized price determination, "market allocation" supplanting state coordinates, and, economic freedom, meaning what is not prohibited is also permitted, replacing economic rigidity. As a result of these high sounding liberalization measures, enterprise autonomy—as enterprise management nebulously understands it— simultaneously translates into both independence from and dependence on the state. That is, enterprise management is independent from the state in decision-making processes when it is expedient, yet it is dependent on the state when difficult-to-

surmount obstacles arise. Price liberalization means monopoly pricing by autonomous enterprises. "Market allocation," despite extensive supply inelasticities, results
in unbridled price increases for essential commodities. Finally, economic freedom
fuels nonproductive speculative activities while circumventing constructive responses
to market signals. All in all, existing institutional arrangements, though inefficient
and restrictive, gave way to an even less efficient, formless disarray. The reason is
that the traditional modi operandi for enterprise management are no longer operative,
while reasonably functional new institutions are not even nascent.

Against the backdrop of the above deliberation, major policy errors may be
classified into two general categories: (1) initiating errors, committed under the most
unfavorable of inherited circumstances; and, (2) propagating errors, precipitated and
intensified by unfavorable developments from the initiating errors. Each is briefly
examined below.

Initiating Errors

The two principal initiating errors are an ill-conceived price liberalization program
and the nearly unconditional letting go of state coordination and control. Without
demonopolizing unsuitable market powers first, rash liberalization policies grant
them the license to freely exercise monopolistic pricing. Without prudential
coordination and regulations during this transitional phase, chaos replaces structural
rigidity. The unprecedented inflationary spiral seriously compromises rational efforts
at an orderly development of market forces.

Hasty price liberalization and rash economic freedom in a traditionally regulated
and controlled economy also create a minority of profiteers and a majority of
casualties. The nonproductive minority accumulates unwarranted wealth while the
working majority teeters near the brink of bankruptcy. Households lose lifelong
savings. Enterprises face escalating instability and uncertainty. Capital replacement
and restructuring approach impossibility, and continual decapitalization becomes the
norm. Production and productivity decrease, while arrears and unpaid leaves
increase. While mounting social tension attends rising levels of pervasive unease,
mistrust in the merits and motive of reform deepens. The ill-gotten wealth,
meanwhile, either remains in the shadow economy, untaxed, or is converted into hard
currencies and leaked into investment opportunities abroad.

Propagating Errors

Economic instability polarizes political forces, magnifies ideological differences,
and helps bring down one government after another. On the governmental level,
political pressures oblige different emphases be placed on incoherent policies and
inconsistent measures at disparate junctures of social and economic crises. Not only
is substantive reform impeded, instability intensifies, while the crises deepen. The

legislative body, for its part, continues spewing forth confusing and defective laws, periodically issuing directives that weaken administrative positions. In an attempt to remedy confusions and flaws in existing legislation, contradictory provisions in conflicting laws multiply, further confounding an already distrustful public and frustrating the few foreign investors still interested in actualizing economic potential on Ukrainian soil.

The most decisive contributing errors reside in the fiscal and monetary spheres. The parliament's proclivity for control denies the nation's central bank its function of directing a rational monetary policy. Furthermore, oblivious to the propagating effects of unwarranted increases in money supplies, the traditional practice of fiat causes parliament to liberally dispense borrowed money for nonproductive purposes. Extra budgetary disbursement with borrowed money helps perpetuate structural deformities, intensifying functional inefficiencies. Instead of exercising fiscal responsibility and monetary discipline for gradually reestablishing macro stability, the state furthers the course of destabilization. Rising public debt accompanies falling currency value, arresting the nation's focus on economic restructuring, draining its energy into crisis management. Thus, instead of effectuating a systemic transformation from ground zero up, Ukraine must now first emerge from below ground level.

The other major contributing factors to destabilization are briefly recapitulated below and provide an overall picture of policy and institutional flaws:

- Ukraine still lacks a comprehensive, cohesive, transparent reform program. Envisioned results from individual reform measures should reinforce overall progress, or, at least not detract from them. Individual policy measures in Ukraine since independence have failed in this respect.
- Confusing, sometimes conflicting, and frequently changed legal provisions exemplify the absence of clear vision, ideological certitude, and political will concerning reform.
- The parliament's reluctance to grant *de facto* operational independence to the banking sector impedes the latter's implementation of a more deliberate and relatively tight monetary policy for reducing the forces of instability and coordinating and leading structural transformation.
- Temporary budget deficits may reasonably be expected in a transitional economy. However, resorting to the mandated easy credits from the banking sector—instead of floating long-term bonds with state-guaranteed repayment of both principal and interest in real values—fuels inflation and destabilizes the domestic currency.
- Ukraine's stalled privatization program owes its origin in part to the state's failure to enforce and secure progress in enterprise restructuring. On the part of enterprise management, there remains a total absence of urgency in internal restructuring. Without meaningful enterprise-level reform, privatization waste and inefficiencies mount, while production and productivity decline. The aggregated effects on the economy render stabilization and recovery more difficult now than before.
- The government has accomplished little in actively promoting increased production and productivity from the nation's most promising sector: agriculture. Increased supply elasticity from the farm sector is a potent source for price stability in the most basic of consumer items,

also providing fertile ground for augmenting the much needed foreign earnings. Moreover, agriculture is the one sector of the Ukrainian economy in which the incremental capital-output ratio promises the greatest of cost efficiencies.

- A close complementary relationship between the nation's privatization and foreign investment laws is necessary. Thus far, Ukraine has not clearly defined the scope of foreign participation in many aspects of the privatization process, including possible foreign participation in financial sector restructuring.

- Although Ukraine has been afflicted with growing underemployment and disguised unemployment, there has been no effective labor policy that can increase labor mobility and multifaceted adaptability. Lost labor productivity, in addition to state disbursements for nonproductive enterprise subsidies, translates into cumulative waste and growing opportunity costs.

- Finally, the executive and legislative branches of the government expend more energy than is necessary on political wrestling matches, leaving less energy available for forming a coalition for economic reforms. The sole casualties have been the nation's economy and the future of its political independence.

Providing a more comprehensive listing of policy and institutional flaws in Ukraine is not essential here. Studying these flaws, however, can help the Ukrainian government set the economy on course toward meaningful reforms. Ukraine and the other newly liberalized economies of the FSU may, with appropriate adaptations, emulate the successful path traversed by the former Czechoslovakia during its early phases of transformation. The ensuing section highlights select lessons that can be derived from Ukraine's own reform experience.

LESSONS DERIVABLE FROM UKRAINE'S REFORM EXPERIENCE

Valuable lessons, although nearly transparent as common sense, flow from the painful experiences of Ukraine's 52 million economic subjects. These costly lessons can benefit decision makers and architects of reform, especially in the newly liberalized economies of the FSU. Since the preceding chapters have already examined individual reform aspects at length, only lessons on the general level are capsulized in this section.

Need for Objectivity

When examining reform options, recognition and acceptance of one's distinctive strengths and weaknesses need ample consideration. During the transitional phase of systemic transformation, recognizing weaknesses should supersede focusing on promising potential. In the case of Ukraine, since it was an integral component of the USSR for seven decades, debilitating deficiencies emanate from internal, as well as external, sources. Externally, all energy-dependent republics of the FSU can fully anticipate a skyrocketing of energy import prices, which by itself would kindle inflationary flames. In addition, the disruption of the interrepublic distributional system, which has created instant macro dislocations, needs adequate assessment. Finally, since all republics of the FSU shared one common currency upon independence, the effects of economic instability in a neighboring republic or a major exchange partner can easily create additional destabilizing forces within a republic's own domestic boundaries.

On the domestic front itself, vague recognition of structural rigidities and functional deficiencies is insufficient. Reform designers must fully evaluate the extensiveness and depth of such rigidities and inefficiencies, on the one hand, and, on the other, inclusively assess the likely impact of economic independence on the furtherance of the same. The collapse of many export markets for parts and semifinished products automatically reduces the salvage value of already inefficient factors to near ground level. Aside from the inflexibility of productive assets, of high capital-out ratios, and low value productivity, policymakers must also appreciate the limits that lack of political consensus, the presence of ethnic tension, and the pervasiveness of institutional deficiencies can place on reform effectiveness. That is, likely impediments or resistance to specific policy proposals must be weighed when determining the pace of reform and scheduling reform measures. Comprehensive, realistic, and in-depth cognizance of what reform efforts might encounter can more objectively and adequately prepare strategists approaching reform design with sensible and pragmatic realism.

Priority of Stabilization over Transformation

Changing course in turbulent waters dictates reduced speed and steady redirection. Alternately expressed, although select reform programs may parallel stabilization measures, the progress of the former is premised on the success of the latter. No free-falling body focuses well on steps for redirection. Without relative economic stability, there can be no substantive results from reform attempts. As in Ukraine, abrupt reform attempts amidst extensive macro disturbances and dislocations have resulted in greater instability, lost ground, and no measurable progress in structural transformation warranting the social and economic cost.

Indispensability of Political Accord

Successful economic reform requires myriads of human, institutional, material, and financial components that complement and strengthen each other's beneficial attributes. Systemic transformation goes wider and deeper into reformulation and reorientation than economic reform. These essential ingredients, therefore, must also be present in the newly liberalized economies, although admittedly in less developed and less functional forms than in the more evolved market-based economies. The most elementary prerequisite for fostering the growth and maturation of these mutually reinforcing elements is political harmony and accord in relative strength. Economic restructuring without political consensus and determination, as in the case of Ukraine, can result in greater structural deformity, functional inefficiencies, and overall weakening of an already enfeebled economy. An appropriate amount of national energy, therefore, must be spent on achieving political reconciliation and securing harmony among political factions before committing the nation to a definitive course of reform actions. Clear and consistent economic laws can then emerge, with the government complementing the legislative mandate by executing a coherent reform program based on national consensus.

Reform Sequencing

The sequencing of reform programs does not mean that distinct policy measures follow one upon another in a linear fashion. For at any given phase of reform, one significant policy without the support of the others reaps the least positive results. Systemic and structural reforms require that all pivotal variables in the endeavor be duly incorporated into the blueprint. With variable proportions of emphasis placed on all major social and economic factors, elements and programs of reform need to move in a quasi-parallel manner.

Relative emphasis and resource commitment to a given policy during a given phase of reform may vary over time. The criterion for placing variable, proportional emphases on diverse aspects of reform is the aggregated efficiency of the entire reform agenda. Efficiency comprises cost minimization, with costs encompassing financial as well as social and political elements, and output maximization. Economically, output may express itself in the external economies that a given program or measure creates, vis-à-vis contributions to stabilization, to aspects of other reform policies and to the effective rise in market forces. Furthermore, output on the social and political levels may be measured by variations in the scales of social calm and political unity.

For distinct economies with unique background forces at work, different priorities and weights need to be simultaneously placed on diverse measures of a unified reform program. The more crucial aspects of reform requiring simultaneous and unified analysis include the following: a legal foundation, financial-sector restructuring, enterprise reform and ownership transference, state revenue and expenditure profiles, income policy and a social safety net, institutional and human resource development, foreign economic relations, demonopolization, and the extent and degree of market regulation of economic activities in place of state coordination at a given stage of systemic transformation. In brief, reform sequencing requires the concurrent and comprehensive weighings of all these policy aspects for maximizing aggregated positive externalities from the program's unified components.

Learning from Lessons of the Past

All economies of the former COMECON organization have attempted economic reforms in the past. Not a single reform program in any of these economies, with the exception of Alexander Dubek's Prague Spring, yielded the desired results. Institutional impediments and bureaucratic resistance decelerated initial reform thrusts and arrested attempts at further progress. Unwillingness, more than inability, contributed to reform failures. In the newly liberalized economies, especially the republics of the FSU, tenacious unwillingness lingers, while inabilities multiply as a result of changed game rules. The vision has changed from reform on a limited scope into transformation on a grand scale. Institutional inadequacies are magnified. Bureaucratic resistance may decline, yet bureaucratic inability simultaneously mounts. Thus inability, more than unwillingness, may now derail reform efforts. In securing the envisioned reform objectives, policy measures need to take into account the possible external effects that can more effectively neutralize bureaucratic resistance, expedite institutional building, and reinforce the enabling elements essential in reform processes.

Securing Confidence from External Economic Entities

The assistance that foreign capital can provide for a smoother and speedier systemic transformation requires no elaboration. There have been only negligible foreign earnings and insignificant foreign capital inflows since Ukraine began its reform. Factors deterring prospective foreign economic entities from entering into the Ukrainian market are legion. Among them are political disunity, social tension, legal ambiguities and inconsistencies, institutional deficiencies, infrastructural inadequacies, currency instability, and privileges or potential gains less liberal than elsewhere in the region. Taking into account its failed improvements on several of these fronts in the near term, Ukraine would benefit from adopting at least consistent and liberal laws regulating foreign economic activities. Sufficient economic incentives may, in part, compensate for incentives Ukraine lacks in other aspects. Delays in strengthening its external sector encourages the potential flow of foreign capital and trade into competing economies outside of Ukraine's domain. Ukraine can ill afford to neglect this one potent ingredient for economic restructuring.

A Rationalized Price Liberalization Program

The first and foremost policy recommendation to any newly liberalized economy by a given international organization has been price liberalization vis-à-vis the shock therapy approach. Ukraine was no exception. The resulting destructive destabilization and avoidable losses have rendered restructuring more arduous than is necessary. Conversely, this is the kind of approach the same organization does not ever recommend to developed economies for correcting their serious economic aberrations. The rapidly growing national debt in the United States is a ready example.

Eventual price liberalization is necessary for efficient market coordination of economic relationships and activities. When formulating an appropriate price-liberalization policy in Eastern Europe, however, decision makers must fully recognize the debilitating effects that hyperinflation can inflict upon all sectors and all aspects of a nation's economy. Given those economies' recent history under the centralized system, price liberalization must begin with nonessential goods enjoying only limited market demand. Simultaneous price liberalization must take place in the most essential, as well as the less essential, goods categories, however, on proportionately limited scales within predetermined parameters, and for a given phase of reform. Instead of budgetary disbursements for wage and pension indexations owing to hyperinflation—or for consumer and producer subsidies due to the same reason—the reduced consumption disbursements by the government may be allocated to the most cost-efficient producers of goods in high demand. Increased production and enhanced supply elasticities therefrom help relieve inflationary pressures from the previously policy-induced distortions. Not only does consumer surplus increase, the lessening of inflationary pressure can permit the acceleration of price liberalization in spheres in which the state initially exercised greater regulatory and coordinating functions.

A rationalized price liberalization schedule arrives at a market-coordinated equilibrium later than the shock therapy approach. The latter arrives at nominal commodity equilibrium sooner because the economy crashes into the abyss swiftly. In such a situation, an exhausted economy lacks purchasing power. Effective demand plummets to an artificial balance. Supple elasticities do not increase, and the contrived equilibrium balances at exorbitantly high price levels. Adverse effects from hyperinflation are well documented. Recovery therefrom is time-consuming and costly. On the other hand, a rationalized approach to price liberalization—taking into full account the objective conditions confronting Ukraine's newly independent economy—minimizes avoidable dislocations while concurrently granting more opportunities for orderly enhancement of supply responsiveness. Increased supply elasticities approach market equilibriums at increased levels of production and consumption, at significantly lower market-determined equilibrium prices. After seven decades of centralized control, the slightly longer time period required for a more orderly arrival at natural commodity balances mitigates social and political tensions, on the one hand, contributing significantly to a more balanced and efficient systemic transformation on the other.

Constructive, Not Destructive Restructuring

Economic reform via systemic transformation targets economic efficiency and growth. The ultimate objective is consumer and social well-being. Circumventing the avoidable gathering of destructive forces is an indirect rule. Fostering constructive elements is a positive norm. In the case of Ukraine, as in most of the newly liberalized economies, advice from some experts abroad has emphasized measures that produce greater destruction of the old than foster functional institutions for the new. The so-called shock therapy, given Ukraine's recent past, is tantamount to the demolishing of the entire existing structure first, then reconstructing a new structure from the ground up. Overlooked is the fact that Ukraine has 52 million hapless occupants impounded within the existing structure. After centuries of foreign domination and seven decades of Soviet rule, a rationally articulated, though slower paced, reform strategy is more suitable for the Ukrainian people. In development economics, the stage of establishing preconditions precedes take-off; so it is with systemic transformation. There should be no tearing down of inefficient—but still functional—support systems before operational substitutes are relatively and securely in place. There should be constructive restructuring, with the dismantling of the old proceeding in a methodical and orderly fashion. A slower and more deliberate approach to economic restructuring nurtures political unity, preserves social calm, and minimizes long-term losses. It accomplishes, in time, a fundamental systemic transformation with minimal destructive shocks to the structure's constituents.

Within the context of the general lessons outlined above, reform strategists and decision makers in other parts of the region may derive specific caveats from Ukraine's experiences with economic restructuring. Other than generalized postulates, there should be no dogmatic approaches to restructuring an economy with historical, cultural, political, and economic background forces that are uniquely its own. Keeping in perspective the *mutatis mutandis* precept, rationalized and flexible adaptation of generalized restructuring principles can, in reasonable time, lead an economy to the promised land.

RECOMMENDATIONS

Taking recent developments in Ukraine as the point of departure, this concluding section summarizes recommendations for possible consideration by Ukraine's decision makers. Because relatively detailed topical analysis has been presented in the preceding chapters, the more cogent recommendations here need be only in an outline format,with the exception of the conducting of a public information and education campaign.

- Extensive consultation with and assistance from legal experts from abroad for improving clarity, consistency, and enforceability of Ukraine's body of economic laws.
- The shock approach toward price liberalization has nearly run its course. It serves no purpose recentralizing price determination. Instead, the government should temporarily freeze prices on consumer essentials at existing levels, until supply responses increase. This would prevent further erosion of consumer purchasing power and reduce the need for consumer and enterprise subsidies.
- More rational budgetary disbursements for an orderly reduction in inefficient resource consumption, for the promotion of constructive competition, and for improved labor mobility via effective job retraining and replacement programs.
- Immediate cessation of the state's intervention in the National Bank of Ukraine's monetary policy operations. Deficit financing should originate from the financial market, paying market-determined rates at constant values.
- Tight monetary policies for reducing instability, accompanied by the NBU's enhanced capability for prudential regulations, including regulations over member banks' lending portfolios.
- Promoting household and enterprise savings by henceforth mandating the payment of principal and interest *to* savers and *by* borrowers on real terms.
- Immediate classification of enterprises into viable, currently inefficient yet potentially viable, nonsalvageable categories. Judicious financial injections therein or withdrawals therefrom, both via fiscal and monetary measures, may be enacted to promote competitive and viable segments of the economy, while prompting the earlier elimination of wasteful resource consumption.
- A more tightly-knit social safety net, in conjunction with a fine-tuned incomes policy, cushioning victims from both the centralized system and recent policy errors.
- Forced acceleration in enterprise restructuring and privatization—including the state's holdings in the banking sector—by extending the scope of effective foreign participation in both.
- With economies of scale and increased competitive efficiency as guidelines, promptly effectuating vertical or horizontal divestiture of monopoly powers.
- Increasing the government's role in reactivating the agricultural sector's vast productive potential. Among other measures, subsidized credits, investment and tax incentives, and organizational restructuring of producing units merit special consideration.
- Immediate focus on expanded foreign economic relations, especially the creation of an environment more conducive to foreign capital inflows.

The final recommendation pertains to the dissemination of information cogent to reform efforts. Ukraine, as all other former economies of Eastern Europe, has inherited a highly evolved propaganda machine from the centralized system. This can be constructively converted into a vehicle for public information dissemination. Definitive, intelligible, and unambiguous communications from the state must include information on the following:

- existing economic conditions;
- the effects of independence on current and future economic relations, both externally and on domestic economic entities;
- the relative strengths and weaknesses, and the promises or likely elimination of the economy's specific subsectors over time;
- short-term and long-term reform objectives;
- a cohesive plan of complementary macro policies, with planned phases and timetables for implementation;
- the economic rationales for introducing publicized policy measures;
- the anticipated potential gains that can be reaped when economic subjects respond within the time period allotted and meet the other conditions the policy measures set forth;
- responsible measures taken at the enterprise level, facilitating constructive responses to various changing economic relations, including necessary organizational, managerial, financial, and physical restructurings;
- the likely market-imposed penalties for nonresponsiveness; and,
- the extent and degree of hardships that will inevitably fall upon consumers and producers for projected durations.

Effective dissemination of such information requires continual, recurrent, and urgent issue. Foreknowledge means economic subjects can expect how much of what to follow, and forewarns enterprise management of the harmful consequences of inertia. It obliges economic entities to assume responsibility for preventing additional hardships as a consequence of apathetic participation in the reform process. It also reduces the state's obligation for sustained subsidies to nonresponsive micro entities. Knowledge is indispensable. In the case of Ukraine's economic subjects, action must also accompany knowledge for the envisioned objectives. An effective public education and informational program can help translate knowledge into responsive and responsible action.

As a concluding note, designing and sequencing policy measures for systemic transformation must incorporate due consideration to a given economy's inherited characteristics. Performance is the ultimate criterion for evaluating a given strategy's appropriateness. Reform architects and decision makers in Ukraine have thus far failed their constituents. Ukraine needs a fresh start, as well as a new resolve. Its 52 million economic subjects deserve better judgments and more discerning policies. Errors have been committed. Painful yet valuable lessons can nevertheless yield constructive results. Micro responsiveness will materialize. A more cohesive, consistent, and rationalized blueprint for an envisioned tomorrow is desperately needed.

References

Allen, W.E.D. *The Ukraine: A History*. New York: Russell & Russell, 1963.

Amodio, Nicoletta. "USSR Legislation on Land." *MOCT*, Vol. 1, 1991a.

—. "Forms of Ownership in USSR." *MOCT*, Vol. 1, 1991b.

Aslund, Anders, Peter Boone, and Simon Johnson. "Ukraine: Ready for a Breakthrough" *Ostekonomisk Rapport*, Vol. 6, No. 8, Stockholm: Ostekonomiska Institute, 1994.

Bilinsky, Yaroslav. *The Second Soviet Republic: The Ukraine after World War II*. New Brunswick, New Jersey: Rutgers University Press, 1964.

Bondar, O. M. "Sytuatsiya ne Beznadiyna: Pryvatyzatsia 'Pide'" (Situation is not hopeless: privatization will 'go'. *Teoretychnyy Ta Naukovo-Praktychnyy Zhurnal (Theoretical and Applied Science JournalTheoretical and Applied Science Journal)*, Kiev: *Informatsia I Rynok (Information and Market)*, 1994.

Boss, Helen. *Ukraine's Economy in Sectoral and Regional Perspective*. Vienna: Vienna Institute for Comparative Economic Studies, 1993.

Boss, Helen, and Peter Havlik. *Russia, Ukraine, and Belarus: Output Slump and Trade Breakdown Set the Stage for Policy Changes*. Vienna: Vienna Institute for Comparative Economic Studies, 1994.

Brzezinski, Ian, and Michael Zienchuk. *Update on Ukraine*, No. 12. Kiev: Council of Advisors to the Parliament of Ukraine, 1993.

Browne, Michael, ed. *Ferment in the Ukraine: Documents by V. Chornovil, I. Kandyba, L. Lukyanenko, V. Moroz, and Others*. New York: Praeger, 1971.

Budekavych, Cabinet of Ministers of Ukraine. *Plan for Urgent Economic Reforms*. Ttranslated by Yarema Havrylyshyn. Kiev: Project on Economic Reform in Ukraine (PERU), 1992a.

—. *The Programme of Economic Reforms and Policy in Ukraine*. Kiev: Ukrainian Government, 1992b.

—. *Plan aktyvnosti uriadu jkrainy* (Plan of action by the Ukrainian government to implement the guidelines of the national economic policy). Kiev: Ukrainian Government, 1993.

Chamberlin, William H. *The Ukraine: A Submerged Nation*. New York: MacMillan, 1944.

Chini, Mekhmet, Alper Bakhchedzhioglu, and Roman Fedorovych. "Import/Export Situation." *Ukrainian Business Magazine*, (SKARB): Vol. 1, 1994.

Chirovsky, Nicholas L. *An Introduction to Ukrainian History*. Vol. 2. New York:

Philosophical Library, 1984.

Decree of the Cabinet of Ministers of Ukraine. *The List of Priority Objects for Attraction of Foreign Investments in the Sphere of Economy.* Kiev: Supreme Rada, 1993a.

—. *On Liberalization of Foreign Economic Activities.* Kiev: Supreme Rada, 1993b.

Decree of the Cabinet of Ministers of Ukraine on Corporatization of State-Owned Enterprises (Associations). Kiev: Supreme Rada, 1992.

Decree of the President of Ukraine. *Regarding Steps to Stimulate Foreign Economic Activity.* Kiev: Supreme Rada, 1992.

Director of Intelligence. *Handbook of International Economic Statistics.* Washington, D.C.: U.S. Government Printing Office, 1992.

Frishberg, Alex. "Ukraine's Political and Economic Reforms." *Ukrainian Legal and Economic Bulletin,* Vol. 2, 1994.

Frydman, Roman, Andrzej Rapaczynski, John S. Earle, et al. *The Privatization Process in Russia, Ukraine and the Baltic States.* London: Central European University Press, 1993.

Iachini, Daniela. "Joint Ventures and the Law on Foreign Investments in the USSR." *MOCT,* Vol.2, 1991.

International Market Insights. *Privatization Progress.* Kiev: State Property Fund, 1995.

International Monetary Fund. *The Economy of the USSR: Summary and Recommendations.* Washington, D.C.: World Bank, 1990.

—. *IMF Economic Reviews: Ukraine.* Washington, D.C.: International Monetary Fund, 1993.

Kuchma, Leonid. *Along the Road of Radical Economic Reform, Address of the President of Ukraine on the Basic Tenets of Economic and Social Policy.* Kiev: Council of Advisors to the Parliament of Ukraine, 1994.

Kvaniuk, Boris. *Presidential Election Has Taken Place. Leonid Kuchma Won.* Kiev, 1994.

Law of Ukraine on Privatization of Assets of State-Owned Enterprises. Kiev: Supreme Rada, 1992.

Law of Ukraine on Privatization of Small State Enterprises. *Small Privatization.* Kiev: Supreme Rada, 1992.

Law of Ukraine on the Leasing of Property of State-Owned Enterprises and Organizations. Kiev: Supreme Rada, 1992.

Law on Business Enterprise. Kiev: Supreme Rada, 1991.

Law on Containing Monopolism and Preventing Unfair Competition. Kiev: Supreme Rada, 1992.

Law on Economic Partnerships. Kiev: Supreme Rada, 1991.

Law on Enterprises in the Ukrainian SSR. *Act of the Ukrainian Soviet Socialist Republic.* Kiev: Supreme Rada, 1991

Law on Foreign Investment. Kiev: Supreme Rada, 1992.

Lukinov, Ivan. *The Inflationary Policy, Its Consequences, and Ways to Overcome the Hyperinflation in Ukraine.* Kiev: Ukrainian Academy of Sciences, 1993.

Manninen, Kevin, and David Snelbecker. "Obstacles to Doing Western Business in Ukraine." *Ukrainian Legal and Economic Bulletin,* Vol. 1, 1993.

Manning, Clarence. *Ukraine under the Soviets.* New York: Record Press, 1953.

Mayetniy, A. "Investment Crisis in Ukraine." *Privatization in Ukraine.* Vol. 3, No.4. Kiev: PERU, 1994.

Ministry of Economy. *Ukraine in Numbers.* Vol. 4. Kiev: Ukrainian Government, 1993a.

—. *Ukraine in Numbers,* Vol. 5. Kiev: Ukrainian Government, 1993b.

—. *Ukraine in Numbers,* Vol. 6. Kiev: Ukrainian Government, 1993c.

—. *Ukraine in Numbers,* Vol. 9. Kiev: Ukrainian Government, 1993d.

—. *Ukraine in Numbers,* Vol. 10. Kiev: Ukrainian Government, 1994a.

—. *Ukraine in Numbers,* Vol. 11. Kiev: Ukrainian Government, 1994b.

—. *Ukraine in Numbers,* Vol. 13. Kiev: Ukrainian Government, 1994c.

—. *Ukraine in Numbers,* Vol. 19. Kiev: Ukrainian Government, 1994d.

Ministry of Statistics of Ukraine. *Ukraina u tsyfrarh u 1993 rotsi* (Ukraine in figures*).* Kiev: Technica, 1994a.

—. *Eksporty (importy) i peresichni tsiny investitsiynykh i spozhyvchykh produktiv v ukraini v 1993 rotsi (*Exports (imports) and average prices for investment and consumer goods in Ukraine in 1993. Department of Statistics of Foreigh Economic Ties, 1994b.

—. *Express Report.* Kiev: Ukrainian Government, 1994c.

—. *Statystychnyy biuleten' za sichen'-liutyy 1993 roku (*Statistical Bulletin) . Kiev: Ukrainian Government, 1994d

—. *Statystychnyy biuleten' za sichen'-liutyy 1994 roku (*Statistical Bulletin*).* Kiev: Ukrainian Government, 1994e.

—. *Ukrainian Foreign Trade January-June 1994.* Kiev: Ukrainian Government, 1994f.

Mycyk, Adam M. "New Procedures Issued for Obtaining Additional Benefits under the Program for Encouraging Foreign Investment," *Ukrainian Legal and Economic Bulletin,* 1994.

National Bank of Ukraine Monetary Policy Administration. *Natsional' nyy bank ukrainy upravlinnia hroshovoyi polityky, Makroekonomichyy ohliad po ukraini za kvartal 1994 roku* Macroeconomic Review of Ukraine, 1st quarter 1994. Kiev: Ukrainian Government, 1994.

National Institute for Strategic Studies. *Strategies for the Development of Ukraine: Contemporary Challenges and Choices.* Kiev: National Institute for Strategic Studies, 1994.

OMRI (Open Media Research Institute). *Daily Digest.* Buffalo: Internet, January 24,1995.

—. *Daily Digest.* Buffalo: Internet, February 10, 1995.

—. *Daily Digest.* Buffalo: Internet, March 2, 1995.

—. *Daily Digest.* Buffalo: Internet, April 4, 1995.

—. *Daily Digest.* Buffalo: Internet, April 10, 1995.

Pavlikovskaya, Lada. *"The Corporatization of Enterprises." Privatization in Ukraine,* Vol. 2, No. 7. Kiev: PERU, 1993.

Popiel, Walter. "Ukraine in Numbers." *Ukrainian Legal and Economic Bulletin.* Kiev: PERU, Vol. 1, 1993.

"Privatization in General." *Privatization in Ukraine.* Kiev: PERU, Vol. 2, no. 6,1993.

—. *State Property Fund: Final Results of 1993 Privatization.* Kiev: PERU, 1994.

Raikhmilovic, Viktor. "Juridical Forms of Enterprise Organization in USSR." *MOCT,* Vol. 1, 1991.

Rehgizzi, Gabriele. "The Joint Venture Company in Soviet Law." *MOCT, Economic Journal on Eastern Europe and the Soviet Union,* Vol. 2, 1991.

Resolution of the Supreme Rada of Ukraine. *On the State Program for Privatization.* Kiev: Supreme Rada, 1994.

Rudekavych, Lesia. "Privatization: Problems and Effectiveness in Practice." *Ukrainian Legal and Economic Bulletin,* Vol. 2, 1994.

Secretariat of the Economic Commission for Europe, Geneva. *Economic Survey of Europe in 1991–1992.* New York: Economic Commission for Europe, 1992.

—. *Economic Bulletin for Europe.* Vol. 44, 1992. New York: United Nations, 1993.

—. *Economic Bulletin for Europe.* Vol. 45, 1993. New York and Geneva: United Nations, 1994.

Shpek, Roman. "My Dovho Shukaly Tu Stezhku...Teper Vona Vidoma" ("We Searched Long for this Path...Now It is Known"). *Teoretychnyy Ta Naukovo-Praktychnyy Zhurnal (Theoretical and Applied Science Journal.* Kiev: Informatsia I Rynok (Information and Market), 1994.

Skredov, Vladimir. "The USSR Property Law: Possible Forms of Development." *MOCT*, Vol. 1, 1991.

State Programme for Encouraging Foreign Investments. Kiev: Supreme Rada, 1993.

State Program for the Privatization of State Property for 1993. Kiev: Supreme Rada, 1993.

State Program for the Privatization of State Property for 1994. Kiev: Supreme Rada, 1994.

State Property Fund of Ukraine. *Approval of Regulation on Procedures for Privatization of State-Owned Enterprises Decree.* Kiev: Supreme Rada, 1993.

—. "The State of Privatization in 1993." *Privatization in Ukraine.* Kiev: PERU, Vol. 3, 1994.

Supreme Rada's Decree on Containing Monopolism. Kiev: Supreme Rada, 1992.

Tremblay, Emil. *The Ukrainian Challenge.* Montmatre, Saskatchewan: Icon Press,1979.

Ukrainian National Information Service. "Foreign Investment," Ukrainian Business Magazine (SKARB): Vol.1, 1994.

Ukrainian Weekly. Jersey City: Ukrainian National Association Inc., January 8, 1995.

—. Jersey City: Ukrainian National Association Inc., January 22, 1995.

—. Jersey City: Ukrainian National Association Inc., February 5, 1995.

—. Jersey City: Ukrainian National Association Inc., March 19, 1995.

Union. "Foreign Investments." *Ukrainian Business Magazine,* Vol. 1, 1994.

World Bank. *Statistical Handbook: States of the Former USSR.* Washington, D.C.: World Bank, 1992.

—. *Ukraine, Country Economic Memorandum.* Vol. 2, Europe and Central Asia. Washington, D.C.: World Bank, 1993.

Zubaniuk, Viktor. "Ukraine's New Investment Policies Look Good, But...," *Ukrainian Legal and Economic Bulletin,* Vol. 2, 1994.

INTERVIEWEES (July 22–August 26, 1994, Ukraine)

Alymov, Alexander	Academician*. Head, Department of Industrial Relations, Institute of Economy, National Academy of Sciences.
Artikuluy, Leonid	Head, Department of Reform and Market Relations, Ministry of Food and Agriculture.
Askanas, Wiktor	Professor of Management, University of New Brunswick, Canada.
Assonov, George	Head, Department of Economic Information, Ukrainian Institute of Science, Technology, and Economic Information.
Besedin, Vasilly	Director, National Economic Research Institute, Ministry of Economy.
Bielienkiy, Peter	Academician*, Ukrainian Academy of Entrepreneurship and Management; Head, Department of Privatization and Entrepreneurship, Institute of Economics, National Academy of Sciences.
Bondar, Interna	Research Professor, Institute of Population Studies and Social Protection, Ministry of Economy.
Borochevsky, Petro	Deputy Director, Ukrainian Research Council for Productive Forces.

Brzezinski, Jan — Director for International Security Programs, Council of Advisors to the Parliament of Ukraine.

Danilenko, Anatoly — Deputy Minister, Ministry of Economy.

Dobrovolsky, Nikolay — Deputy Director, Department of International Economic Relations, Ministry of Economy.

Dorofeyev, Nina — Head, Department for Monetary Policy, National Bank of Ukraine.

Doroguntsov, Valery — Deputy Director, Budgetary Board, Ministry of Finance.

Flissak, Nataly — Director, Department for Legislative Drafts on Indirect Taxation, Ministry of Finance.

Gerasimchuk, Mykola — Deputy Director, Institute of Economics, Ukrainian Academy of Sciences.

Ivanov, Voldymyr — Deputy Director, International Division, National Bank of Ukraine.

Kalitich, Georgi — Academician*, Ukrainian Academy of Information Systems; Deputy Director for Research, Ukrainian Institute of Science, Technology, and Economic Information.

Karpov, Vladimir — Director, Statistical Research Institute, Ministry of Statistics.

Khurmanets, Galina — Head, Department of Agricultural Production, Ukrainian Institute of Science, Technology, and Economic Information.

Kryzhanovsky, Boris — Senior Researcher, Ukrainian Research Council for Productive Forces.

Kul'chitskiy, Stanislav — Deputy Director, Institute of History, National Academy of Sciences.

Kvasniuk, Boris — Senior Researcher, Department of Political Economy, Institute of Economics, National Academy of Sciences.

Lukinov, Ivan — Academician*; Vice President, National Academy of Sciences; Director, Institute of Economics, National Academy of Sciences.

Mararenko, Alexander — Deputy Minister, Ministry of Foreign Affairs.

Masiuk, Andrew — Director, International Management Institute of Kiev.

Mashkin, Anatoly — Deputy Director, Department for the Restructuring of Property Ownership Rights, Ministry of Economy.

Maslykov, Yevgeny — Senior Researcher, Department of Price Formation and Market Infrastructure, Institute of Agrarian Economy, Ukrainian Academy of Agricultural Sciences.

Melnik, Lidiya — Deputy Director, Department of Foreign Investment, Ministry of Economy.

Messel-Veselyak, Victor — Deputy Director, Institute of Agrarian Economy, Ukrainian Academy of Agricultural Sciences.

Moguilevich, Roman — Deputy Director, Department of Scientific Research, National Institute of Economic Programs, National Academy of Sciences.

Murashyn, Guennady — Deputy Director, Institute of State and Law, National Academy of Sciences.

Nagivnjak, Peter — Director, Research Department of Market Reforms, Statistical Research Institute, Ministry of Statistics.

Novotorov, Alexander — Senior Researcher, Ukrainian Research Council for Productive Forces.

Oksanych, Olexandr	Head, Department of Energy and Resource Conservation, Institute of Economics, National Academy of Sciences.
Parakhousky, Boris	Head, Department of Welfare Studies, National Institute for Strategic Studies.
Parfenceva, Nelja	Director, Department of Methodology for Data Collection and Information Processing, Statistical Research Institute, Ministry of Statistics.
Paskhaver, Boris	Head, Department of Agro-Industrial Economic Relations, National Academy of Sciences.
Pastushenko, Anatoly	Head, Department of Social Development Problems, Ministry of Economy.
Pirozhkov, Serhiy	Director, National Institute for Strategic Studies.
Pitzyck, Myroslav	Deputy Minister, Ministry of Statistics
Radiuk, Victor	Deputy Director, Department for Legislative Drafts on Direct Taxation, Ministry of Finance.
Romaschenko, Oleg	Head, Department of Instructional Resources, Professional Retraining Institute, Kiev.
Rudchenko, Alexandr	Head, Department for Market Relations Development, Ministry of Economy.
Sabluk, Peter	Director, Institute of Agrarian Economy, Ukrainian Academy of Agricultural Sciences.
Sangursky, Vladimir	Coordinator for Scientific Research, Ukrainian Institute of Science, Technology and Economic Information.
Schur, Mikhail	Head, Department of Analysis and Forecasting, Institute of Agrarian Economy, Ukrainian Academy of Agricultural Sciences.
Sedletsky, Oleg	Head, Department of Industrial Restructuring and Production, Ukrainian Institute of Science, Technology, and Economic Information.
Shevchenko, Yaroslava	Head, Department of Labor Relations Law, Institute of State and Law, National Academy of Sciences.
Shokun, Valery	Deputy Director, National Institute of Economic Programs, National Academy of Sciences.
Siry, Mikolay	Research Coordinator, Institute of State and Law, National Academy of Sciences.
Sordet, Bernard	Advisor to the Minister of Economy.
Suslov, Victor	Chairman, Finance and Banking Committee, The Supreme Council of Ukraine.
Trachenko, Olexandre	Deputy Speaker, The Supreme Council of Ukraine.
Tyvonchuk, Stepan	Head, Department of Scientific-Technological Progress and Information Management, Ministry of Agriculture; President, Ukrainianagricultureservis Association.
Urchishin, Vladimir	Academician*, Institute of Agrarian Economy, Ukrainian Academy of Agricultural Sciences.
Valovy, Yri	Head, Department of Economic Analysis and Forecasting, Ministry of Food and Agriculture.
Vlasyuk, Alexander	Head, Department of Systems Modeling and Forecasting, National Institute for Strategic Studies.
Vovkanyhc, Stepan	Head, Department of Sociological Research, Institute of Economics, National Academy of Sciences.

Wasylyk, Myron	Executive Secretary, Council of Advisors to the Parliament.
Yermoshenko, Mykola	Director, Ukrainian Institute of Science, Technology, and Economic Information.
Zienchuk, Michael	Advisor to the Minister of Economy.

---

*The title "Academician" in Ukraine indicates that an individual has attained the highest level of academic achievement within his/her respective sphere of expertise.

Index

About the Author

RAPHAEL SHEN is a Professor of Economics at the University of Detroit Mercy. Dr. Shen is well published on subjects dealing with the liberalization of Eastern European economies and governments including *The Polish Economy: Legacies from the Past, Prospects for the Future* (Praeger, 1992), *Economic Reform in Poland and Czechoslovakia: Lessions in Systemic Transformation* (Praeger, 1993) and *Restructuring the Baltic Economies: Disengaging Fifty Years of Integration with the USSR* (Praeger, 1994).

ISBN 0-275-95240-1